Migration and Covid-19

Migration and Covid-19: Gender Perspective

Dr. A. Ranjithkumar
Ms. M. Eswari
Dr. Anji A

KALPAZ

First Published, 2020

Published by

Kalpaz Publications
C-30, Satyawati Nagar,
Delhi – 110052
Ph.: 011-47034999, 9811692060
www.kalpazpublications.com
E-mail: kalpaz@hotmail.com

Printed at: Gyan Press, Delhi.

Cataloging in Publication Data—DK
Courtesy: D.K. Agencies (P) Ltd. <docinfo@dkagencies.com>

Migration and Covid-19 gender perspective / Dr. A. Ranjithkumar, Ms. M. Eswari, Dr. Anji A.
pages cm
Contributed articles.
ISBN 9789353246181

1. Migrant labor—India—Social conditions. 2. Migrant labor—India—Economic conditions. 3. Women migrant labor—India—Social conditions. 4. Women migrant labor—India—Economic conditions. 5. Covid-19 (Disease)—Social aspects—India. 6. Covid-19 (Disease)—Economic aspects—India. I. Ranjithkumar, A., editor. II. Eswari, M., editor. III. Anji, A., editor.

LCC HD5856.I4I87 2021 | DDC 331.5440954 23

Contents

Introduction

The outbreak of Covid-19, Acute Respiratory Syndrome Respiratory disease caused by corona virus 2 (SARS-CoV-2), at the latter half of 2019, has grown into becoming a deadly pandemic. Unlike previous outbreaks of MERS and SARS, Covid-19 has a very high transmission rate. This particular nature Covid-19 has spread global fear and put everything on a standstill affecting drastically the economies of many countries. The onset of the disease in late 2019 and its manifestation in the year 2020 has propelled rapid transmission of the virus and has led to World Health Organisation to deem the disease as a pandemic. As the understanding of the disease is in its infancy there is widespread disparity on Covid-19 knowledge and epidemiology of the disease. In Wuhan, China, Covid-19 was first reported and then spread around the world. To control the spread of Covid-19, the global community has been reported to be declining.

On 24 March 2020, Indian Government, as a preventive measure against the Covid-19 epidemic, restricted the movement of a total of 1.3 billion people in India and ordered a nationwide lockdown for 21 days. Nationwide lockdown involves 4 phases; Phase 1: 25.03.2020–14.04.2020 (21 days), Phase 2: 15.04.2020 – 03.05.2020 (19 days), Phase 3: 04.05.2020 – 17.05.2020 (14 days), and Phase 4: 18.05.2020–31.05.2020 (14 days). After a nationwide lockdown, the government released the lockdown; Opening 1.0: 01.06.2020 – 30.06.2020 (30 days), Opening 2.0: 01.07.2020 – 31.07.2020 (31 days), Opening 3.0: 01.08.2020 – 31.08.2020 (31 days), Opening 4.0: 01.09.2020-30.09.2020 (30 days), Opening 5.0: 01.10.020 – 31.10. 2020 (31 days), and Opening 6.0: 01.11.2020 – 30.11.2020 (22 days). During the nationwide lockdown, migrant workers were affected.

During the Covid-19 epidemics, migrant workers in India faced many difficulties with the closure of plants and work environments in the country, large numbers of migrant workers were needed to manage the impact of wage shortages, food shortages and their future. Following this, a significant number of them and their families were starving. Many of them were locked up at the time and began to return home without any mode of transportation. Accordingly, the Central and State Governments took different measures in their favour and then formulated the transport for them. More than 300 unstable professionals kicked the bucket for being locked up, with reasons such as starvation, suicides, fatigue, street and train accidents, police ruthlessness and denial of the best medical opinion.

According to the World Economic Forum, 139 million passengers are expected in the country. The International Labour Organisation (ILO) expects that about 400 million professionals will be lifted out of poverty due to epidemics and lockdowns. Most travellers in the country start from Uttar Pradesh and Bihar, which travels through Rajasthan and Madhya Pradesh. The urban communities of Mumbai and Delhi attract a large number of intermediaries. Although most men move for work, women move because of marriage. There are a significant number of migrant workers per day working in the aggregation and development industries. Since many of them work in the normal area, they are regularly denied adequate medical care, food, shelter and contraception. They are generally from the countryside, yet work in urban communities for most of the year. Many had no investment funds and lived in plant dwellings that were closed due to locks. Moreover, despite the state Migrant Labour Act of 1979, there was no focal library of unstable experts.

According to research distributed at the Royal Geographical Society, the most notable handled workers were from regions such as Odisha, Jharkhand and Chhattisgarh, in which the characteristic properties of the tribal people were removed by the Pariahs. Moreover, the lowest paid workers for hard work have earned a place with the reactionary classes, mainly from the Dalit and Adivasi population. The study shows that groups of temporary workers supported them by keeping their homes and interacting with them when they were unable to work from time to time or when they were ready to work during this time. According to the 2011 Census of India, Maharashtra has the highest number of intermediaries. On March 20, Pune, Pimpri-Chinchwad, Mumbai metropolitan area and Nagpur forced its state government to lock up, leaving interim experts without any work.

At that time thousands of people congregated at train stations and stations, looking for transport to the places where they grew up. All auto offices were closed as the cross country was locked. When locked up, a handful of state migrant workers tried to revisit their home state. As public transportation offices were suspended, passengers began to walk toward their home state.

Accordingly, transport and shramik exception trains were allowed by the central government subject to inter-state coordination. Covid-19 is a caused by a new corona virus. 'Go' stands for corona, 'VI' for virus and 'D' for disease. Previously, the disease was referred to as the '2019 Novel Corona Virus' or '2019-nCoV'. Covid-19 virus is a new type of virus that is linked to the same family of viruses as acute respiratory illness (SARS) and some types of colds. Symptoms of Covid-19 include fever, cough, and shortness of breath. In more severe cases, the infection can cause pneumonia or respiratory difficulties. Very rarely, the disease is dangerous. These symptoms are similar to the flu (influenza) or the common cold, and are more common than Covid-19. This is why testing is needed to confirm whether someone is linked to Covid-19.

The virus is spread by direct contact with an infected person's respiratory tract (caused by coughing and sneezing). Individuals can be affected by touching surfaces contaminated with the virus and by touching their faces (e.g., eyes, nose, mouth etc.). The Covid-19 virus can survive on the surface for hours, but simple disinfectants can kill it. The elderly and those with chronic medical conditions such as diabetes and heart disease are at increased risk of developing severe symptoms (World Health Organisation, 2020). Corona virus disease 2019 (Covid-19) is defined as a disease caused by a novel corona virus called "acute acute respiratory syndrome corona virus 2 (formerly known as SARS-CoV-2; formerly 2019-nCoV)", which was first identified among respiratory outbreaks Found in Wuhan, China (Cennimo, 2020).

Migration is defined as "the process by which people travel to a new place, usually in large numbers" (Cambridge University Press, 2020). International organisations have warned that millions of workers will lose their jobs as a result of the lockdown. Its impact will be huge in poor and developing countries. Global unemployment, at 190 million, could see a sharp rise as businesses lay off workers and reduce working hours. For those working in the informal sector, often in poorer and developing countries, the impact of their lack of social security, such as unemployment benefits, can be devastating. International Labour Organisation (ILO), UNO The company estimates that four out of every five (81 percent) of the 3.3 billion global workforce will be affected by partial or complete layoffs. "Workers and businesses are facing catastrophe, in both developed and developing economies," said ILO Director – General Guy Ryder. "We have to move fast, decisively, and together. The right urgent, measures, could make the difference between survival and collapse."

In worst-affected sectors, employees are often low-skilled and low-wage, such as construction workers. About 1.25 billion people, who make up almost 38% of the global workforce, work in sectors that deal with severe stress, including in hotels, restaurants and shopping malls. The ILO says the retail and wholesale sector, which employs 482 million people worldwide, will be worst affected. "In India, with a share of almost 90% of people working in the informal economy, about 400 million workers are at risk of falling deeper into poverty during the crisis," the ILO said in recent report. As the Covid-19 expansion is progressing globally, we are trying to explore the issue of migrant labour in India during the lockdown.

List of Contributors

1. **Dr. A. Ranjithkumar:** Research Associate, Department of Women's Studies, Allaggappa University, Karikudi
2. **Dr. Anji A:** Teaching Faulty (Ad-hoc), Dept. & Research Centre for Women's Studies, Karnatak University, Dharwad
3. **M. Eswari:** Research Associate Centre for Women's Studies, The Gandhigram Rural Institute-Deemed to be University Gandhigram
4. **Swapna Sikha Das:** Research Scholar, Department of Education, Tezpur University, Napaam, Assam, Pin-784028
5. **Dr. Remmiya Rajan P.:** Assistant Professor, Zamorin's Guruvayurappan College
6. **Dr. Noohi Khan (AP II):** Amity School of Applied Sciences, Amity University Lucknow, UP, India
7. **Chandrakala Ghosh:** Department of English Asutosh College Shreya Chakrabarty, Assistant Professor of English, Rampurhat College
8. **Sulaiman KM:** PhD Scholar, Department of Migration & Urban Studies, International Institute for Population Sciences, Mumbai, India
9. **Afsal K:** IIPS Mumbai, Deonar (PO), Mumbai-400088. Ph: 7678022812
10. **Biplab Debnath:** Assistant Professor, Department of Political Science, Tripura University, Suryamaninagar - 799032
11. **Aswathikrishnan U.R:** School of International Relations and Politics, Mahatma Gandhi University, Kottayam, Kerala

12. **Nidhin C:** School of International Relations and Politics, Mahatma Gandhi University, Kottayam, Kerala
13. **Dr. Reena Malik:** Assistant professor, Chitkara Business School, Chitkara University, Punjab, India
14. **Dr. Shourini Banerjee:** Assistant Professor, Dept of Visual Communication, The American College, Madurai-625002, Tamil Nadu
15. **Sumedha Chaudhuri:** PhD Research Scholar, Dept of English, Ranchi University, Ranchi- 834008, Jharkhand
16. **S. Balaganapathy:** PhD Research Scholar, Dept of Media Sciences, Anna University, Chennai- 600025, Tamil Nadu
17. **Ms. Sophia Sharon:** Assistant Professor, Department of Humanities, Mount Carmel College - Bangalore
18. **Fariza Saidin:** Department of Education & Psychology University of Science and Technology, Meghalaya
19. **Tajbina Yasin:** Department of Education & Psychology, University of Science and Technology, Meghalaya
20. **Ms. S. Durga Devi:** MA in Political Science, UGC NET, Assistant Professor at Mount Carmel Autonomous College
21. **Anil Kumar:** Postgraduate student, Department of Political Science, Maharishi Dayanand University, Rohtak, Haryana
22. **Dalip:** Maharishi Dayanand University, Rohtak, Haryana
23. **Ms. Shabnam Yesmin:** Faculty, Department of BBA, Dispur College
24. **Neelofer Habib:** Ph.D Research Scholars, Department of Sociology, University of Kashmir
25. **Dr. Salima Jan:** Research Scientist, Department of EMMRC, University of Kashmir
26. **Prantik Basak:** PhD research scholar in Political Science, Rabindra Bharati University; 171/B, G.T Road, Ballavpore, Serampore, Hooghly-712201
27. **Alka Rani:** PhD, Department of Zoology, Kumaun University, Nainital, UT, India

28. **Abhishek Gupta:** PhD Department of Zoology, Chaudhary Charan Singh University, Meerut, UP, India
29. **Gayadhar Malik:** PhD Research Scholar, Department of Political Science, Utkal University, Bhubaneswar, Odisha, India
30. **Dr. K. Puspham**: D.Lit, Assistant Professor in Sociology, The Tamil Nadu Dr. Ambedkar Law University, Chennai
31. **Dr. S.K. Ramani, Assistant Professor (SG) in Sociology**, The Tamil Nadu Dr. Ambedkar Law University, Chennai

1

Issues and Challenges of Migrant Worker during National Lockdown: Indian Experience

Dr. Anji A & Dr. A. Ranjithkumar

Abstract

Migrant workers in every state in India lived in very poor conditions during national wide lockdown. All Indian states have failed to take action to provide timely food for migrant workers. We cannot deny that lockdown was the major reason to push factors of migrant workers to go to their native places to meet their basic needs like food. Migrant workers do not have enough money to travel to their hometowns. They walked long distances on foot and by-bicycle in a similar situation with their family members including children and aged people. In this context, the study seeks to discuss the issues and challenges of migrant workers during national lockdown.

Introduction

The world's biggest lockdown has forced migrants to walk hundreds of miles home in India, and they are faced many difficulties during the national lockout. With companies, factories, and workplaces shut down due to the lockdown imposed in the country, many migrant workers had to deal with the loss of basic needs, loss of income, food shortages and uncertainty about their future. Following this, many of them and their families went hungry. Millions of them then began walking back home, with no means of transport due to the lockdown. In response, the Central and State Governments took various measures to help them, and later arranged transport for them. Save Life Foundation said that from during national lock down from March 25 to May 31 there were at least 1,461 accidents over the course of the nationwide lockdown - from March 25 to May 31 - in which at least 750 people were killed, including 198 migrant workers. There were 1,390 who got injured, according to the data (Save Life Foundation: 2020). At the same time, there is no data available on the deaths and job losses among migrant workers due to the imposition of lockdown during Covid -19 pandemic said by the Government of India. The present study tries to discuss issues and challenges of migrant workers during national lock down in India.

Concept of Migration

Before looking at the problems of migrant workers, it is good to first look at the need for an understanding of migration. WHO said that Migration is "The movement of a person or a group of persons, either across an international border, or within a state. It is a population movement, encompassing any kind of movement of people, whatever its length, composition and causes; it includes migration of refugees, displaced persons, economic migrants, and persons moving for other purposes, including family reunification". John R Weeks defined as any permanent change in resident (Weeks 2008: 264). The migration involves the two aspects; 1. Changes of residence and 2. Crossing of a predefined administrative boundary and also it involves two areas namely place of origin and place of destination (IIPS : 2008). According to Demko, migration is the most complex component of population change (Sinha 2005:4.3). Goldscheides defined migration as any permanent change in residence. It involves detachments form the organization of activities one place and the movement of the total round of activities to another (Goldscheides 1971: 64).

The United Nations Multilingual Demographic Dictionary defines migration as "spatial mobility or geographic mobility is concerned with the quantitative aspects of moves made by individuals in geographic space. The distinguishing characteristic of **migration** is that it involves a change in usual place of residence and implies movement across an administrative boundary. The administrative unit left by the migrant is the place of origin or place of departure; the unit to which the migrant goes is the place of destination or place of arrival" (UN: 1956). Ram B. Bhagat rightly pointed out that Push factors like low income, low literacy, dependence on agriculture and high poverty are cited as some examples associated with place of origin. On the other hand, high income, high literacy, dominance of industries and services, are the pull factors associated with place of destination (Bhagat 2009:17).

The migration is important to policy makers and it may be considered as symptoms of basic social, economic, and political change. However migration influences mortality and fertility which are manipulating public policy. The concept of migration can be divided into two types namely internal and international migration. Internal migration is migration of persons within a home county and international migration takes place across international boundaries. Hence in this aspect, the present study discussed internal migration in India during national lockdown. Internal migration in India is primarily of two types: Long term Migration which results in the relocation of an individual or household, and Short term Migration involving back and forth movement between a source and destination.

The Census of India defines a "migrant by place of birth—as a person who is enumerated in a place (village or town), which is different from their place of birth. However, mig-rants by place of last residence provide a better account of the extent of internal migration. The concept of mobility or migration concerns the movement of persons from one place to another. A considerable part of this movement is incidental to carrying on the activities of daily life – commuting to and from the place of work, shopping, visiting, travel for business or pleasure, to name a few. However, they are to be distinguished from the type of mobility that involves a sustained or permanent residence in the place of destination. It is this latter type of mobility that is envisaged by the concept, migration (Census of India: 2011).

Bhagat said that there are three types of internal migration namely intra district, inter-district, and inter-state migration (Bhagat 2009:7). He also pointed out intra state migration and inter-state migration can be divided into four types such as rural to rural, rural to urban, urban to rural, and urban to urban (Bhagat 2009:10). The reasons for migrations are work and employment, business, education, marriage, moved after birth, and moved with households (Bhagat 2009:11). IIPS said that the reason for migration are marriage migration, labour migration or migration of people for work, employment etc., migration for prosperity, refugees migration arising due to political reasons, migration due to natural calamities, return migration, and brain-drain, migration of professional from developing to developed countries (IIPS:2008).

Covid-19 has spread around the world due to international migration which is closely related to internal migration. According to the World bank report 'COVID-19 Crisis Through a Migration Lens', nationwide lockdown in India due to COVID-19 has impacted nearly 40 million internal migrants. Around 60,000 moved from urban centers to rural areas of origin in the span of a few days. The magnitude of internal migration is about two-and-a-half times that of international migration. Internal migrants have faced issues in health services, food, cash transfer and other social programmes. They are vulnerable to the loss of employment and wages during an economic crisis. Lockdowns in labour camps and dormitories would increase the risk of contagion among migrant workers. The state boundaries became the sites of violent migrant-police encounters, as police resorted to beating migrants for having violated the lockdown orders. Thousands of them, without any means of transport left to their villages back on foot, dying of starvation, fatigue, and road accidents. Though, on May 1, 2020, the Central government introduced special Shramik trains to take urban migrants back to their villages, due to train cancellations and exorbitant fares, these special trains brought little relief to urban migrants (journalofindia:2020). But the government does care for rural migrant workers those who are working in the informal sectors. But the government was not paying attention to rural migrant workers working in the informal sector.

Internal Migration and Covid -19

Lock down was announced nationwide on March 24 for a period of 21 days. All state Boundaries were sealed and even district boundaries too, traffic was stopped, factories, shops, restaurants and all kinds of economic activities were closed, except for essential services. This proved to be a nightmare for hundreds of thousands of migrant workers who lost their livelihoods overnight and became homeless and helpless. The immediate challenges facing these migrant workers are related to food, shelter, loss of wages, fear of infection and anxiety. As a result, thousands of them began to flee from various cities to their native places. Many migrant workers lost their lives on the way due to hardship, hunger, accident and some committed suicide (Bhagat :2020).

No data have been maintained for internal migration during covid-19 and it means that the government does not care about migrant workers. According to the report on COVID-19 Crisis through a Migration Len, The lockdown in India has impacted the livelihoods of a large proportion of the country's nearly 40 million internal migrants. Around 50,000–60,000 moved from urban centers to rural areas of origin in the span of a few days. The government set up camps with basic provisions to provide shelter to these migrants in cities and districts of destination, transit, and origin.

This study seeks to understand what problems migrant workers face during the national lockdown and the migrant worker suffers from psychological problems, which is very dangerous for them. A study on COVID 19 pandemic: Mental health challenges of internal migrant workers of India written by Ranjana Choudhari (2020) and the study said that internal migrant workers suffer from high levels of anxiety and fear due to various concerns about COVID infections, and they need psycho-social support. the continued relocation of millions of migrant workers to their own villages is detrimental to mental health and Rural India in particular is likely to commit suicide in the future due to the high economic burden of unemployed migrant workers (Choudhari 2020:2).

The Migrant workers also face social isolation and mental challenges during the Covid-19 epidemic and they face malnutrition due to lack of access to nutritious food. The fact is that most migrant workers work in the informal sector and they are living in an unhygienic and polluted environment that can be vulnerable to health problems both physical and mental. Migrant workers work on construction sites, metro projects, quarries, and mines and highway projects live in hazardous environments and are affected by air and water pollution that can lead to kidney and lung disorders. Few case studies have been presented in this study to understand issues of migrant workers.

Case Study

Case -1

Ravi (name changed) aged 47 working as manager in a private company. His salary is Rs. 18500/- and he migrated Chennai from Tenkasi district of Tamil Nadu for his employment. After an unplanned lockdown by the government of India, the company directed all employees including Ravi also. Ravi and his friends approached the company for vehicle arrangement and the company has denied their request. He asked travel agents and too much money has been demanded which is more than his monthly earning salary. He decided to go to native place by walk and he walked more than six hundred Kilometers, nearly eight days he took for his journey. During his journey he faced physical and mental problems such as leg pain, back pain, headache, sleeping disorder, no proper food and water, and so on. After reaching his native, he faced nutrition problems and later a few days he took nutrition food which is made in house.

Case -2

In 2016 Meena (name changed) aged 36 started a tailoring shop in Vellore District of Tamil Nadu. Her husband passed away in 2015. After her husband's death, she has been maintaining his family expenditure for this purpose she migrated from rural to urban and she has three children and her mother in law also staying with them. Children are studying in school. Meena's income is nearly Rs.25, 000/ - per month from the tailoring shop. After lockdown she suffered a lot. Meena said that the lockdown made very traumatic changes in my business and also my family, and I never faced this kind of pathetic economic situation in past days". It is noted that she has borrowed money from her relatives to run the family. She has expressed that women facing economic shocks are more likely to take on high-risk work for their economic survival. Covid-19 is an additional burden of working women. It is observed that Migrant workers faced financial difficulties due to the national lockdown which also led to their health problems being affected.

Conclusion

The Supreme Court has received several letters and representations from different sections of society highlighting the problem of migrant workers and on May 26th 2020 the Supreme Court directed the union and state government to ensure the adequate transport arrangement, food and shelters are immediately to be provided by the Centre and State Governments free of costs. The most vulnerable and worst hit by the Covid-19 Pandemic Lockdown are the women, children and migrant workers like construction workers, painters, delivery boys, cooks, cleaners and factory workers etc. Because, lack of proper planning in handling the crisis of which is mentioned above groups puts a question mark on the performance of the government during Covid-19 Pandemic. This huge section of India's life force is being deprived of their rights as equal citizens. The suspension of trains which is being considered as the cheapest means of transportation forced migrants whose pockets were short of money and were more vulnerable to the virus due to the lack of hygienic accommodations to take the desperate measures to reach the safest place. Mismanagement by the both Centre and State governments left no option for these stranded women, children, and migrant workers etc., to use the life threatening measure. The unplanned declaration of national lockdown in the country made it very difficult for migrant workers to seek help.

National level lockdown has a great impact on the economic conditions of underdeveloped and developing countries. Lot of people in India have lost their jobs and have become unemployed and millions of migrant workers are forced to return to their villages after losing their jobs. Many migrant workers have lost their jobs and lost their way of life. In India from 29 April 2020, the migrant workers gradually began to return to their home states. Creating employment opportunities for returning workers is a challenge to the government. After the intervention of the court, the union and state governments arranged transport for migrant workers.

References

1. Anoop Khanna (2020): Impact of Migration of Labour Force due to Global COVID-19 Pandemic with Reference to India, Journal of Health Management, vol. 22(2), pp. 181–191.
2. Asha A Bhende and Tara Kanikar (1978): Principles of Populations Studies, Himalaya Publishing House, New Delhi.
3. Bhagat R. B (2009): Internal Migration in India: Are the Underclass More Mobile? Paper presented in the 26th IUSSP General Population Conference held in Marrakech, Morocco, 27 September- 2 October 2009.
4. Bhagat R.B. (2008) "Assessing the Measurement of Internal Migration in India", Asian and Pacific Migration Journal, Vol. 17, No. 1, pp. 91-102.
5. Bidita Dhar & Bhagat R. B. (2020): Return migration in India: internal and international dimensions, Migration and Development, DOI: 10.1080/21632324.2020.1809263.
6. Irudaya Rajan S et. al (2020): The COVID19 Pandemic and Internal Labour Migration in India: A 'Crisis of Mobility' Indian Society of Labour Economics, pp. 1021-1039.
7. Jacob S. SIEGEL and David A. Swanson (2004): The Methods and Materials of Demography, Elsevier Academic Press, Londan, UK.
8. John R Weeks (2008): Population: An Introduction to Concepts and Issues, Wadsworth Cengage Learning, Belmont, USA.
9. Ranjana Choudhari (2020): COVID 19 Pandemic: Mental health challenges of internal migrant workers of India, Asian Journal of Psychiatry, pp. 1-4.
10. Ranjithkumar A (2020): Rural and Urban Disparities of Scheduled Caste Population: A Study with Special Reference to Viluppuram District, Tamil Nadu, Journal of Social Science Research, Vol. 16, pp. 13-32.
11. Shakil Ahmed et. al. (2020): COVID-19 lockdown in India triggers a rapid rise in suicides due to the alcohol withdrawal symptoms: Evidence from media reports, International Journal of Social Psychiatry, Vol. 66, Iss.8, pp. 827-829.

2

Impact of Covid-19 among Migrant Women Workers in Dindigul District: An Analysis

M. Eswari

Women migrant workers face a higher risk of losing their livelihoods, having their labour and human rights violated and contracting Coronavirus. They are likely to work in the informal economy, especially domestic service and the care sector, with insecure contracts and no paid leave or ability to work from home. They are also more likely to be engaged in short-term, part-time work. Their jobs are generally excluded from contributory social insurance schemes, which mean limited or no social safety nets to compensate for lost income and limited or no access to healthcare and maternity protection.

For many of the 8.5 million women migrant domestic workers, the onset of the pandemic has led to dismissal from jobs, with their health and safety ignored and even violated. For live-in migrant workers, losing their jobs also means losing their place to live. The onset of travel restrictions has increased financial challenges and uncertainty, with many stranded far from home.

The economies of many countries around the world are sustained by the remittances sent home by women migrant workers. Remittances provide a lifeline for families and communities in their countries of origin, especially during times of crisis. Given the economic downturn caused by the impacts of Covid-19, women migrant workers are sending fewer remittances, further exacerbating the vulnerabilities of families that depend on this income.

The consequences of the Covid-19 pandemic on women migrant workers in situations of vulnerability are severe. Covid-19 could cause 25 million jobs to be lost globally, with women migrant workers particularly vulnerable. Due to the pandemic, 8.5 million women migrant domestic workers on insecure contracts are facing income loss and much greater risks of abuse and exploitation, particularly those who cannot return home owing to travel bans and border controls.

Objectives

- To study socio-economic status of women migrant workers.
- To study the reasons for women to migrate.
- To find the impact of Covid-19 among the respondents.

Study area

Dindigul District was selected as the study area. This study covers Aathoor block.

Sampling

Simple random sampling was used to select the sample. Totally 100 respondents were selected randomly as the sample from Athoor blocks. The respondents are rural women from the age group of 18 years and above.

Research design

A non-experimental descriptive research strategy has been chosen for this study as the most appropriate method to the objectives of the study.

Tools for Data Collection

A structured interview schedule was prepared. The interview schedule consist components like Personal details, socio-economic and legal status of the respondents. This interview schedule comprises both close ended and open ended questions.

Analysis and interpretation

The analyses are made using Statistical Package for Social Sciences (SPSS). Percentage table were prepared to analyze the data.

Data Analysis and Interpretation

Table 1: Distribution of the Respondents by Age

Sl. No.	*Age of the Respondents (In Years)*	*Number of Respondents*	*Percentage*
1.	Below 20 years	5	5
2.	21 - 30 years	20	20
3.	31 - 40 years	25	25
4.	41 - 50 years	38	38
5.	51- 60 years	12	12
	Total	**100**	100.0

Table 1 shows the age of the respondents, 38 percent of the respondents belong to 41 - 50 years, 25 percent of the respondents belong to 31 - 40 years, 20 percent are 21 - 30 years old, 12 percent belongs to 51 - 60 years and 5 percent of the respondents belongs below 20 years old.

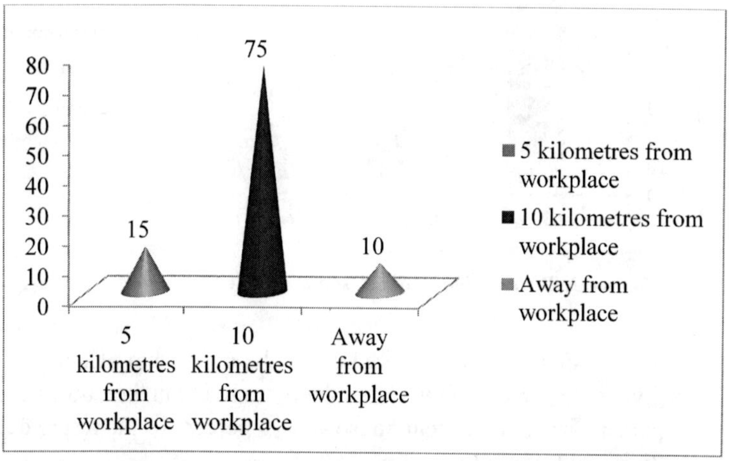

Figure 1: Distribution of the Respondents by working place to residence.

The present figure shows the residence of the respondents. 15 percent of the respondents are residing within 5 kilometres from the workplace, 75 percent of the respondents are residing within 10 km from the workplace. Only 10 percent of the respondents are residing away from the workplace.

Table 2: Distribution of the Respondents by Type of House

Sl.No.	*Type of house*	*Number of Respondents*	*Percentage*
1.	Hut	10	10
2.	Tiled	44	44
3.	Concrete	24	24
4.	Asbestos	22	22
	Total	**100**	**100.0**

The Table 2, the respondents were asked about the type of house, 44 percent of the respondents living in tiled house, 24 percent of the respondents are living in concrete house, 22 percent of the respondents are living in asbestos house and 10 percent of the respondents are living in Hut house.

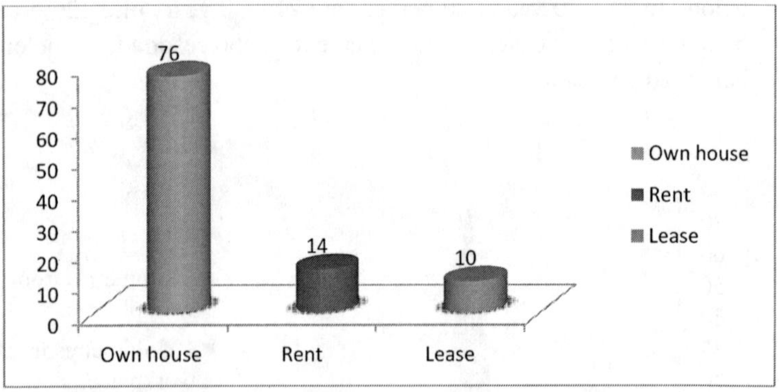

Figure 2: Distribution of the Respondents by Ownership of House.

The respondents were asked about the ownership of house they are living, 76 percent of the respondents are living in their own house, 14 percent are living in rent house and 10 percent of the respondents are living in lease house.

Table 3: Distribution of the Respondents by Marital Status

Sl.No.	*Marital Status*	*Number of Respondents*	*Percentage*
1.	Unmarried	08	08
2.	Married	71	71
3.	Separated	02	02
4.	Divorced	02	02
5.	Widow	17	17
	Total	**100**	**100.0**

The Table 3 discloses the marital status of the respondents. 71 percent of the respondents are married, 17 percent of the respondents are Widow, 8 percent of the respondents are Unmarried, each 2 percent of the respondents are separated from their house and divorced.

Table 4: Distribution of the Respondents by Educational Qualification

Sl.No.	*Educational Qualification*	*Number of Respondents*	*Percentage*
1.	Illiterate	38	8
2.	Primary school	25	25
3.	Secondary school	26	26
4.	Higher secondary school	04	04
5.	Under Graduate	03	03
6.	Post Graduate	02	02
7.	Diploma	02	02
	Total	**100**	**100.0**

The Table 4 discloses the educational qualification of the respondents. Among the 100 respondents, 38 percent of the respondents are illiterates, 26 percent of the respondents have completed their secondary education, 25 percent of the respondents have completed their primary school level, 4 percent of the respondents have completed their Higher Secondary school, 3 percent have UG holders and each 2 percent are Diploma holders and PG holders.

The Fig. 3 mentioned the occupational status of the respondents. Among the 100 respondents, 31 percent are private employee, 22 percent of the respondents are Coolies, 17 percent of the respondents are government employee, 18 percent of the respondents are seasonal worker, 12 percent are domestic workers.

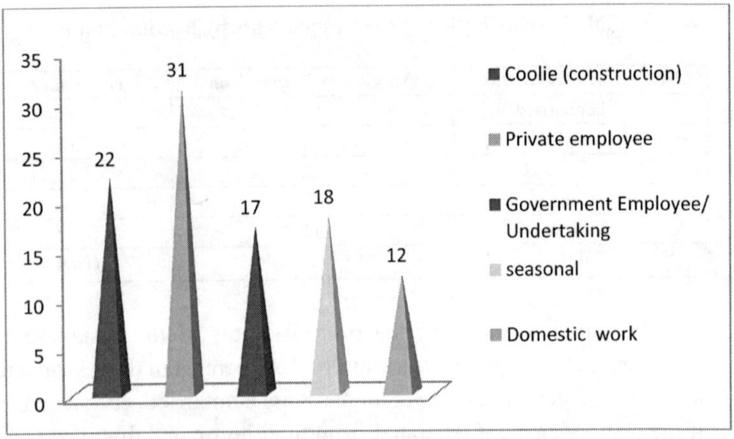

Figure 3: Distribution of the Respondents by Occupation.

Table 5: Distribution of the Respondents by Occupation of Husband

Sl.No.	*Occupation of Husband*	*Number of Respondents*	*Percentage*
1.	Coolie	30	30
2.	MNREGA	12	12
3.	Private employee	22	22
4.	Government Employee/ Undertaking	10	10
5.	Self employment	12	12
6.	Not applicable	14	14
	Total	**100**	**100.0**

The Table 5 mentioned the occupational status of the respondent's husbands. 36 percent of the respondents husbands are Coolies, 22 percent of the respondent's husbands are working in Private employees, each 12 percent of the respondent's husbands are self-employee and working in MNREGA, 14 percent of the respondents are unmarried, Separated, Divorced and Widows and 10 percent of the respondents husbands are Government Employees.

The following Table 6 shows the monthly income of the respondent's family. 64 percent of the respondents earn less than Rs. 2000, 19 percent in not applicable like unmarried, widow and separated. 11.0 percent have earned Rs. 2001 – 3000, each 1.4 percent of the respondents have earned Rs. 3001 – 4000, earned Rs. 4001 – 2 percent earned Rs. 5000 and 5001 and above.

Table 6: Distribution of the Respondents by Monthly Income

Sl. No.	*Monthly Income(In Rupees)*	*Number of Respondents*	*Percentage*
1.	Below 2000	64	64
2.	2001 - 3000	11	11
3.	3001 - 4000	02	02
4.	4001 - 5000	02	02
5.	5001 and Above	02	02
6.	Not Applicable	19	19
	Total	**100**	**100.0**

Tabl 7: Distribution of the Respondents by Livestock at Home

Sl.No.	*Live stock at Home*	*Number of Respondents*	*Percentage*
1.	Have	22	22
2.	Do not have	78	78
	Total	**100**	**100.0**

The Table 7 indicates that the livestock at home, 78 percent of the respondents have livestock like Cow, Goat and hen in their house and 22 percent of the respondents do not have any livestock in their house.

Table 8: Distribution of the Respondents by Type of Family

Sl.No.	*Type of Family*	*Number of Respondents*	*Percentage*
1.	Joint Family	34	34
2.	Nuclear Family	66	66
	Total	**100**	**100.0**

The above table indicates that the type of family of the respondents, 66 percent of the respondents are in Nuclear family and 34 percent of the respondents are in Joint family.

The following Fig. 4 indicates that the family members of the respondents, 64 percent of the respondents said they have four members in their family. 18 percent of the respondents have five members in family, 9 percent of the respondents have six members, 4 percent of the respondents have seven members and 5 percent of the respondents have eight and above members in their family.

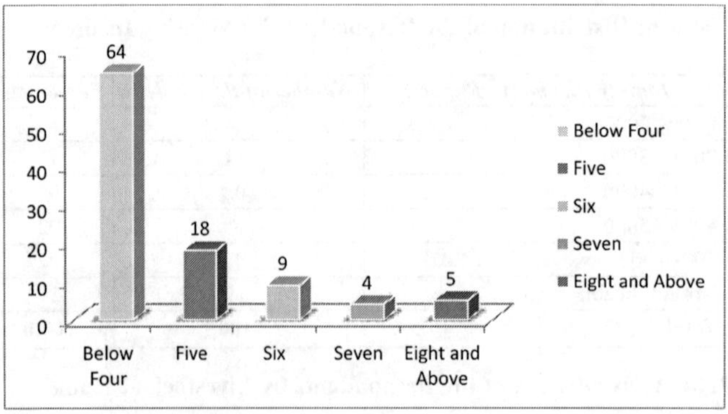

Figure 4: Distribution of the Respondents by Number of Family Members.

Table 9: Distribution of the respondents by Reasons for Migration

Sl.No.	*Reason for migration*	*Number of Respondents*		*Percentage*
		Yes	*No*	
1.	Unemployment	37	18	100
2.	Poverty	26	27	100
3.	Earn Income	52	48	100
4.	Other	29	71	100
	Total	**100**	**100**	**100.0**

The Table 9 indicate that, 52 percent of the respondents said that they have migrated for earn income for support of the family 37 percent of respondents said that due to unemployment and 26 percent of the respondents said that they have migrated for poverty reduction.

Table 10: Distribution of the respondents by Negative Impact of Covid-19

Sl. No.	*Impact*	*Number of Respondents*		*Percentage*
		Yes	*No*	
1.	Loss of livelihoods/ Poor and inhuman living condition	82	18	100
2.	Reduced payment/ Lack of work	73	27	100
3.	Stresses on care and domestic work	72	28	100
4.	Limited freedom of movement	29	71	100
5.	Lack of social protection and health care	62	38	100
6.	Domestic violence	56	44	100
7.	Feeling of Inferiority as unemployment	73	27	100
8.	lack of Finance for children's education	57	43	100

The Table 10 shows that, impact of Coivd-19 among women migrant workers, 82 percent of the respondents suffered from loss of livelihood/ poor and inhuman living condition during the pandemic due to pandemic loss their income, 73 percent of the respondents felt that they lost their job and reduced their payment also, 72 percent of the respondents suffered from stress on care and domestic work during the pandemic, 22 percent of the respondents said that limited freedom of movement during the pandemic, 62 percent of the respondents said that they los their job due to lack of social protection and healthcare, 56 percent of the respondents suffered from domestic violence due to loss of work/poverty and 73 percent of the respondents felt that inferiority as unemployment and 57 percent of the respondents suffered lack of finance crises for children's education.

Major findings

Less than fifty (38 percent) of the respondents belong to 41 - 50 years followed by 25 percent of the respondents belong to 31 - 40 years. Most of the (75 percent) of the respondents are residing within 10 km from the workplace. 15 percent of the respondents are residing within 5 kilometres, only 10 percent of the respondents are residing away from the workplace. Nearly fifty (44 percent) of the respondents living in tiled house followed by 24 percent of the respondents are living in concrete house.

Most (76 percent) of the respondents are living in their own house followed by 14 percent are living in rent house. Most (71 percent) of the respondents are married followed by 17 percent of the respondents are Widow. 38 percent of the respondents are illiterates followed by 26 percent of the respondents have completed their secondary education and 25 percent of the respondents have completed their primary school level.

Less than fifty (31 percent) of the respondents are private employee followed by 22 percent of the respondents are Coolies and 17 percent of the respondents are government employee. 36 percent of the respondents husbands are Coolies and 22 percent of the respondent's husbands are working in Private employees.

More than fifty (64 percent) of the respondents earn less than Rs. 2000 followed by 19 percent have not earned any income. Most (78 percent) of the respondents have livestock like Cow, Goat and hen in their house and 22 percent of the respondents do not have any livestock in their house. 66 percent of the respondents are in Nuclear family and 34 percent of the respondents are in Joint family.

Fifty (52 percent) of the respondents said that they have migrated for earn income for support of the family followed by 37 percent of respondents said that due to unemployment and 26 percent of the respondents said that they have migrated for poverty reduction.

Majority (82 percent) of the respondents suffered from loss of livelihood/ poor and inhuman living condition during the pandemic due to pandemic loss their income, most (73 percent) of the respondents felt that they lost their job and reduced their payment also, 72 percent of the respondents suffered from stress on care and domestic work during the pandemic, 22 percent of the respondents said that limited freedom of movement during the pandemic, 62 percent of the respondents said that loss their job due to lack of social protection and healthcare, 56 percent of the respondents suffered from domestic violence due to loss of work/poverty, 73 percent of the respondents felt that inferiority as unemployment and 57 percent of the respondents suffered lack of finance crises for children's education.

Conclusion

Overall, socio-economic condition of the women migrant workers is not good. The reason is that they face problems both at home and work place during the pandemic. At home they perform all kinds of domestic work without remuneration whereas at work place they have a very heavy work load with less remuneration during the lockdown. Because they belonged to the economically underprivileged group and most of them live in rural areas. The working conditions of migrant women workers are appalling with long working hours and absence of job security. Because there is variation in their wage structure and their wage level is very low as compared to the other workers. On the other hand, they are bound to do this work due to low education and poor financial background.

Often, they are considered as traditional and low skilled workers according to the requirement of the market. This again lowers their wage. They also have to take care of their children at home and at the same time they have to work to support their families. In fact, they are doing double the amount of work and paid less than half when compared with their male counterparts. The women engaged in outside work face such difficulties such as sexual harassment and abusive language.

Maternity benefits and childcare, which are crucial for their mental and physical well being, are denied, because of which they often lose their jobs. Pension and a minimum insurance cover for unorganised sector workers remain pipe dreams. The real challenge is to ensure that the labour laws and social security schemes that exist for the diminishing number of workers in the organised sector are extended to the 90 percent workers in the unorganised sector and then actually implemented. It urgently needs social policy to protect the rights of women migrant workers in the newer as well as older forms of work in the unorganised sector.

References

- Conell, John (1984). Status on subjugal women Migration and Development in the South Pacific. International Migration Review, 18 (4): 966.
- Devi, Lakshmi (1998). "Status of Immigrant Women Workers from India to the Middle East", in Prakash, B. A (ed.), op.cit, pp. 57-74.
- Dey Soumi (2014). The Situation in Contractual Work at Domestic Sphere: A Study of the Paid Female Domestic Workers of Howrah, West Bengal, India: International Research Journal of Social Sciences, Vol. 3(7), 36-42, July (2014).
- Gathia, Joseph A. 1983. Women and child workers in the unorganised sector. New Delhi: Concept Publishers.
- Geetha, K.T. (2010). Women in Informal Sector-A Case Study, IJBEMR, Volume- 1, Issue-2, December 2010, pp. 23-26.
- Kamala Kanta Mohapatra (2012). "Women Workers in Informal Sector in India: Understanding the Occupational Vulnerability", International Journal of Humanities and Social Science, Vol. 2, No. 21; November.
- Tripathi, S. N. and Das, S. Informal Women Labourer in India. Discovery Publishing House, New Delhi, 1991.

3

Downswing of the Tea Industry in Assam and the Plight of the Labourers Amid Covid-19 Pandemic (2020)

Swapna Sikha Das

Abstract

Due to Covid-19, the work sector is being profoundly affected throughout the nation and has brought a threat to public health, the economic and social setting the long-term livelihoods and wellbeing of millions. The pandemic has highlighted the real working and living conditions of labour forces. They are struggling to survive and need protection of their rights like never before. The tea industry in India with which is an important commercial cultivation in India is in a downswing. Corona virus in India is threatening worldwide tea supplies. Many gardens are in deep trouble and fear to loss a enormous amount of crops. Growing bushes, low productivity, high production cost, low quality, low market demand, lack of economic support for small growers, and repeated falling of price in both domestic and international markets, etc. is witness by the industry during the pandemic.In Assam, the gardens remained completely barred and the industry is hit hard during the weeks of lockdown, owing to Corona virus pandemic. The industry is extremely vulnerable to disruptions and this Covid-19 now also threatens to exacerbate the conditions of vulnerable labour population of tea gardens with disastrous circumstances and impacts. Many tea garden labours already suffer from weak immune systems and suffer from various infectious diseases. These labours are unable to access clean water or adequate housing and have much less hygiene maintained. It is observed that these gardens of Assam suffer from poor quality and discontinuous water supply, sanitation, electricity and most live in overcrowded housing quarters. This paper is an attempt to have an overview of the present condition of the Assam's tea garden industry and the labours associated in these gardens during the pandemic of Covid-19 and providing some suggestions for making the situation better and to throw light for further development of the overall industry.

Keywords: *Tea Industry, Tea Garden Labourers, Covid-19, Assam.*

Tea Industry of Assam and its Labour Population

According to Industries and Commerce Department, Assam; Tea industry in India is the oldest industry; about 180 years old. It is an integral part of the Indian economy. The Indian tea industry employs around 1.2 million permanent workers as tea garden labours (Katakee, 2020). In North East India, the main regions are the Brahmaputra valley and the Barak Valley in Assam, Darjeeling, Dooars and Terai regions in West Bengal and Tripura, are the largest tea growing region in the world (KKHSOU, 2018-19). The Assam tea industry has 800 tea gardens with over 10 lakh workers. In 2019, Assam produced 1390 million Kgs of tea and exported 250 million Kgs of tea around the globe (Tea Association of India, 2020). The total area under tea in Assam is 312,210 hectares. India's largest tea research centre managed by the Tea Research Association is situated in Jorhat, Assam, started in 1911 at Tocklai (Jorhat).

Tea gardens in Assam have been providing job opportunities to a large section of the people since ancient time as it is a labour intensive industry. The tea garden labourers come under the Plantations Labour Act and Rules,1951 and under the Act it is mandatory to make effective arrangements by the managements for sufficient supply of drinking water, a sufficient number of latrines and urinals, Medical facilities, Canteens, Crèches, Recreational facilities, Educational facilities, Housing facilities under the provision of this Act (Labour & Welfare Department, Assam). But it is very unfortunate to know that, the labourers in the tea gardens of Assam are the most exploited class in the organised sector of economy. Labourers on tea plantations are denied their rights to a living wage and decent working and living conditions (Benarji & Robin, 2019). Though tea is popular all over the world, very few know about the exploitations taking place inside the tea industry.

Tea garden labourers are often found in miserable conditions with poor socio-economic problems from generations. The causes of such conditions are deeply rooted in the history and development of the Indian tea industry, creating inequality of power between the women and men and thus leading to poverty and deprivation. In most gardens, labourers do not have access to basic necessities of life. Women labourers are the lowest paid group among the workforce and trade union corruption in the gardens has develop deprivation and denial among them. Labours most often suffer from diseases such as diarrhoea, jaundice, eye problem, asthma, coughs, tuberculosis,typhoid and allergic reactions to dust and chemical. And this pandemic at present has bought a bleak future staring at them.

1. Tea Industry in Assam amid Covid-19

The Assam tea industry, one of the biggest industry in the world has suffered a major hinder due to the Covid-19 crisis. It has shown the way to a financial crunch for the industry.With export and import activity restrictions in the tea market, managements are bound to undertake emergency comeback measures to avoid the spread of Covid-19 in such areas. Tea plantation in Assam is a seasonal activity. The peak seasons for tea leaves plucking and production in Assam is from mid-March to late November, due to which there is high risk of Covid-19 transmission due to the high concentration of people on the estates and in the factories. As the plucking has got disrupted amidst the lockdown all over the nation, it has lead to overgrown the tea leaves which are of no use for harvesting. At present, the industry has incurred a loss of around Rs 1,059 crore in revenue. The total revenue loss of Assam tea industry due to lockdown = 80 million kgs × Rs 152.26 per kg = Rs. 1,218 crore (Tea Board of India, 2020). The price for Assam tea has already gone up by Rs 70 which used to be sold at Rs 150 per kg and now it is being sold at Rs 210 to 220 per kg (Das, 2020). The loss of Assam tea is a huge chunk of the total loss in the entire industry of India.

From April (2020) based on the guidelines of the *Ministry of Home Affairs*, India; tea gardens of Assam have started carrying out tea production and marketing again, but the lockdown of pandemic has impacted tea producers and planters livelihoods significantly. The Assam government allowed 50 percent of its workforce for factory operations in the gradens with proper sanitisation measures and social distancing guidelines. At present, the entire labour force is employed on a rotation basis. Crop losses continue because of the limitations on the workforce in the gardens. Due to prolonged lockdown the plantations have to be skiffed (removal of overgrown tea leaves). Skiffing operation increase extra cost and will require two to three weeks for recovery to bring the tea bushes into a proper condition. The present circumstances has resulted in high prices of green leaf and fluctuating supplies for the production-ready factories (Singh, 2020). Huge economic loss and danger in the livelihood of lakhs of labourers is witnessed in this situation. Another major problem is with migration of people from different parts of India due to the Pandemic. In some cases, labourers who have returned back to their own place or who have low immunity have been tested positive in tea garden areas. Now the tea industry cannot afford to close the gardens again, so the Tea Associations are trying hard for implementing all measures strictly (Tea Association of India, Assam branch).

Transportation cut off and the closing down of the tea auction caused restrain to the domestic supply to the other states and the deficit in the market and the failure of proper execution system to pass raw bushes from the gardens to the processing centers and factories to the markets have left the industry towards an unsecured destiny (Business & Human Rights Resource Centre, 2020). Moreover, at present the new damages caused by the floods in different parts of Assam, the tea industry is witnessing a severe decline in production and marketing, making the lives of labourers more pathetic.

2. Plight of the Tea Garden Labourers of Assam due to lockdown amid Covid-19

For all the migrant labourers and other workers the Covid-19 pandemic and lockdown has unleashed an unprecedented threat to their life. The plight of migrant workers and labourers is witnessed during the lockdown as they are struggling to make their ends meet. In the lockdown period, one portion of people are staying at home safely and has the opportunity to work from home with proper digital facilities, while another section of the country is without proper food, water, home and sanitation and travelling days and long distances to reach the safety of their own place and home from another place.

It is notable that tea garden labourers in Assam and other parts of the nation have been living in highly deprived conditions that include unfair wages, inadequate water and sanitation facilities and poor education and healthcare facilities. They are far away from the mainstream society. These labourers in tea gardens are fully dependent on tea garden from generations and if in any circumstances the gardens gets close they cannot survive. Half of the workforce in the garden constitutes the women class(nearly 60%) and they are the ones primarily engaged in the indispensable work of leaf plucking and other factory works. Workers earn an illegally low daily wage of Rs. 167 per day (Sen, 2020). Now the wages have been further minimised by the management due to the Corona pandemic and lockdown happening, being aware of the prevailing life conditions of the labourers inside the tea gardens, we can make out that the tea garden labourers do not have enough savings for basic needs because of their low wage. It has been found that the tea garden managements had not paid any wages during the total lockdown period. It is at present felt that state government is lacking political upholding of the fundamental right to life of the tea garden workers. Now that the whole system has slow down, the trade unions bodies need support from the central and state government to secure the labourers during this indefinite pandemic period. The tea management authority are ignorant towards supporting and helping the labourers in this time of want. One reason that has pushed the tea labourers across the regions back to work is hunger and poverty. Tea garden workers with no other means of survival made workers fear for their livelihoods in this pandemic.

The Tea Board continues to look at the plantation crisis purely on the marketing ends and most of the times fail to fulfill its regulatory role as enshrined in the Tea Act, 1953. The Tea Board has been ignoring the wages and provident funds. In unparalleled times like this, government is trying to ensure that labourers are paid full during the lockdown. In this Pandemic, Assam government has announced a 20 percent bonus for all those workers who are working in Assam Tea Corporation gardens, but the tea companies have been maintaining that they would be able to give only 8.33 percent as bonus due to the deepening financial crisis in the tea sector (Northeast Live, 2020).

Objectives

(i) To know the current status of tea industry in Assam in view of the Covid-19 crisis.

(ii) To examine the socio-economic condition of the tea garden labourers in the time of Covid-19 pandemic.

(iii) To suggest necessary steps towards the tea garden industry and its labourers for their sustainable safeguard amid Covid-19.

Methodology

The study is based on the secondary data. Data are collected from e-newspaper, blogs, government reports, articles, etc.

Observation

When observed, it is very disappointing that the labourers in some part of Assam repeatedly alleged that the authority of the tea estate has not paid full wages to the labourers despite the Central Government issued a direction in the matter. So, although the Assam government has made specific orders for quick payment of wages and necessary facilities, demands are raised by different labourers' union in several tea gardens because labourers are not being paid their wages and supplied with rations by their managements. The labourers in the tea gardens are in dire circumstances and facing extreme poverty. Thousands of tea plantation labours in north-eastern state of Assam protested at the end of April 2020, demanding payment of unpaid wages during the Corona virus lockdown (Talwar, 2020). Labourers in some tea estates regions are complaining that they have not received their wages, despite government guidelines that they should be paid in full during the lockdown period.

In this pandemic and during the nationwide lockdown happening from March 24th, 2020, the supply of daily groceries and drinking water to the tea estates had been interrupted. Moreover, the hospitals were also closed down totally, no doctors were available and treatment was not possible. The conditions of children,women in the gardens were most pathetic. The labourers have huge account of unpaid bonus and wages. Electricity facilities are been disrupted as huge bills are pending.

The pandemic is a huge health risk to the labour population, as it does all over the world. Since screening rates are still limited in some regions and most importantly no vaccine is there, it could come at the irretrievable cost of human life.

Recommendation to fight the consequences of Covid-19

(a) As the tea industry is facing financial difficulties due to poor production and marketing throughout the pandemic, the government has to and must support tea companies for their smooth running and ensure that labourers are living a safe and healthy life during this difficult period within the gardens.

(b) Provision for living wages during the continued difficult period, donating sanitizers, PPE kits, clean water and soap, neccesary rations and increased Covid screening test and basic healthcare facilities are some of the very basic measures that need to be taken up to keep labourers safe from the virus spread.

(c) Management should actively engage in forming voluntary health teams and carrying out massive awareness programmes to educate the workers to take preventive measures.

(d) Social distancing has to be made mandatory among the work force and protective gear are to be used by tea garden managements.

(e) There should be launce of new and better technology to increase productivity, reducing cost and ensuring quality competitiveness of tea after the pandemic crisis gets over.

(f) Management should continue to provide ration packs to the families in the tea garden areas.

(g) The government officials should make arrangements to get medical supplies for the labourer in the gardens.

(h) The surroundings and households have to be sprayed with disinfectants. And the labourers living in the small kutcha houses provided by tea garden management should be less crowded.

Conclusion

The 2020 year has been challenging for consumers, producers, and businesses across the globe. So, now there is urgent need to control the spread of the virus and protect the lives of the nation so that together we can emerge strong and build the economy of the nation together. It is now necessary to focus on '*Lastest Transformation and Renew Strategies*' to build their resilience and ensure lasting recovery. Efforts to address the various crises must be continued.

References

- Banerji, S., Willoughby, R., & Nandy, A. (2019). *Addressing the human cost of Assam tea: An agenda for change to respect, protect and fulfil human rights on Assam tea plantations*. Oxford: Oxfam GB for Oxfam International.
- Borkokoty, A. (2020, June 15). Covid-19 deepens existential crisis for Assam tea sector; stiff competition, rising costs and diminishing prices threaten 180-year-old industry [Web log post]. Retrieved July 28, 2020, from https://www.firstpost.com/india/covid-19-deepens-existential-crisis-for-assam-tea-sector-stiff-competition-rising-costs-and-diminishing-prices-threaten-180-year-old-industry-8484361.html?cv=1
- Das, A. (2020, June 1). How has Covid-19 impacted Assam's tea industry? *Times Now News*.
- *Impact of Covid-19 Emergency response in tea supply chain*. (2020). Retrieved from https://www.idhsustainabletrade.com/impact-of-covid-19-in-tea/?cv=1.
- Nagar, A. (2020, April 8). Indian Tea Plantation Workers Look to the World Bank to Prevent a Coronavirus Disaster. *The Diplomate*.
- Dowerah, S. S. (2012). Health Security Facilities Among the Tea Garden Labourers: A Myth or Reality: A Study on the Tea Gardens of Dibrugarh District, Assam. *International Journal of Scientific Research, 2*(12), 522-523. doi:10.15373/22778179/dec2013/166.https://labour.assam.gov.in/portlets/plantation-workers?cv=1

- Das, M. (2020, June 03). First flush gone in lockdown, Bengal and Assam tea industries face Rs 2,100 cr loss. Retrieved August 16, 2020, from https://theprint.in/india/first-flush-gone-in-lockdown-bengal-and-assam-tea-industries-face-rs-2100-cr-loss/434344/
- Katakee, N. (2020, June 24). Tea Workers in a Tough Spot [Web log post]. Retrieved August 14, 2020, from https://www.oxfamindia.org/blog/tea-workers-tough-spot
- Karmakar, R. (2020, April 15). Assam tea group pegs Covid-19 lockdown losses at Rs. 1,218 crore. *The Hindu*. https://www.thehindu.com/news/national/other-states/assam-tea-group-pegs-covid-19-lockdown-losses-at-1218-crore/article31347920.ece
- K. (2020, April 15). "Markets closed, no work or money at home": How the Covid-19 lockdown is affecting tea garden workers in West Bengal. *Adivasi Resurgence*. Retrieved August 14, 2020, from http://www.adivasiresurgence.com/markets-closed-no-work-or-money-at-home-how-the-covid-19-lockdown-is-affecting-tea-garden-workers-in-west-bengal/
- Nag, C. B. (2019, September 13). Adivasis and the Indian State: Abysmal wages, ineffective labour unions leave tribal tea garden workers high and dry. *First Post*. Retrieved August 14, 2020, from https://www.firstpost.com/india/adivasis-and-the-indian-state-abysmal-wages-ineffective-labour-unions-leave-tribal-tea-garden-workers-high-and-dry-7331001.html
- Tea labourers. (2020, May 12). Retrieved August 14, 2020, from https://bhrpc.wordpress.com/tag/tea-labourers.
- Sen, S. (2020, May 11). Covid-19 Has Pushed India's Already Suffering Tea Plantation Workers into Deeper Crisis. *The Wire*. doi:https://thewire.in/labour/covid-19-lockdown-tea-workers-labour
- Saikia, S., Misra, S., & Mishra, B. (n.d.). *Tea Garden Labours and Their Living Conditions: A study on Sarusarai Tea Garden of Jorhat District of Assam*. Retrieved fromhttp://www.internationalseminar.org/XV_AIS/TS%205B/8.%20Mrs.%20Sangeeta%20Saikia.pdf?cv=1
- Talwar, S. (2020, May 14). SC Seeks Govt.'s Response On Challenge To Non-Payment Of Wages To Tea Garden Workers During COVID Lockdown. Retrieved July 28, 2020, from https://www.livelaw.in/top-stories/sc-seeks-govts-response-on-challenge-to-non-payment-of-wages-to-tea-garden-workers-during-covid-lockdown-156733
- Singh, B. (2020, April 29). Covid-19: Complete lockdown hits tea industry hard in Assam. Https://economictimes.indiatimes.com/news/politics-and-nation/covid-19-complete-lockdown-hits-tea-industry-hard-in-assam/articleshow/75437962.cms?utm_source=contentofinterest&utm_medium=text&utm_campaign=cppst. *Economic Times*.

- Pandemic & Flood: Assam Tea Industry Sees 48.32% Decline in Production. (2020, July 13). *Guwahati Plus*.Retrived from -https://www.guwahatiplus.com/daily-news/pandemic-flood-assam-tea-industry-sees-48-32-decline-in-production
- Parkin, B., & Terazono, E. (2020, April 15). The Next Covid-19 Casualty May Be a Nice Cuppa. Retrieved August 16, 2020, from https://www.ozy.com/the-new-and-the-next/the-next-covid-19-casualty-may-be-a-nice-cuppa/306375/?utm_source=OZY
- https://industries.assam.gov.in/portlet-innerpage/about-tea-industries

4

The Impact of Covid-19 on Kerala Economy

Dr. Remmiya Rajan P.

Abstract

The Covid-19 pandemic is creating a frightening challenge for the world economy. The impact of the catastrophe is expected to severely curtail the economic growth rate of the Kerala economy. It is hurting the livelihoods of defenceless groups, the poor, the informal sector and the micro, small and average sectors. The state government must encounter the challenges of unprecedented decline in labour market, income and production coupled with brutal deficits in its revenues. It is Government's immediate main concern to plan a strategy for economic recovery without any interruption.

Keywords: *Impact, Pandemic Covid-19, Kerala Economy, Economic growth.*

Introduction

Kerala has placed in the 10th position among largest economy in India (Ministry of Statistics and Programme Implementation, 2019). Kerala economy was subjugated by service sector. Kerala's is story of amazing success in the sphere of social development, tarnished by a lethargic industrial development that has braced the state to the middle rungs of the inter-State income-ladder. Covid-19 is having an irresistible effect on the economy. It has affected human life and employment frequently among the defenceless groups. The impact of the Covid-19 pandemic is creating a frightening challenge for the world economy. It is hurting the livelihoods of defenceless groups, the poor, the informal sector and the micro, small and average sectors. The Covid-19 catastrophe is expected to severely curtail the economic growth rate of the Kerala economy. Kerala's GSDP was about rupees 9.78 trillion in 2020-21 (Kerala Budget Analysis, 2020-21). It has embellished all sectors of the economy and has dealt with a shock which could be observed from the Table 1.

Table 1: Loss in different sectors in Kerala due to lockdown

Sectors	*Percentage of loss in first Phase*	*Percentage of loss in second Phase*	*Percentage of loss in third Phase*
Agriculture	74	55	47
Industry	88	82	71
Service	79	69	58

Source: Kerala State Planning Board 2020.

The table reveals that there is a heavy forfeiture in different sectors due to Covid-19 and lockdown, so it is pertinent to study the problem in detail.

Rationale of the study

As Covid-19 remains to cause pandemonium on markets throughout the world, the impact of the virus will have on the economy of a state like Kerala in days to come could be mightier than one could twig. Veterans in the sector of finance are saying that the virus is all set to break the back of a number of sectors that bring core revenue to the state and there by push Kerala further into economic stagnations, the likes of which has not been seen in recent times. The Kerala State Planning Board has arranged a report that gauge the pandemic loss which reported estimated a loss of about Rs 80,000 crore in gross value added (GVA) to the Kerala economy in Q1 of 2020 (April - June) (Kerala Budget Analysis, 2020-21).

Objectives of the study

1. To analyse the effect of Covid-19 on Agriculture sector
2. To analyse the effect of Covid-19 on Industrial sector

3. To analyse the effect of Covid-19 on Service sector
    (a) To analyse the effect of Covid-19 on Tourism and Hospitality industry
    (b) To analyse the effect of Covid-19 on Education
    (c) To analyse the effect of Remittances due to migrant returnees
4. To analyse the government package to overcome Covid-19

Methodology of the study

The collected data from *Secondary Source* such as *Times of India, Hindu* etc. *Descriptive Analysis* was used to demonstrate the extent of effect on the economy.

Analysis and interpretation

1. *To analyse the effect of Covid-19 on Agriculture sector:* Even though the primary sector has been contributing the Gross Domestic Product (GDP) in a deteriorating manner the Lockdown has gone downhill the situation. The agriculture sector in Kerala has been facing challenges with regard to its developments. Agriculture sector take part the major role in providing food, nutrition and livelihood to the public.

Covid-19 has drastically brought upshot on total losses in agriculture crop husbandry including plantation crops are estimated to be Rs 1,570.75 crore in March and April 2020 (Kerala State Planning Board 2020). The agricultural labourers whose wage has being estimated to be about Rs 200.30 crore (Economic Times, 2020)) but now it is showing a decline graph due to Covid-19, will lead a shrink in production sector which will be crucial to state because globally job losses are being reported in every second, we have to care about that an ample portion of its migrant workers could come back to the state. It is a decisive problem to the state that there will be more mouths to feed, and the state take advance preparation to feed everyone. Kerala had set up a special scheme to ensure its food security; 'Subhiksha Keralam' is being visualised as a massive people's campaign to attain self-sufficiency in food production. The major aims of the programme are to make farmers financially sound, keep interest among youngsters towards farming and rehabilitating the returned migrants by providing new vision towards the scope of agriculture in modernised future.

2. To analyse the effect of Covid-19 on Industrial sector: The contribution of manufacturing together with construction sectors is about 27%. (Ministry of Commerce and Industry 2019) Kerala has large number of small scale industries; unfortunately all are stagnant condition since the produced items are not sold due to Covid-19 constraint. The small scale enterprises come in the manufacturing, trade and service sectors together contribute a sizable amount to the SDP and provide job opportunity to many people. There will be a problem of working capital in future, because in pandemic period the working capital were used to provide wages to the labour class instead of keeping it for future production. To overcome these type of crises occur in the small scale industries due to corona, the banks have announced moratorium for repayment; moreover the government have to introduce some special schemes for the welfare of small scale industries by providing financial aid to preserve the industry sector.

3. To analyse the effect of Covid-19 on service sector

(a) *To analyse the effect of Covid-19 on Tourism and Hospitality industry:* Tourism sector of Kerala underwrites almost 10 percent of the State Domestic Product (SDP), which has been the worst hit sector (decreased down to 2%) since 2018 because of the greatest victim of the two floods occurred in the last two consecutive years; and also the outbreak of Nipah virus. Government has reported a loss of US$ 300 million in the domestic tourism of the country. Kerala has generated 45000 crores from tourism in the last year. The impact of Covid-19 has been very high on our tourism our losses would amount to Rs. 20,000 crore (Kerala State Planning Board, 2020) this year. Around 38,000 foreign tourists were in the state when the first lockdown was announced, to cancel village tours of around 2800 foreign tourists and 1220 domestic tourists after the crisis started. This loss alone has cost us nearly 45 lakh. Kerala tourism industry has demanded a revival package from center and state government. In order to set back the tourism sector, the government has planned to conduct five levels meeting with SLBC (State Level Bankers Company) to provide the financial support. Hospitality Sectors will be the hardest hit. The last five months while the hotels are shuthoteliers anticipate the following months might be tough for the hospitality industry with no definite vision of recovery. It is time that the government realises the involvement of the hotel industry, predominantly heritage hotels, not only to the GDP, but also to employment. The consequences of this pandemic disease are visible in Kerala as many of the hotels are temporarily shut down others are not able to find sufficient fund for their daily essential functions. The segment of hotels and restaurants which depend on the tourism sector are the real victims of the Covid-19. To overcome the situation government has planned to invite the Kerala migrant executives and workers of IT and Management companies and provide resorts to 'work at home' in an enjoyable manner.

(b) *To analyse the effect of Covid-19 on Education:* Kerala has taken special care to develop an education system that is inclusive and universally accessible. The state has achieved a zero dropout rate, though with a few exceptions in some pockets of tribal population. Kerala still requires some serious interventions to enhance academic quality at school as well as in higher education levels, to achieve universal standard. Unfortunately the structure of schooling and learning was crucially affected by the shutting down all the educational institutions temporarily as a measure to prevent the spread of Covid-19. Government of India is looking at the outlook of tumbling up to 20 percent of the arranged syllabus to make up for the lost school days and ensure that the academic year ends on time in schools. The online learning system effected poor students since they are unable to access online learning facilities like internet, computer, mobile phone etc. Only a handful of private schools could adopt online teaching methods. Government of Kerala is telecasting video classes for the school students in an organised manner during class hours. Some schools provide opportunity to students to interact their teachers to clear doubts in the same day through online, unfortunately very less students only can able to access these opportunity because of the lack of online learning facility. The students, in addition to the missed opportunities for learning, no longer have access to healthy meals during this time and are subject to economic and social stress. To avoid this government take care to provide the mid-day meal kit to students home, but it is progressing at a snail's pace. Covid-19 has significantly disrupted the higher education sector as well, which is a critical determinant of a country's economic future. MHRD has already sent directives to Universities to start online core courses on 'Swayam' platform. All the higher education institutions started online classes systematically but to some extent it is in veil because of the negative attitude of the students; most of the students entering in the online class only for attendance and muting the video and doing other activities. A large number of Indian students enrolled in Universities abroad, especially in countries worst affected by the pandemic, United State, Australia, United Kingdom, Canada, and China. Covid-19 pandemic-impacted higher education will be different mainly in the mode of teaching and evaluation. It is imperative for teachers to be formally accustomed to the art, science and methods of ICT-based pedagogy to become effective in virtual teaching.

(c) *To analyse the effect of Remittances due to migrant returnees*: World Migration Report 2020 put in the picture that out of the total population of 272 million international migrants, almost 17 million (6%) of them are Indians (World Migration Report, 2020). This consists of students, labour's and their family members. When comparing international Indian migrants, Keralites are far more than any other state peoples. So the return to native of international migrants due to Covid-19 will affects Kerala more because a large number of migrants were lost their jobs. Kerala could lose Rs 13,000 crores in remittances as over 4 lakh register to return from abroad. The NRKs, whose remittances to the tune of $14,935 million bolstered Kerala's badly hit finances, are befuddled by the State's hasty U-turn. Immigrants from Kerala still account for 19%, the highest share of India's total remittances worth $78,609 million in 2019 that helped the country becomes the world's top remittance economy. About 2.5 million Keralite working in Gulf countries, USA and the Europe; 85% of these people are working in Gulf, where is an oil crisis too. The state will lose around 15 percent, or Rs 12,750 crores, of its annual remittances. (Economic Times 2020) Before Covid-19, a Gulf returnee without a job had only lost his economic value. "The very same people who used to celebrate his yearly visits now perceive him as a disease-carrying agent." (Economic Times 2020). Now day the returned migrants are not only perilous but also risky to our society.

4. **To analyse the government package to overcome Covid-19**

- The state government has declared 20,000 crore Covid-19 package for the state
- Two months welfare pension in advance
- Subsidised meal package at Rs 20
- Rs 500 crore health package
- 2 months welfare pensions in advance
- 1320 Cr for providing 1000 assistance to families not eligible for welfare pensions.
- 100 Cr for free food grains to families in need.
- 50 Cr for Subsidised meals at 20
- Loans worth 2000 Cr through Kudumbashree
- 2000 Cr for the employment guarantee programme
- State government will clear arrears by April; it will amount to 14,000 Cr.
- Fitness charge relaxation for Autos, Taxis
- Tax relief for passenger vehicles
- Relaxation in bill payment deadline for electricity- water utilities.
- Entertainment taxes reduced for cinema halls. ***(The official website of Chief Minister of Kerala, 2020)***

Conclusion

Globally the pandemic Covid-19 has cruelly interrupted livelihoods and nastily disrupted the financial foundation. In Kerala, during the period of the lockdown the financial activities in most sectors have come to a grinding halt. The state government must encounter the challenges of unprecedented decline in labour market, income and production coupled with brutal deficits in its revenues. It is Government's immediate main concern to plan a strategy for economic recovery without any interruption.

References

1. Kannan, K.P. & Hari, K.S. (2002). "*Kerala's Gulf connection: Emigration, remittances and their macroeconomic impact* 1972-2000".
2. Patrick, Martin (2020). "*SARS-Cov-2: Impact on Kerala Economy"* Centre for Public Policy Research Independent. In-depth. Insightful
3. www.thehindu.com "*How can India contain the economic impact of Covid-19*".
4. Agan Mohan, M. (2020). *Travel and tourism industry in India, statistics and facts*. https://www.statista.com/topics/2076/travel-and-tourism-industry-in-india/
5. KPMG . (2020). "Coronavirus: India's GDP growth may fall below 3% if lockdown extends" Report *Business Today*. https://www.businesstoday.in/ current/economy- politics/coronavirus-india report/story/400135.html Google Scholar
6. The Economist. (2020). "*The new coronavirus could have a lasting impact on global supply chains*". https://www.economist.com/international/2020/ 02/15/the-new-coronavirus-could-have-a-lasting-impact-on-global-supply - Google Scholar.
7. Sujathan, P.K., & Azad Parambangal P., (2020). "*Social Impact of Lockdown in Kerala: A Case Study*" https://ssrn.com/abstract=3587603 or http:// dx.doi.org/ 10.2139/ssrn.3587603.
8. Ministry of Labour and Employment (2019). *"Report of the Expert Committee on Determining the Methodology for Fixing the National Minimum Wage,"* Government of India.

5

Covid-19 and its Impact on Education

Dr. Noohi Khan (AP II)

Abstract

There are different types of coronavirus such as Severe acute respiratory syndrome coronavirus 2(SARS-Cov-2) and Middle East respiratory syndrome (mers-Cov-2), Covid-19. Severe acute respiratory syndrome coronavirus 2(SARS-Cov-2) and Middle East respiratory syndrome (mers-Cov-2) are treated by controlling their symptoms but there is currently no therapy approved for Covid-19. A lenient to acute breathing disease that is due to by a coronavirus which is transformed chiefly by contact with contagious materials like breathing droplets or with things and is distinguished by feeling asthmatic, high fleve, cold, swollen throat, loss of smell, loss of taste and at the end people suffers from pneumonia and respiratory failure. This disease was first identified in Wuhan, China in December 2019. In this paper we discuss causes, cure, history and how this disease effects on Indian economy. The major modification in teaching during the pandemic is classroom teaching gets online teaching. Online teaching is also called Asynchronous online teaching. In this chapter we discuss what is asynchronous teaching, methods of Asynchronous online teaching, advantages, and disadvantages of asynchronous online teaching.

Keywords: *Corona, epidemic, economy, virus, covid-19, Pandemic, teaching, e-learning.*

Introduction

In anatomy Corona is a part of body resembling or likened to a crown. Study shows that this disease spreads from person to person among those in close contact. The virus layout by breathing blobs released when anyone with this virus croak, runny nose or talks. These blobs can be draw in or land in the mouth, nose of a human being close by. It can also layout if a human being press a outside part with the virus on it and then touches his or her mouth, nose or eyes. Covid-19 can be determine by using the blood, cell, or mouth spit or it can be also try out by use of cotton swab to recover a sample from the inside of your nostrils. The test of Covid-19 are performed by the CDC, some state fitness departments and hospitals. Go and talk to doctor if you have any indications discuss earlier. Your physician will counsel you on whether you should stay in house and monitor your symptoms.

Coronavirus such as severe acute respiratory syndrome coronavirus 2(SARS-Cov-2) and Middle East respiratory syndrome (mers-Cov-2) are curable by controlling its symptoms but there is no cure approved for Covid-19.

Therapies which are used to treat Covid-19 are

(1) Breathing support, mechanical ventilation.

(2) Steroids to reduce lung swelling.

(3) Antiviral medicines.

(4) Blood plasma transfusions.

The clinical features of Covid-19 are as follows-

The most common are fever, cough and breathing difficulties.

The critical cases are respiratory failure, severe acute respiratory infections, kidney failure, death.

The Rare is Diarrhea, virus-specific effector memory T cells typically home to the mucosal surfaces they had previously encountered with a common Cov, i.e., upper and lower respiratory tract.

Objectives

To know the Impact on education due to Covid-19

The major modification in teaching during the pandemic is classroom teaching gets online teaching. Online teaching is also called Asynchronous online teaching. More than 300 million students worldwide specially kids are having their education disrupted by the spread of Coronavirus. Schools, colleges and universities have not faced this level of disruption in generations, but unlike any time in the past, we have the ability to continue education even when schools, colleges and Universities close. During this pandemic classroom teaching gets online teaching. Asynchronous Online teaching is the education that takes place over the Internet. It is also called as "e-learning" or e-education. However, online learning is one type of "distance learning".

Due to Covid-19 schools' colleges and Universities shut all across the world. Over 1.8 billion children are out of the classroom. They suffer more than the college students the result of this, education has changed dramatically, whereby teaching is undertaken on online platforms. Research suggests that online learning has been shown to increase retention of information, and take less time.

Since the Covid-19 pandemic has disrupted the normal lifestyle of people across the globe, the virtual world has come to the rescue. Amongst many institutions' schools have also shifted their base to virtual platforms to conduct classes online. Consequently, catering to the needs of all stages of education from pre-primary to university level, online education has emerged as an alternative to ordinary face-to-face classes. The Central government has recently launched the PM e-VIDYA platform, with 12 new DTH channels, one for each class to reach out to all strata of society.

Teaching is of two types:

(1) Synchronous teaching: Offline teaching or classroom teaching.

(2) Asynchronous teaching: Online teaching or e-classroom teaching.

Methodology

To know what is Asynchronous Online Teaching [5]

Asynchronous Online Teaching is the teaching which is based on Computer or laptop-based teaching or learning, Web-based learning, Internet based teaching, electronic learning (e-learning), m-learning (mobile learning), computer-aided distance learning etc. Asynchronous

Online Teaching is electronically supported learning fully depends upon the Internet for teacher and student interaction and the distribution class materials, taking quizzes, MCQ, Google forms Viva-voce. Online education includes Pre-audio lectures, audio, video, text in the form of pdf, word file, power point presentation, virtual training environments and live chats with Teachers and professors. Online learning is a rich learning environment with much more exibility than a traditional classroom system. There are various online platforms which are used by schools, colleges and Universities.

Such as MS teams, Zoom, Google classrooms, WebEx meet, Learning module systems etc. There are various online portals which are conducted various online courses workshops and faculty development programmes such as Swayam Prabha, NEPTL, Boditree powered by IIT Bombay, National digital library, e-pathshala, PM e-VIDYA platform

Tools of Asynchronous Online Learning: The are following tools which are teachers used in online teaching:

(1) Teaching with video platforms like zoom, Google classrooms, MS teams etc.

(2) Live video and audio chatting with learners.

(3) Using LMS, Moocs, Power point presentation, Uploading Text.

(4) Using video conferencing tools.

(5) Virtual office hours.

(6) Mobile and internet availability.

(7) Upload lecture videos and chat transcripts

Each of these tools encourages live participation and interaction.

Instruction for Asynchronous learners

Online courses that allow learners to view online lectures, view and download course materials, and collaborate with teachers and peers on their own schedule are called asynchronous courses. Lectures might be pre-recorded or presented on a programme like Microsoft PowerPoint, perhaps with instructor voice-over. Many teachers more than one technology, which could include the following tools:

(1) Downloadable pre-recorded lectures.
(2) PowerPoint presentations with or without voice-over.
(3) Communication via Emails or WhatsApp with learners.
(4) Off-hour support tools like virtual tutoring centers and virtual resource centers.

Advantages of Asynchronous Online Teaching:

(1) Increased flexibility of time and location.
(2) Information sharing.
(3) Isolated environment.
(4) Internet and Digital information literacy.
(5) Online education can streamline some administrative aspects of teaching.

Limitations and Disadvantages of Asynchronous Online Teaching:

(1) Access to use technology and internet.
(2) Instructor and learner feels lonely and isolating experience.
(3) Overloaded information.
(4) Teaching feedback is limited.
(5) Cheating prevention during online examination.
(6) Lack face to face communication with students.
(7) Lack of quality Assurance.

Software used in online teaching: LMS is the tool to constitute and conduct online courses, anchor a basic classroom, allot assignments, and behold learner progress—with the help of our laptop, tablet, or phone. There are following learning module system software's which are commonly used in online teaching and they are totally free.

(1) Google classroom: It is the software which is completely free for schools, colleges and institution. Google Classroom permits instructor to form teams of classes, apportion and grade assessments. It gives permissions for students, guardians, are customizable. In this software there is a option of sharing screen with students. Teachers can easily share their screen with students.

(2) Talent LMS: Talent LMS is a cloud-based **learning management system (LMS)** which aids little as well as midsize businesses cart training to worker, clients, and partners. Talent LMS is liked by 5,600 plus business firms because it's set up is easy and can be handle, easy to learn, and even easier to master. On the self-paced learning side, instructor can drift existing courses, or form whole new courses from blemish, then depose customised learner paths to prescribe how and when learners can deplete them.

(3) iTunes: Apple users may acknowledge long time iTunes U as the company's predesigned athenaeum for free teaching material, but the application also work as an online education tool that hold up course building, allocating assignments, ranking, and course analysis. Educator can transfer and share course content with learners in a variation of arrangement, including records, images, and videos. Students can also grip webcast, exercise books, and other assets already accessible in iTunes U. eye to eye chat performance is incorporate, as is the capacity to see when learners have observed or completed homework.

(4) Microsoft teams: It is the software which is similar to Google classroom and it is completely free for schools, colleges and institution, corporate. Microsoft teams is a special feature of Microsoft. It permits instructor to form teams of classes, staff apportion and grade assessments. It gives permissions for students, guardians, are customisable, in this software there is a option of

(a) Sharing screen with students. Teachers can easily share their screen with students.
(b) Sharing Power point presentation.
(c) Special feature of virtual Whiteboard App. Whiteboard app has a pen support option. With the help of pen, you can write or erase anything.
(d) Another special feature is One Note. OneNote is a multifaceted note-taking tool that is built into Teams and can be used for a variety of lessons and activities.

Fast meeting Application

Fast meeting is the Number 1 video conferencing app in China. It gives highly-well organised, easy and cost-effectual outcome for online meeting, training, faculty development programmes, workshops, webinars. You can get immediately connected with your worldwide teams for actual video communication and data transferring through your laptops or mobile devices easily!

It differentiate itself with completely a lot of characteristic, including:

(a) **Fluent HD Video and Audio.** It gives 1080P high clarity video standard and the non-devasting volume transference of labial accompaniment by various advanced audio technologies, this app delivers the "eye to eye" enveloping meeting occurrence.

(b) **Fast Data Sharing.** Fast meeting can transfer files, PDFs, Power point files or video files, all of them can be presented to all participants simultaneously.

(c) **Various Interactive Options.** Various roles to have class chats, private chats and raise hands to speak, with multiple communication ways such as texts, videos and audios.

(d) **Feature-Rich Meeting Controls.** Rich features for meeting controls like multi-level management, recording, roll call, subtitles and video loops, etc. to deliver an on-the-spot meeting experience.

(e) **Cross-Platform.** Enjoy online meetings on Windows, Mac, iOS, or Android system. And connect people via different devices seamlessly without any hassle.

Articulate Storyline

Articulate Storyline is one of the best online classroom software that brings online training to life. It helps trainers create online eLearning courses quickly and easily. It gives students the power to interact with teachers as if they were in the same environment/room. The software comes with outstanding features that allow trainers to build highly interactive mobile and online courses.

Easyclass

Easyclass live online class platform helps educators in not just taking online classes but also managing content sharing for course material, assignments, etc. The software used for virtual classrooms can also monitor the performance of students through grades, quizzes and exams and provide timely feedback for improvement.

The list of the best online classroom software is just endless. However, those mentioned and explained above are just but a few and worth a trial. While most educators often spend plenty of money trying to find the best online course software, it is essential to note that there are some that are free to use. As a rule of thumb, it is highly advisable that you explore all these platforms and check out their features before subscribing to use them.

Virtual software used in 2020 for Online Education:

(1) ez talks: ez Talks Webinar virtual classroom software is a web and video conferencing tools for creating slideshows, presentations, whiteboard and other video/audio files. Use the virtual classroom platform for quick file and screen sharing in order to keep the entire team aligned with current as well as upcoming tasks.

Key features of ez Talks Webinar:

(2) Instant messaging

(3) Audio conferencing

(4) Interactive whiteboard

(5) Video webinar

(6) Meeting control

(7) Room calendar sync

Pricing: ez Talks virtual classroom software pricing starts at around 755 per host per month.

(2) Moodle: For live online classes is a learning management system. Modular Object-Oriented Dynamic Learning Environment or Moodle is used by educators to create customised lessons for learners. This live online classes software sends automatic notifications/alerts as well as provides multimedia integration. Plug in management and all in one calendar are this virtual classroom software's additional advantages.

Key features of Moodle:

- Manage user roles and permissions

- Detailed reporting and logs
- Multilingual capability
- Outcomes and rubrics
- Mass enrolment and secure authentication
- Intuitive text editor
- Peer and self-assessment

(3) Learn cube platform: Learn cube platform for corporate trainers, language institutes and tutoring organisations is used for uploading lesson material and multimedia content on website for courses and classes. The virtual classroom software free trial is also available to familiarise users with online teaching, training and tutoring courses.

Key features of Learn Cube:

- Interactive whiteboard
- Quality audio/video services
- Custom branding options
- Conversation mode
- Private/group classes
- Class review
- Scheduling
- Reporting
- Content marketplace

(4) Tutor Room: Tutor Room is an online teaching software for organising virtual classrooms with scheduling, live demos, updated courses, etc. You can take advantage of the software for virtual classroom management system by utilising its bright homepage that further help receive a short glance of upcoming classes.

Key features of Tutor Room:

- Credit cost for each class
- Booking button
- Backend resource upload
- PDF samples
- Tutor profile

- Backend scheduling
- Credit weight
- ABC credit system
- Backend management system

Analysis and Discussion

Asynchronous education provides Instructor with the flexibility to improve and update their skill set while working simultaneously. Online teaching helps them everyone updated about the new technologies. Asynchronous **online teaching** is a time saving teaching and cost effective process for anyone. The study revealed that, online teaching has many benefits as compared to the conventional teaching in the classroom environment. online teaching has many protest like lack of positive compliment from learners and lack of the proper technology to effectively conduct online learning, these restrictions can be reduce by improve the E-Leaning systems and the use of online discussion forums and new web based software's. In the last, online learning is beneficial to the learners, educators and the organisation providing these courses. I would therefore recommend that asynchronous online teaching be furnished on all learning organisations and investigate on how to improve this teaching method should be delivered out.

References

1. ARS-CoV-2 viral load in upper respiratory specimens of infected patients. Zou L, Ruan F, Huang M, et al. *N Engl J Med.* 2020; (published online Feb 19.) Doi:10.1056/NEJMc200173.
2. Clinical features of patients infected with 2019 novel coronavirus in Wuhan, China. Huang C, Wang Y, Li X, et al. Lancet 2020;395:497-506.
3. Clinical course and risk factors for mortality of adult inpatients with Covid-19 in Wuhan, China: a retrospective cohort study. Zhou F, Yu T, Du R, Fan G, Liu Y, Liu Z, Xiang J, Wang Y, Song B, Gu X, Guan L, Wei Y, Li H, Wu X, Xu J, Tu S, Zhang.
4. Clinical course and risk factors for mortality of adult inpatients with Covid-19 in Wuhan, China: a retrospective cohort study. Zhou F, Yu T, Du R, Fan G, Liu Y, Liu Z, Xiang J, Wang Y, Song B, Gu X, Guan L, Wei Y, Li H, Wu X, Xu J, Tu S, Zhang Y, Chen H, Cao B. Lancet. 2020 Mar 11. pii: S0140-6736(20)30566-3. doi: 10.1016/S0140-6736(20)30566-3.

5. Epidemiological and clinical characteristics of 99 cases of 2019 novel coronavirus pneumonia in Wuhan, China: a descriptive study. Chen N, Zhou M, Dong X et al. https://pubmed.ncbi.nlm.nih.gov/32007143/.
6. Genomic characterisation and epidemiology of 2019 novel coronavirus: implications for virus origins and receptor binding. Lu R, Zhao X, Li J, et al. Lancet 2020;395:565-574. https://pubmed.ncbi.nlm.nih.gov/32007145/.
7. Early transmission dynamics in Wuhan, China, of novel coronavirus-infected pneumonia. Li Q, Guan X, Wu P et al. N Engl J Med. 2020; (published online Jan 29.) Doi:10.1056/NEJMoa2001316 https://pubmed.ncbi.nlm.nih.gov/31995857/.
8. Epidemiological and clinical characteristics of 99 cases of 2019 novel coronavirus pneumonia in Wuhan, China: a descriptive study. Chen N, Zhou M, Dong X et al. https://pubmed.ncbi.nlm.nih.gov/32007143/.
9. Persistent shedding of viable SARS-CoV in urine and stool of ARS patients during the convalescent phase. Xu D, Zhang Z, Jin L, et al. Eur J Clin Microbiol Infect Dis. 2005; 24: 165-171 https://pubmed.ncbi.nlm.nih.gov/15789222/.
10. Severe acute respiratory syndrome-related coronavirus: the species and its viruses—a statement of the Coronavirus Study Group. Gorbalenya AE, Baker SC, Baric RS, et al. *bioRxiv.* 2020; (published online Feb 11.) (preprint). Doi:10.1101/2020.02.07.937862 https://www.biorxiv.org/content/10.1101/2020.02.07.937862v1.
11. Neurological Manifestations of Hospitalised Patients with Covid-19 in Wuhan, China: a retrospective case series study. Mao L, Wang M, Chen S, He Q, Chang J, Hong C, Zhou Y, Wang D, Li Y, Jin H, Hu B. medRxiv 2020.02.22.20026500; https://www.medrxiv.org/content/10.1101/2020.02.22.20026500v1.

6

The Stifled Voices of Female Migrants: Mirroring the Migrant Crises in Art and Literature

Chandrakala Ghosh

Abstract

Hit hard by the unprecedented attack of Covid-19, the world is reeling under severe economic, social and psychological crises. Trying to protect and safeguard itself, the centre often overlooks the multifaceted issues and problems placating the lives of its marginalised population of which the refugees and migrants form an extensive part. This paper aims to focus on the refugee and migrant crises at the wake of the pandemic, culturally centering it to the popular artistic expressions, with an attempt to highlight the ways the migrant and refugee crises, specifically the problems faced by the female migrants and refugees, can be effectively taken care of by the governing centre.

Keywords: Migrant Crises, Covid-19, Sexual Exploitation, Rohingyas, Female Migrants, Exile

Introdution

Song Kang-Ho (Bong Joon-ho, 2019) asked his son to keep the windows of their semi-basement living quarters open when the fumigators came to their neighbourhood for a routine round. They kept the windows open, not caring that sulfuryl chloride has the potential to kill an average adult on sufficient inhalation. When one realises that they might have to starve to survive throughout the foreseeable (and unforeseeable) future, they tend not to care about these. While writing the paper, the realisation dawned upon us that belonging to financially affluent families, we won't understand how it feels to be unsure about the roof over our head or the next meal. Picking up on this uncertainty, French philosopher Simone Weil opines: "To be rooted is perhaps the most important and the least recognised need of the human soul." (Weil, 1952, p. 41) It is from this uncertainty that the political construct of exile is forced upon millions of innocent civilians: a construct whose achievements are "permanently undermined by the loss of something left behind forever". (Said, 2000, p.1)

The problem of Migrant Crises

On September 02, 2015, photo journalist Nilüfer Demir made global headlines with the hash-tag 'KiriraVuyanInsanlik' (humanity washed ashore) and picture of a three year-old, whose body had washed ashore on a beach of Bodrum, Turkey. Although the toddler was found with his face buried in the wet sand, he was identified as Alan Kurdi, one of the 370,000 (Quinn, 2016, p. 275) Syrians who did not survive the perilous journey from Syria to Europe, to escape from the disastrous civil war.

In 2015, UNHCR had reported that more than 65 million people were forcibly displaced, globally (www.unhcr.org/news/latest/2016/6/5763b65a4/global-forced-displacement-hits-record-high.html). Like, Alan Kurdi's family, millions of other citizens had placed their lives in the hands of unscrupulous smugglers, because they were confused about what was safe and trust-worthy anymore. These smugglers gambled not only with their own lives, but also with the lives of the people on-board. The usual 8-seater boat was occupied by 20 adults and 1 child (Kurdi) the day they departed from Syria. Subsequently, these boats had undergone recent renovation, in which cheaper materials were used to build the trunk, notwithstanding the decreased tensile strength of the body. This runs parallel to the Sewol Ferry Incident that occurred during the wee hours of April 16, 2014, when an over-occupied motor vessel overturned and sank down near Jeju Island, killing 304 passengers, out of which 250 were high-school students, who were on their way to a field trip.

"Migrants are often described using water images – floods, waves, flow – metaphors that dehumanize and strip them of their identity, while representing migrants as a homogeneous group." (Quinn, 2016, p. 277). We tend to forget that each and every survivor has a story, a voice, and an identity. We tend to overlook the fact that these individuals are not merely blobs of fleshes. Standing where they are today; they are braver than most of us will be in this lifetime, even if they have to live in holes (Auden, 1939). They certainly don't deserve to be identified as a refugee: an idea that is "a historical construction that privileges political and ideological considerations over economic and ecological ones." (Galllien, 2018, p.721).

As per our deduction, the mental health condition of the migrants can be divided into four sects, which made us construe a pertinent theory: the Theory of Four D's. Desperation, because the migrants are unsure of what tomorrow has in hold for them; Displacement, as finality is assured by giving in the inevitable; Dejection (and fear) while moving out (rather, illegally being smuggled out) in herds like cattle in unsafe boats and vehicles, and being forced to live in conditions worse than slums; Depression (with a sense of perpetual estrangement) because no matter how much one feels at home in a foreign land, it will never be their home. Since this is universally true, we can witness these emotions in any migrant, anywhere in the world. Let's look at the oriental side, and take the Rohingyas for example.

In the state of Rakhine, Myanmar, the Rohingyas have faced decades of systematic discrimination, uprooting and targeted violence. In August 2017, the largest and fastest refugee influx into Bangladesh was witnessed. An estimated 745,000 Rohingyas – including more than 400,000 children – have fled into Cox's Bazar. Inhuman atrocities against the Rohingyas included burning entire villages, families' massacre, and brutal rapes of the Rohingya women. As of March 2019, over 909,000 stateless Rohingya refugees reside in 34 extremely congested camps in Ukhiya and Teknaf Upazilas. The Kutupalong-Balukhali Expansion Site hosts approximately 625,000 Rohingya refugees in a meager span of 13 km^2, with a population density of 46,000/km^2 (www.unocha.org/rohingya-refugee-crisis)

The Reflection of Migrant Crises in Literature

The presence of such inhuman living conditions in a neighbouring country as proximate as that of Bangladesh immediately reminds us of Art Spiegelman's Pulitzer-winning graphic novel *Maus*, where with the brilliant strokes of the artist's brush, Spiegelman has unfolded the unthinkable living conditions in the Jewish ghettoes and the concentration camps that Artie accesses through his father Vladek's traumatic memories of his camp life (Spiegelman, 2003). The constant, hammering comparison of the Jews to mice (*Maus* is mouse in French) and other rodents that need to be exterminated as soon as possible, loom around throughout the novel as a sinister motif. It is recorded, that upon their arrival in Auschwitz, the Jews were shaved from head to toe, before being bathed in industrial pesticides and insecticides, with a hope of racial cleansing (Jews were supposed to be of an inferior race than the Aryan Germans), much like that of the Rohingyas.

This subjective, auto-narrative mode is challenged in French cartoonist Horst Rosenthal's 1942 comic book, *Mickey au Camp de Gurs*, which was conceived and created during his confinement at the Gurs internment camp in France. Here, the subjective perspective of the camp-dweller is subverted and entrusted through an objective perspective of Mickey Mouse, who comes to visit Gurs camp, without the slightest knowledge of the life there and is bewildered beyond his wits as the atrocities unfold with a tinge of comicality in it. The living conditions, food rationing, and lack of basic provisions for livelihood: everything is presented through the flummoxed gaze of Mickey, who finally decides to flee back to the United States, an option that the creator of the book did not have, and had to perish at the camp (Rosenthal, 2014).

In his critically acclaimed text on the introduction to logotherapy, the psychotherapeutic method of coping with the Nazi atrocities in the Jewish extermination camp, *Man's Search for Meaning*, Viktor Frankl states: "Those who have a *why* to live can bear with almost any *how*"(Frankl, 2014, p.132) . This observation of Frankl turns into a conviction as we come across Will Eisner's tenement stories, where he brilliantly depicts the lives of the migrant European Jews, who took refuge in the tenements of Bronx in the States. (Eisner, 2005)

Eisner's graphic tales are replete with instances of sexual harassments, often faced by female migrants in their daily ordeal of striving for better living conditions. This problem, which is a burning issue in the migrants' lives as well as the refugee camps, has been candidly highlighted by comic-journalist Joe Sacco in his 1996 American Book Award Winner graphic novel, *Palestine*. The text begins with several references of sexual exploitation and harassment meted out to the female Palestinian refugees in course of their everyday conflicts with the Israelites (Sacco, 2003). Similar instances have also been referred to in his *Safe Area Gorazde*, where the Serbio-Bosnian ethnic conflict has rendered the Bosnian women entrapped at Gorazde to suffer regular sexual exploits (Sacco, 2007).

Gendering of Migrant and Refugee Crises

Amidst the chaos of uprooting and displacement, which form the core of migrant life, the aspect of gender adds another dimension to the suffering. To understand the everyday struggle that a female migrant faces, we might resort to black feminist Patricia Hill Collins' concept of 'double bondage'(Collins,1990) or Gayatri Chakraborty Spivak's notion of 'double marginalisation'(Spivak, 1999). The intersectionality of nationality and gender identity adds up to the sufferings of the female migrants, which stretches beyond the permissible limits of human imagination.

According to a census conducted by the UNFPA in 2015, almost half of the 244 million migrants and 19.6 million refugees are women (www.unfpa.org/migration). Even though women are often the first responders in a crisis, refugees and migrant women's needs, priorities and voices are often missing from policies designed to protect and assist them. Today, 50% of the world's refugees are women and girls; yet only 4% of projects of UN inter-agency appeals were targeted at women in 2014, and 0.4% of the entire funding fragile states went to the women's groups or women's ministries from 2012 to 2013 (www.unwomen.org./en/news/in-focus/women-refugees-and-migrants).

According to UN reports, at least 1 in every 5 of displaced women is estimated to have experienced sexual violence (www.unwomen.org./en/news/in-focus/women-refugees-and-migrants). Along with sexual violence, other major issues faced by female migrants are sexual exploitation and trafficking. Women and girls account for 71% of all human trafficking victims, according to a 2016 report by the United Nations Office on Drugs and Crime. Consequently, displacement owing to conflict or natural disaster accelerates the vulnerabilities of the female migrants. Chaos and breakdown of the protection systems result in the increase in vulnerability. Lack of shelter, overcrowding in camps, poorly lit public toilets increase the risk of gender-based violence. Under extreme hardships, refugee families often adapt coping mechanisms which can jeopardize women's and girls' welfare. A UNFPA supported study found alarming rates of child marriage among some vulnerable Syrian refugee populations (www.unfpa.org/news/five-reasons-migration-feminist-issue). Again, perpetual pregnancy of the female migrants due to lack of access to sexual and reproductive healthcare, antenatal services and safe childbirth is another problem faced by most women migrants.

According to IOM's World Migration Report 2020, migrant women represent around 74% of the service industry, mainly as domestic help (www.iom.int/wmr). During Covid-19 outbreak, mobility and travel restrictions are jeopardising the job prospects of migrant women. As this eventually leads to an increased dependency on the employer, it results in the removal of women from social protection services.

When the isolation from the health crisis ends, the economic consequences can expose women to sexual exploitation, which had occurred during the Ebola outbreak of 2013-2016. Women migrants are also forced to subject themselves to inhuman working hours and conditions just to secure employment, as migrant female workers are often the bread-earners of their families. Female migrants are often targeted as a vent to the aggression of male migrants (owing to loss of job in the current scenario), and they are not allowed to seek shelter elsewhere due to social restrictions.

A woman has to go through triple the amount of difficulties and problems than a man her age just because she is born physiologically different. As two fellow women who have had to face a few of the difficulties that constitute a migrant woman's daily life, we have tried to come up with some probable solutions that can make her already tough life comparatively easier.

Probable Solutions

The female migrants should be ensured protection against domestic violence, i.e. protection from male migrants. Protection of female migrants from sexual exploits at workplace through legal assistance should be ensured. A minimum wage for female migrant workers (which should be sufficient for supporting a family) should be ensured and offices should strictly stick to this regulation (especially in India, where the concept of minimum wage doesn't exist, yet). Stringent punishment should be meted out to the practitioners of gender-based discrimination at a migrant job centre. We should ensure fixed working hours (preferably during the day) for the female migrant workers so that safety measures can be accessed by them during an emergency. Employment option for the female migrants should be diversified so that they can choose job-mobility over insecurity in the Covid-19 situation. Female migrants should have a regular access to feminine hygiene products and the State must sponsor free gynecological check-ups to the female migrants at regular intervals. State-sponsored healthcare and health protection gears should be made available to the female migrant workers as they might often have to support their entire family with her meager income.

As it is often seen, that due to the governmental blind-eye towards the migrants, the migrant females are entrusted with the full responsibility of their children, whereas the male stays aloof. The State should ensure aid in child support so that the female migrant is not forced to take up whatever job comes in her way, in the post-Covid-19 scenario. The State should also distribute ample quantities of birth control measures to prevent a mass-scale population explosion amidst unhygienic migrant quarters in the current pandemic crisis, as the procurement of prenatal and postnatal might be impossible in the given situation.

Separate unions must be formed for the female migrants which will voice their grievances and present their problems to the State; these organisations should be strictly apolitical.

Even though it is a long-term process, State sponsored programmes against misogyny and xenophobia must be launched regularly for the complete obliteration of the discrimination and hatred faced by the female migrant.

Conclusion

As art tries to soothe even the most bereaved, we hope that art provides a home to our fellow migrants as well. Art mirrors life – the raw, naked truths of the happenings around us can be captured best by none other than artistic expression. The migrant and refugee crisis that is an everyday happening in the contemporary world, often escapes our attention by the virtue of our distance (physical and psychological) from the epicenter of the occurrences. Art intervenes at this juncture and destabilises our apparent stupor, forcing us to pay heed to the suffering humanity among us.

Theodor Adorno, in his autobiography in exile, Reflections of a Damaged Life says that he believes the "only home truly available now, though fragile and vulnerable, is in writing." (Adorno, 2006, p. 240).

Ironically, the most necessary solution to the migrant crisis is an outburst, a revolution. Quoting Nighat M. Gandhi, "failed fantasies fuel revolution" (Gandhi, 2013, p. 3). *Home* is a dream, a fantasy that every migrant dreams of, and now, this dream has been deferred for too long. It is only a matter of time before they explode.

Migrants think that they are parasites because they belong nowhere, because they have adapted themselves to feel at home with the sense of estrangement. It is our responsibility as the privileged to make them realise that they are not parasites; that their identity is not tied with their exile, that humanity and human rights exist beyond political boundaries, greed and dictatorial power.

I would like to conclude with an excerpt from Said's *Reflections on Exile*, about his meeting with Urdu's most prolific contemporary poets, Faiz Ahmed Faiz, who was exiled (much like Palestinian poet Mahmoud Darwish) during the militaristic dictatorship of Zial-ul-Haq:

> "Only once, when Eqbal Ahmed, a Pakistani friend and a fellow exile came to Beirut, did Faiz seem to overcome his sense of constant estrangement. The three of us sat in a dingy, Beirut restaurant late one night, while Faiz recited poems. After a while, he and Eqbal stopped translating his verses for my benefit, but as

the night wore on, it did not matter. What I watched required no translation: it was an enactment of a homecoming expressed through defiance and loss, as if to say, 'Zia, we are here'." (Said, 2000, p. 175).

References

Adorno, Theodor. (2006). *Minima Moralia: Reflections of a Damaged Life.* London, UK: Verso.

Auden, W.H. (1939). 'Refugee Blues'. Retrieved from https://allpoetry.com.

Collins, Patricia Hill. (2000). *Black Feminist Thought: Knowledge, Consciousness and the Politics of Empowerment.* London, UK: Routledge.

Eisner, Will. (2005). *The Contract With God Trilogy: Life on Dropsie Avenue.* NY, US: W.W.Norton & Company.

Frankl, Viktor. (2014) . *Man's Search for Meaning.* London, UK: Rider.

Gallien, Claire. (2018). 'Refugee Literature: What Postcolonial Theory Has to Say'. *Journal of Postcolonial Writing,* Vol. 54, *No.6.* Abingdon, UK: Routledge.

Gandhi, Nighat M. (2013). *Alternative Realities: Love in the lives of Muslim Women.* Ahmedabad, India: Tranquebar Publishers.

Quinn, Eugene. (2016). The Refugee and Migrant Crisis- Europe's Challenges. *Studies: An Irish Quarterly Review,105*(419), 275-285.Retrieved July 10,2020, from http://www.jstor.org/stable/24871398.

Rosenthal, Horst. (2014). *Mickey au Camp de Gurs*. Paris, France: Memorial de la Shoah.

Sacco, Joe. (2003). *Palestine.* London, UK: RHUK Publishers.

Sacco, Joe. (2007). *Safe Area Gorazde.* London, UK: RHUK Publishers.

Said, Edward. (2000). *Reflections on Exile*. Massachusetts, US: Harvard University Press.

Sin-ae, Kwak (Producer), & Joon-Ho, B. (Director). (2019). *Parasite*. [Motion Picture]. South Korea: CJ Entertainment.

Spiegelman, Art. (2003). *Maus*. New Delhi, India: Penguin.

Spivak, Gayatri C. (1999). 'Can the Subaltern Speak?'. *A Critique of Postcolonial Reason: Toward a History of the Vanishing Present.* Massachusetts, US: Harvard University Press.

Weil, Simone. (1952). *The Need for Roots.* England, UK: Routledge.

7

Covid-19 and Gulf Return Migration: A Testing Time for Kerala

Sulaiman KM, Afsal K

Abstract

Just after the global Covid-19 outbreak, 413,000 Non-Resident Keralites (NRKs) living outside India have registered to return to Kerala. The pandemic and the consequences of lockdown have had self-evident impacts on remittances to Kerala from Gulf countries and an unemployment crisis among NRKs. Kerala may have to supplement the anticipated drop in the remittances with other revenue. Furthermore, enhancing the talents of returning migrants can be mobilised to sectors suffering from a deficit of human resources and may also facilitate further international migration to new destinations or to the Gulf itself. For quite some time in Kerala, return migration and integration strategies have lost their pertinence. This moment could be an opportunity to re-orient these strategies to address the current demands. The study reveals the migration and return migration pattern of Kerala people and also covers the socio-economic impact of return migration including return migration due to the Covid-19 pandemic.

Keywords: *Return migration; Kerala; Gulf; Covid-19; Reintegration; Policies.*

Introduction

The outbreak of Covid-19 pandemic has brought into focus the major international migration corridors India shares with the globe, including the Gulf, Europe, and North America. Many of Stage 1 imported cases in India came through these corridors as emigrants returned to their families. Based on news reports related to Indian emigrant workers and significant recruiters in the Middle East countries reveals a frantic desire to return to their home regions. A sound understanding of emigrant corridors is crucial if we are to successfully pre-empt the spread of the corona virus in the coming months. India has the highest number of international migrants in the world, according to the World Migration Report, 2020. Out of the total population of 272 million international migrants, almost 6 percent (17 million) of them are Indians and Kerala international migrants contribute 3 million. This includes students, workers and their family (spouses, parents, etc.).

Many studies have been conducted on international migration from Kerala as well as about return migration (Prakash, 2013; Zechariah et al. 2012). The international migration from Kerala is mainly toward the Gulf region, it is a temporary migration and contract worker's migration, the contract workers are not able to change the jobs, and they have to return completion their contract (Zachariah et al. 2002). The flow of International return migrants started during mid-1980s from Gulf region due to completion of developmental and infrastructural works, many of unskilled and semi-skilled labourers were impelled to depart from abroad (Shekhar, 1997). By the end of 20th century construction phase of the Gulf was over and the demand of local citizen for a larger share of employment market was getting strong (Zachariah et al., 2004). During 2000-2014 periods the increase of return migrants to Kerala was due to the impact of unexpected economic recession in the world and new employment policies in Gulf region (Prakash, 2013; Zechariah et al., 2015; Zachariah et al., 2011).

Since the start of the Covid-19 crisis, India has evacuated its citizens multiple times, first from China and then from Italy, totalling about 842 rescued, according to a press release of 9 March. In the last few months, there has also been considerable return migration from countries in Europe, America, and the Gulf. In Kerala, for instance, conversations with migrant welfare workers reveal that anywhere from 40,000 to 80,000 Gulf emigrants returned in the lockdown phase and have been quarantined. In the last few weeks, 413,000 Non-Resident Keralites (NRKs) living outside India have registered to return to Kerala due to the pandemic. So far, 150,000 Indians have registered with the Indian Embassy in the United Arab Emirates to return. Half of those registered are NRKs. The majority are blue-collar workers, willing to return to India due to the loss of their jobs.

NRKs, as the largest migrant community in the Gulf, have suffered the most from job losses and pay cuts.As the Gulf countries slowly lockdown non-essential industries, migrants were facing the loss of job and income are desperate to return to their motherland. Many already have returned, over the past one month, leading to a spur in Covid-19 cases in Kerala, in particular. The Covid-19 crisis has already highlighted Kerala's active international migration network, with India's first three cases in January 2020 being imported ones from Wuhan, China.

Return migration is a predictable feature of short-term or contract migration. Return migration may be defined as the process whereby people voluntary or involuntary return to their country or region. United Nations Statistics Division for Collection data on International migration (UNSD, 1998), return migrants are persons returning to their country of citizenship after having been international migrants (Whether short term or long term) in another country and who are intending to stay their own country for at least a year. Return migration failed to get adequate attention from researchers and policy makers. It was a great unwritten chapter in the history of migration process. The impact of return flows is very severe to the state of Kerala as well as to the migrants in the form of declining remittance, unemployment, demographic changes, reintegration and rehabilitation problems and policies, etc. There is extensive debate on the adverse impact of return migration on economy and demography of Kerala.

Objective

This paper is trying to understand the migration and return migration pattern of Kerala people from Gulf based on Kerala migration survey-2018 and 2014 conducted by the Centre for Development Studies Trivandrum and existing literature in this area. This paper also covers the socio-economic impact of return migration by highlighting the current wave of return migration due to the Covid-19 pandemic from Middle East region.

Data source and methodology

Kerala migration survey-2018 and 2014 surveys represent the entire state with the potential of generating estimates at taluk level. A scientifically designed household survey based on a census based sampling frame is adequate for characteristic disaggregated analysis. The 1998 survey covered 10,000 households; the exercise expanded to include 15,000 households in 2008 and has incorporated 25,000 households in 2018. Over the last two decades, KMS has provided estimates of emigration, return emigration, out-migration, return out-migration, remittances and average costs of migration. KMS data also provides valuable information on key aspects of Kerala society, such as household composition, consumption, gender, and social groups.It is widely regarded as the first, most reliable and authentic source of data on international migration for researchers and policymakers. The analysis was done by using SPSS 20 software and the descriptive statistics methods were used.

Results

Trend in Migration and Return Migration

The emigration of Keralite to the Gulf countries although started with a few thousands in 1973, has continuously increased and has been making far reaching impact on the development scenario of the Kerala economy. The major type of migration of workers from Kerala to the Middle-East is contract type and they are expected to return home at the end of the contract period. Emigration of workers from Kerala to the Gulf region has made significant impact on the economy of Kerala for the last four decades. Kerala is the largest supplier of migrant workers to the Gulf Cooperation Council (GCC) countries, accounting to nearly 2.5 million. Gulf remittances also contribute to a major part of the annual GDP of the state. In the year 2018, Kerala received approximately INR 30,717 crores as Gulf remittance (Table 1).

As per the 1998 study on Kerala migration (Zachariah et al., 2001), the stock of return migrants in that year was more than seven lakhs. During 2003 to 2008 unexpected increase in both emigration and return emigration as well as the remittances also, the global economic crisis periods not deeply affected emigrants from Kerala in Gulf countries but there was a negative impact on emigrants in developed countries as well for female migrants, during this period majority of returnees were from UAE followed by Saudi Arabia and Qatar. The trend of return migrants during post global crisis period 2008-2011, were decreased from 11.6 lakhs to 11.5 lakhs while it was 8.9 lakhs in 2003 (Zachariah et al., 2010; Zachariah et al., 2011; Zachariah et al., 2012; Prakash, 2013). After 2011, returnees increased for 11.5 lakhs to 12.5 lakhs (Fig. 1).

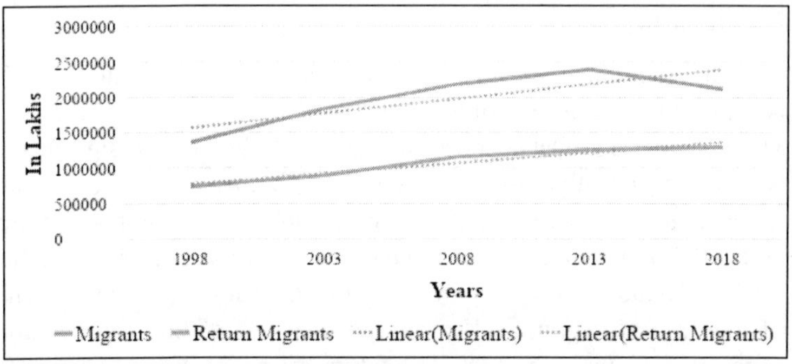

Source: Kerala Migration Surveys 1998-2018.

Fig. 1. Trends is Kerala-Gulf migration and return migration.

Majority of the return migrants were above 35 age as well male than female, but the proportion of female return emigrants were primarily increased during the economic crisis period (Zachariah et al. 2012). By considering the marital status of returnee above 70 percent were married in contrast to their first time of migration, they were not married. The educational quality of migrants was better than the general population. Still, the number of return migrants with low-level of education such as primary, secondary and higher secondary were more as compared to highly educated emigrants. Based on religion, Muslims are 44 percent followed by Hindus 39 percent and Christians 16 percent (Zachariah et al., 2015).

Destination

Table 1 shows the percentage of migrants, people returned in the time of the 2018 recession and return migrants by destination countries, and the number of Covid-19 cases in those countries reported by

June 7. Nearly 90 percent of the Kerala emigrants going towards the Gulf countries. United Arab Emirates (UAE) have the highest share of Kerala migrants, 39 percent, while 23 percentage of Kerala international migrants are in Saudi Arabia. Oman and Qatar have become the destination for nearly 20 percent of Malayalee migrants. The most significant number of return emigrants coming from Saudi Arabia, followed by UAE and Oman, mainly due to new labour policies. In the last three years, especially, after the Nitaqat crisis, Saudi Arabia has lost about three percentage points in its share (KMS Report, 2014).

The mentioned six major destination countries in that Table 1 accounts the four percent of the total Covid-19 cases in the world, and Saudi Arabia and Qatar are mostly affected. One of the significant waves of return migration was experienced before was in the time of the economic recession of 2008. According to Kerala Migration Survey 2008, 173,339 people returned due to the recession. Mainly from the UAE and Saudi Arabia, they were together contributing the 69 percent of total return migration. Kuwait was also one of the major return exporter's migrants in 2008. The return migration due to Covid-19 will rise the same challenges raised by 2008 return migration due to economic recession to Kerala.

Table 1: Percentage of migrants and return migrants by destination countries and number of Covid-19 cases

Countries	*Migrants Percentage*	*Migrants Returned*	*No of Covid-19 cases by June 7*	*Percentage of migrant returned (recession 2008)*
United Arab Emirates	39.1	33.1	38,808	46.4
Saudi Arabia	23	38.0	101,914	22.7
Oman	8.6	12.0	17,486	6.9
Qatar	8.7	4.9	70,158	5.3
Kuwait	6	4.3	32,510	10.5
Bahrain	3.8	4.7	14,763	2.6
Others countries*	10.8	3.1		5.6
Total	**100**	**100**	**4%(World)**	**100**

Source: Kerala Migration Surveys 2008, 2018.

Reasons for Return

The principal cause for the return of emigrants to Kerala was labour-related issues such as expiry of the contract, compulsory repatriation, low salary, non-payment of wages, harsh behaviour of the employer and lousy work atmosphere (Prakash, 2013; Reshmi, 2008). The critical reasons for return were contract expiry, the low wage at the destination, ill health, new labour policy and problems at home, Nitaqat issues and compulsory expatriation. (Zachariah et al., 2012; Zachariah et al., 2015; Rasheed, 2017). Figure 2 shows the reasons for return of Kerala migrants from the Gulf region both in 2014 and 2018. 2014 was used to show the importance of Nitaqat issue, one of major crisis Kerala migrants faced after the 2008 economic recession.

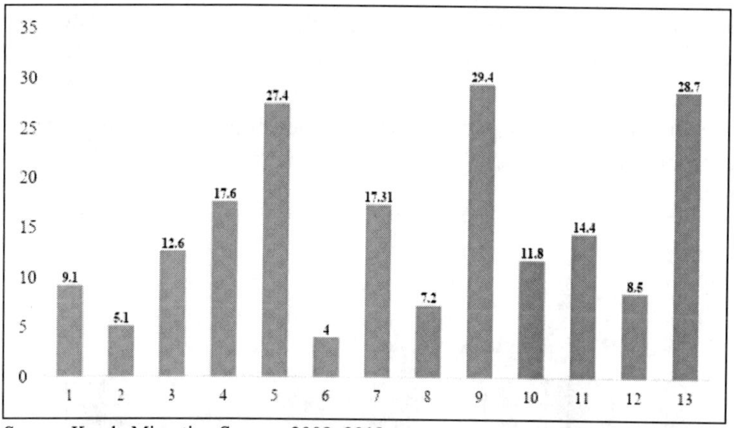

Source: Kerala Migration Surveys 2008, 2018.

Fig. 2: Reasons for Return Migration from Gulf Region (in Percentage).

Work and related financial issues are acting as primary reasons for return migration from the Gulf region. From 2014 to 2018, the percentage of people returning because the loss of job was increased six times (Fig. 2). Whereas in 2014 the proportion of returns from Saudi Arabia were high (KMS, 2014), due to compulsory expatriation, and Nitaqat issues (4 percentage people returned from Saudi Arabia (Fig. 2), as well as other fixed reasons such as poor working conditions, low wage and problems at home. Those returned due to Nitaqat issues were mainly working in the private sector and engaged in self-employment sector. The new rule impelled the companies to replace the local citizen for foreign citizen and the propensity of return with low-level education and worked in the semi-skilled and unskilled sector were very high (Zachariah et al, 2015).

Remittances and Migrant Households

The migrant's dependency is high in Kerala. When a person migrates, the whole family became mostly depended on them. It is explained in fig. 3 that shows the household use of remittances received. It shows that 37 percent of remittances used for household day to day expenses, 15 percent for household asset purchase and eight percentage of remittances spend on children's education. Around 13 percentage of remittance used to pay back the debt and only 19 percentage of remittance went into saving (Fig. 3). Together 60 percentage of total remittances directly spend on household need shows the dependence of households on the money sent by the migrant. It is essential to know how many families are depended on remittance or having the migrants or return migrants.

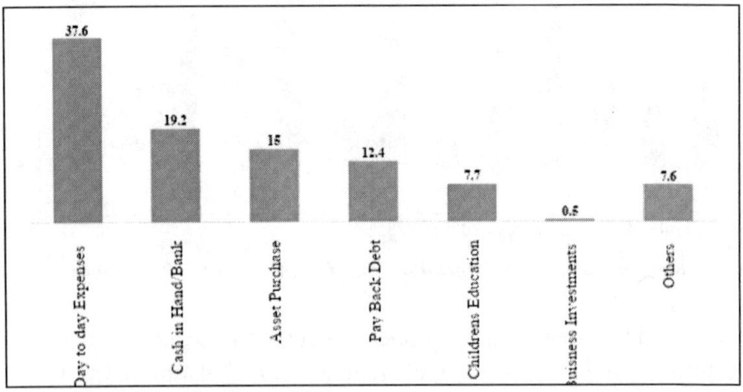

Source: Kerala Migration Survey 2018.

Fig. 3: Household use of Remittance 2018.

Table 2 shows that in Kerala 24 out of 100 households have at least one migrant, and in district-wise Malappuram having migrant in 40 out 100 households, contributing the 20 percentage of the total migrants from Kerala to the Middle East. Besides that districts like Kollam, Pathanamthitta, Kottayam and Kannur having more than

30 out of 100 households with the migrant outside.The maximum number of return migrants are in Malappuram district followed by Trivandrum, and the minimum amount of return migrants were in Idukki followed by Wayanad. Malappuram again homes for 24 percentage of the total return migrants to the state, out of 100, 32 households having the return in migrant while Kerala has return migrants in 14 out of 100 families. In Kollam and Kasaragod, more than 20 households out of 100 have return migrants. Nearly eight percentage of migrants returned in the time of 2008 great economic recession, and major migrant-sending districts have an equal share of returnees in that time (Table 2). Most of the emigrants had returned after just one-episode migration and the average period of duration at abroad was seven years (KMS Report, 2020).

The reason for dwindling of return migration in some districts of the southern region in 2018 was due to decline of return, especially skilled migrants from western and Gulf countries and decrease of female returnees from abroad (Zachariah et al., 2012; Zachariah et al., 2015; Prakash, 2013). After the economic recession of 2008, from 2011 to 2018 the number of return emigrants primarily increased especially form Saudi Arabia due to Nitaqat Law (which is a plan implanted by Saudi Government to increase the number their citizen in all enterprises and companies) this law mainly affected the semi-skilled, unskilled labours and self-employed persons.

Table 2: Migrants, Return Migrants and Remittances Received in Kerala

District	*Percentage of Emigrants*	*Emigrant/ 100 Household*	*Percent of Return Migrants*	*Return Migrants/100 Household*	*Percentage of Migrant returned (Recession 2008)*
Trivandrum	6.5	15.2	7.2	10.4	16.7
Kollam	11.3	32.8	12.8	22.6	6.9
Pathanamthitta	5.2	31.9	4.2	15.8	3.9
Alappuzha	6.4	23.6	7.7	17.3	6.1
Kottayam	7.9	31.3	3.2	7.9	3
Idukki	1.6	11.3	0.5	2.1	0
Ernakulam	2.5	5.8	1.8	2.6	3.9
Thrissur	11.4	27.9	7.3	10.9	13.5
Palakkad	4.2	12.2	4.5	7.9	11.3
Malappuram	19.1	42.1	23.9	32.1	14.1
Kozhikode	7.6	19.7	11.7	18.5	11
Wayanad	1.4	14.5	0.9	5.7	0.5
Kannur	11.8	38.8	7.3	14.7	6.5
Kasaragod	3.2	21.3	6.9	28.4	2.8
KERALA	**2121887**	**24**	**1294796**	**14.6**	7.7

Source: Kerala Migration Surveys 2008, 2018.

Life after Return Migration

Return migration by various reasons has serious consequences on the life of migrants. The life after return in home society directly depends on the nature and context of their return migration. The impact of forced or involuntary return makes their life more vulnerable with the immediate loss of jobs and not having pre-departure planning to home society. There are many cases where the average NRK returning home after decades do nothing and sink into depression. The state is also struggling with a compound range of socio-economic problems faced by Gulf returnees without having systematic supporting mechanisms and policy plans. Return migrants are likely to be more vulnerable with exoticism with the changing socio-cultural and economic environment of the home society due to their long time absence as a migrant in another country. Majority of the migrants from Kerala are skilled, unskilled or semiskilled labourers.

Transition in occupation and employment sector from before emigration to after return to home is one of particular part which could help to study the impact of emigration on occupations in Kerala, in contrast to occupational mobility, majority of return emigrants joined in same sector before migration and they mainly were worked in non-agricultural sector and private sector after return, the percent of worked in self-employment sector were highly increased among return migrants. The incidence of unemployment among the return emigrants were high and majority of returnees faced economic and employment problems after return (Zachariah et al., 2011; Zachariah et al, 2012; Prakash, 2013; Reshmi, 2008).

The present labour market system has a rapid change over the last few years, and trained and untrained employments are being filled with immigrant workers from other states of Uttar Pradesh, West Bengal, Bihar and Tamil Nadu. This affects the economic reintegration of return migrants after the return. The present low wages in Kerala comparing to Gulf will also change the total financial management of family after the return. Moreover, the entrepreneurial opportunities compared to other states are very low in Kerala. This leads to many migrant returnees forced to remain unproductive for the rest of their life. On the whole, the investment activity of the return emigrants was minimal after the return. Very few had tried to start any kind of economic activity. Other than a few trading shops, taxi services or agricultural processing establishments, the return emigrants of Kerala did not get involved in any sort of investment activity. Those who did try were not very successful (Zachariah, Rajan, 2011)

The proportion of savings as well the investment of remittances was very less among migrants and utilisation of remittances were mainly for construction of building, daily expense and marriage. The earnings, expenditures of return migrants decreased as compared before return. (Rasheed, 2017; Zachariah et al., 2012). Rehabilitation programme for return migrants from government's side didn't helped to improve their living standard (Zachariah et al. 2001). The Study suggest to framework multidisciplinary policies which will address all problems of return emigrants such as information based policies, economy incentive policies and institution based policies (Jabir, 2014). However, another positive aspect of emigration is that return emigrants have acquired several skills while working abroad. These include various kinds of technical skills, marketing skills, managerial/ supervisory skills and financial management skills (Zachariah et al, 2011; Zachariah et al, 2012).

Due to current Covid-19 outbreak, the problems of return migrants and their reintegration into family, society and current economic system has become an avoidable issue in Kerala. The government and other many NGOs/INGOs are involved in the process of successfully reintegrating migrants to their home societies. The government has planned specific schemes and policies to return migrants on an emergency basis. The migrants also have some coping strategies and resources that make them more adaptive with the unfriendly environment in the home country.

Discussion

Kerala and the Pandemic

Kerala a small state in India, the land that proclaims itself as "God's Own Country" is a heaven for tourists who make a beeline to the backwaters, palm-fringed sunset beaches, lush hills of the Western Ghats, and the spice plantations on the mountain slopes. Kerala has been known around the globe as a model for preventing the spread of Covid-19. Global media have been pouring praise on the state's success (BBC, 2020). Kerala reported the first three cases of coronavirus in India in late January, all three victims being Indians who had studied in Wuhan. Later on Kerala received people from Italy too with positive cases including a whole family tested positive. The state soon began implementing mandatory quarantines for visitors arriving from abroad and from outside of the state, weeks before the Centre instituted similar measures across the country. A detailed guideline to deal with a new Coronavirus was issued by the Department of Health and Family Welfare of Kerala on 5th January 2020, much earlier than the first case detection in India. Importation and transmission-based approach for Testing Strategy on January 26th 2020, even before the first case of Covid-19 was reported in the state (Gov. of Kerala, 2020).

The critical situation is that Kerala is a small state (38,863 sq.km), but it homes for 35 million people makes it 819 people per square kilometer, eight most densely state in India. Other than people living in closely Kerala has 25 lakh migrants, who frequently travel to their native land. In addition to that, international travelling is a part of Kerala culture, which is connected to the rest of the world through four airports serve around 17 million passengers annually. Finally, Kerala has 2.5 million migrant labourers from other states. Simply Population density, affluent non-resident Keralites and thriving tourism all raise the risk for an outbreak in Kerala. However, the containment strategies adopted by Kerala have helped in slowing the spread of infection into the community by the end of May (GoK Dashboard, 2020). Study also suggests that the head start that Kerala had in preventing the spread of the disease in the initial phase may help the state in dealing with the next wave of the disease (Kumar, Gulia, 2020).

Kerala opted for a combination of massive testing, quarantine and support of the poor with positive short-term effects (Joseph CD, Al-Aghbari Asa'ad A, Jang SY, Ramirez TR, Vincent J, Joshi A, et al, 2020). By January itself, the government started promoting using the face masks. On February 3, the state government declared Covid-19 as state calamity and drafted measures to be followed. By the beginning of March, government introduced more precautionary measures by shutting down the schools and colleges and asking all religious and other groups cancel all gatherings, including marriages, to encourage social distancing (Live mint, 2020). On the nutritional point of view, free meals delivered for school children at their home. The government also instructed internet service providers to improve the bandwidth to encourage work from home (Indian Express, 2020).

Return Migration in the time of Pandemic and Challenges

As the Middle East countries slowly shut down non-essential industries, migrants facing job loss and no income are desperate to return. Many already have, over the past month, leading to a spike in Covid-19 cases in the state, in particular. The Covid-19 pandemic has already highlighted Kerala's strong and active international migration networks, with India's first three active cases in January 2020 being imported ones from Wuhan. Subsequently, a new outbreak of cases erupted in Kerala at the end of March, with the northern districts of Kasaragod and Kannur registering the more active cases. 44 out of 63 new cases reported between 22-24 March came from the Gulf.

KMS (2018) data shows that Malappuram and Kollam rank the highest in terms of emigration as well as return migration (Table 2). Kasaragod and Kannur, rank relatively lower in-migration and return migration compared to other districts but like the other districts, share the most robust migration linkages with UAE and Saudi Arabia (worst affected in the GCC). Kasaragod's high case point maybe because of its special relationship with Dubai: the district, with 121 cases as of 1 April, sends emigrants to the textile sector of Deira Naif, Dubai, from where almost every return migrant has been testing positive, according to a 25 March report in The Lede.

Even though return migration is a predictable feature of temporary or contract migration, information to gauge its magnitude and impact is sparse. In the case of Kerala, government authorities do not record the number of return migrants. Yet, it is nonetheless clear that the Covid-19 has imposed additional burdens on state agencies to screen and trace recent returnees from the Gulf while taking steps to avoid rumours that might lead to the latter facing social rejection and discrimination. Moreover, return migrants who have lost their jobs will add to unemployment rolls in Kerala. Previous similar situations that have resulted in sudden job loss and large-scale returns from the Gulf (e.g., the economic recession of 2008 and Saudi Arabia's Nitaqat policy, 2012) do not necessarily provide a bright idea to how much less how good returnees in the current context will be re-absorbed into their communities, what the impact of their reintegration will require of the Government of Kerala and local authorities, and what the latter's response capacities are.

In the last few weeks, 413,000 Non-Resident Keralites (NRKs) living outside India have registered to return to Kerala due to the pandemic. Why people returning by losing their job and income matters? Take the case of Malappuram, One in three households here is an NRK household. It boasts the highest number of migrants, nearly 4 lakh, and gets 21 percent of Kerala's total remittances. But the flow of returnees is the highest too—almost a quarter of the total, with about one in four households having a returnee. The phenomenon of migration is not individual, but also concerned with migrants' families, as families of migrants in Kerala have long been depending on remittances to meet their expenses. Before the crisis, migrants would remit to support their spouses and family, to meet children educational and medical expenses, and to repay loans. Therefore, families of migrants are also directly affected by the return of migrants due to the pandemic.

It raises another critical question that is it only affecting the families with migrant returned in the time of pandemic? The answer is simple, and it directly affects three groups of people that included person returned in the time of the pandemic. Three groups are:

1. *Migrants who have returned to Kerala for breaks/leaves before the pandemic:* These people are stuck and are in danger of losing their livelihoods and having no source of income in the last few months. The prevailing situation halted large infrastructure projects in the Gulf and caused oil prices to fall drastically. As the Gulf is facing a severe economic crisis, it may not recruit migrants shortly. This will hit Kerala's economy and migrants' livelihoods the hardest.
2. *Migrants returned in the time of Pandemic:* Migrants returned in the time of lockdown, due to loss of job and even with voluntary retirement due to the instability they faced in the

destination. Most of them have lost their source of income and rethink about their future endeavours. This group also includes the early migrants who went to the Middle East for a short time visit in search of the job by making investments (taken as loan or debt).

3. *Migrants at the destination who lost the income source but not returned*: These migrants are running out of money and are unable to go out for work. In some cases, workers were not provided with adequate financial support for food or rent, but they believe it's better to stay back and wait till a hard time to pass than returning to the homeland that cost a considerable amount.

The experts expect that from above three groups all together more than 3 lakh people will be losing their jobs, it accounts for 16 percent of the current Kerala migrant at Gulf region. It will directly affect the migrant or remittance depended households and the state economy as well. There is an interconnection between migrants and remittances. Remittances are the lifeblood of Kerala's economy and have been steadily increasing over the last two decades. But the real global economic slowdown triggered by the pandemic may lead to loses in remittances. It is estimated that 15% of Kerala's annual remittances are expected to decline, as the crisis has further heightened the livelihood concerns of returning migrants and NRKs remain in the Gulf. It is pertinent to mention that most of the Indians abroad who are infected by Covid-19 are in the Gulf countries. Due to shutdowns or quarantines, their earnings have decreased, their families are facing a difficult time, and their remittances have been affected.

Return migrants, the majority are employed either on a part-time or full-time basis. Studies on return migrants (2014) shows that nearly one-fifth of the return migrants are unemployed. Similarly, from self-employment and wage employment, they get only a small amount as monthly income. Studies also observe that the socio-economic status of 40 percent of return emigrants due to emigration to Gulf countries have not improved. Two-thirds of households have created several financial problems. Similarly, migrations of the head of the household create social tension and problems for return emigrant households. Emigration has adversely affected the education, as well as character formation of the children and, has created mental stress and challenges to wives of emigrants. Return emigrants also feel that they are isolated from society due to emigration. Return emigration also produces a mild or moderate recession in the economic activities in the localities having a high concentration of immigrant households.

Conclusion

The return of a large number of migrants in this health emergency will create severe economic consequences, especially in employment, unemployment, consumption, savings and investment and in the general wellbeing of the people. So, the State and Central Government also should give high priority to the issues of return migration and rehabilitation of return emigrants. Though the state Kerala could plan more policies and implement programmes on the other side, it affects a lot of challenges in the reintegration process of returnees. The current unhealthy economic scenario due to Covid-19 of the state carries a significant role in making challenges. The nature of problems and difficulties may be personal or situational. Though the own issues like lack of adjustment with family or home society is not a big problem, the challenges regarding the excessive return migration and lack of alternative systems become a significant challenge to the government and other related departments.

The pandemic and the consequences of lockdown have had self-evident impacts on remittances to Kerala from Gulf countries and an unemployment crisis among NRKs. Kerala may have to supplement the anticipated drop in the remittances with other revenue. However, the more significant consequence will unfold over the coming months. Only then can we understand how far this pandemic has hit Kerala's remittance economy. While the Kerala government has organised medical facilities for returning NRKs, it will need to do more to overcome financial difficulties due to the loss of livelihoods. Kerala may see these returning workers as a possibility since their skill sets can be mobilised in sectors suffering from a deficit of human resources. Furthermore, enhancing the talents of returning migrants may also facilitate further international migration to new destinations or to the Gulf itself. However, this proposal would require comprehensive research to examine the best feasible ways for the economic integration of the returning NRKs. For quite some time in Kerala, return migration and integration strategies have lost their pertinence. This moment could be an opportunity to re-orient these strategies to address the current demands.

References

GoK Dashboard. Kerala fights Covid-19 [Internet] (2020). Available from: *https://dashboard.kerala.gov.in/index.php*

Government of Kerala D of H and FW. Testing Strategy: Strategy for Covid-19 testing in Kerala state (2020). Available from: *https://health.kerala.gov.in/2020/06/*

Gulia, KK, Kumar VM. Reverse quarantine: Management of Covid-19 by Kerala with its higher number of aged population. Psychogeriatrics [Internet] (2020). Available from: *http://www.ncbi.nlm.nih.gov/pubmed/32497386*

Jabir, M.M. (2014). Reintegration of Return Migrants in Kerala: Policy Initiatives and Challenges, *International Journal of African and Asian Studies* - An Open Access International Journal Vol.4 2014

Joseph, CD, Al-Aghbari Asa'ad A, Jang SY, Ramirez TR, Vincent J, Joshi A, et al. Mass media and publications from six countries. J Chem Inf Model [Internet] (2017). 53(9):1689–99. *Available from: file:///C:/Users/User/Downloads/fvm939e.pdf*

LiveMint. Covid-19: Kerala shuts down schools and colleges. (2020). Available from: *https://www.livemint.com/news/india/covid-19-kerala-cm-announces-shutting-down-of-schools-and-colleges-11583832113627.html*

News B. Coronavirus: How India's Kerala state "flattened the curve." (2020). Available from: *https://www.bbc.com/news/world-asia-india-52283748*

Prakash, B. A. (1998). Gulf migration and its economic impact: The Kerala experience. *Economic and Political Weekly*, 3209-3213.

Prakash, B. A. (2013). Return Emigration of Indian Emigrant Workers from the West Asia.

Rajan, S. I., Kurusu, V., & CK, S. P. (2015). Return of Diasporas: India's Growth Story vs Global Crisis. In *India Migration Report 2014* (pp. 110-124). Routledge India.

Rasheed, C.K. (2017). International Return Migration to Kerala: *A Socio-Economic Analysis International Multi-Disciplinary* E-Journal.

Reshmi, R.S. (2008). Labour Migration of Women from Kerala: Socio-Economic Impact on Migrants and Their Families. *Unpublished Ph.D. Thesis*, IIPS Mumbai.

Service EN. Kerala gives internet boost to help people brave Covid-19 vigil. (2020). Available from: *https://www.newindianexpress.com/states/kerala/*

2020/mar/11/kerala-gives-internet-boost-to-help-people-brave-covid-19-vigil-2115440.html

Shekhar, TV (1997). Migration and Social Change, *Rawat Publication*, New Delhi.

Web Desk TW. Kerala's Covid-19 response puts "so-called first world" to shame: British economist. (2020). Available from: *https://www.theweek.in/news/india/2020/04/13/kerala-covid-19-response-puts-so-called-first-world-to-shame-british-economist.html?fbclid=IwAR2tOR6mzrOAavm 9ZvSm-oNps_K_dwHBAILc4RvFWNdgZeylrq9ooenAY_U*

Zachariah, K. C., & Irudaya Rajan, S. (2015). Dynamics of emigration and Remittances in Kerala: The Kerala Migration Survey 2014 (No. 115). Working Paper.

Zachariah, K. C., & Rajan, S. I. (2004). Gulf revisited economic consequences of emigration from Kerala: emigration and unemployment. *Kerala Migration Report.*

Zachariah, K. C., & Rajan, S. I. (2010). Impact of the global recession on migration and remittances in Kerala: new evidences from the Return Migration Study (RMS). *Kerala Migration Report* 2009.

Zachariah, K. C., & Rajan, S. I. (2011). From Kerala via Kerala via the Gulf: emigration experiences of return emigrants. *Kerala Migration Report 2011.*

Zachariah, K. C., & Rajan, S. I. (2012). Inflexion in Kerala's Gulf Connection: Report on *Kerala Migration Report 2011.*

Zachariah, K. C., Mathew, E. T., & Rajan, S. I. (1999). Impact of migration on Kerala's economy and society. *International Migration.* 59(1), 23-41.

Zachariah, K. C., Mathew, E. T., & Rajan, S. I. (2001). Social, economic and demographic consequences of migration on Kerala. *International migration*, 39(2), 43-71.

8

Examining State's Response to the Covid-19 Pandemic: Implications for Labour Migrants in India

Biplab Debnath

Abstract

The Covid-19 pandemic had an unprecedented social, economic and political impact in our society. Nation-states' response to the pandemic challenged the very principles of globalisation and liberalisation that has affected our lives for the past few decades. India's immediate response to the pandemic was stringent, justified as a necessity to control the spread of the virus in a country with the second largest population in the world. While every section of the society felt the effects of the pandemic, one segment that was reduced to the most vulnerable position, both as a result of the pandemic and government policy response towards the same, were the migrant labourers in India. The chapter highlights the impact of Covid-19 on labour migrants in India, relegated to one of the most vulnerable sections in society. The chapter begins with a general assessment of labour migration in India, followed by an analysis of the process of reverse migration that the pandemic induced nationwide lockdown initiated. The next section provides an analysis of the economic, health and human right implications of the migrant labourers in the context of the government's response to the pandemic. The final section examines the government welfare measures initiated in short to medium term along with a few recommendations that might be crucial for the wellbeing of this segment of the society.

Keywords: *Covid-19, migrant workers, India, human rights, lockdown.*

The Covid-19 pandemic is having an unprecedented impact on the process of globalisation exemplified through cross-border movement of goods and people. Numerous aspects of liberalism, in rapid ascendance over the last few decades, have come to a sudden halt. Nation-states became insular and overtly nationalistic; borders, domestic and international, is in prominence once again after decades of 'irrelevance' as globalisation proponents would put it; and nation-states responded the pandemic with a series of policy measures which cuts through the very notion of integration that is the hallmark of a liberal economy. All of these happened in response to a pandemic that has taken shape as the biggest global challenge of the century.

India's reaction to the pandemic was nothing less than extreme. After a *Janta Curfew* on 22 March, the government declared 21-days nationwide lockdown effective from 25 March 2020, which was subsequently extended twice till 31 May. The lockdown in India was the most stringent in the world (Hale et al., 2020), that involved severe restrictions on the movement of people along with public health measures such as social distancing, isolation and quarantine of individuals. The government invoked the Epidemic Diseases Act 1897, one which empowered the state to take such regulatory measures that deem necessary to prevent the outbreak of epidemic disease (Government of India, 1897: 2). With 500 Covid-19 positive cases at the time of the 1st lockdown, the rationale for invoking the act was to flatten the Covid-19 growth curve and avoid the dreaded possibility of the pandemic spreading in a country of 1.2 billion people with a high population density of 450 people per square km greatly dependent on an inadequate public health infrastructure (Biswas, 2020a).

While the Covid-19 pandemic is having an unprecedented political, economic, social and health impact across individuals and nations, some sections of the society were especially reduced to the worst-off condition. The objective of this chapter is to provide an analysis of one such vulnerable section, the labour migrants in India, whose travails have sparked off one of the biggest humanitarian crisis witnessed in India in recent times. The work is analytical in nature using the data from a few surveys conducted on stranded workers and internal migrant labourers, along with their accessibility to the state welfare schemes, on the first few months of the lockdown. The chapter also situates the condition of internal migrants in global institutional reports on the ethical implications of a pandemic spread in general and Covid-19 in particular.

Internal Migration in India

The total migrant population in the world is estimated to be 1 billion (one in seven of the world population) of which 272 are international migrant and 763 million internal migrants (WHO, 2020a). Despite being the primary drivers of economic growth across the world, the pandemic has relegated migrant labourers to one of the most vulnerable sections of the society with severe health and livelihood repercussions. Almost 1.6 billion informal economy workers, nearly half of the global workforce, have been affected by lockdowns enforced by nations across the world with a decline in earnings of 60% of informal workers – 82% in lower middle income and lower-income countries, 28% in upper-middle-income countries and 76% in high-income countries (ILO, 2020a: 1-2).

The process of migration falls under two categories in terms of national borders - internal (within-country) and international (across nations) migration. Within internal migrants, there are three more categories in terms of time-period and residence - short-term/seasonal, semi-permanent and permanent migrants. Short-term or seasonal migration occurs for a few months, either for a slack season at home or peak demand at the destination and are cyclical in nature (Tumbe 2014: 3). For instance, India witnesses a massive flow of seasonal migrants from different parts of the country to the agricultural regions during the harvesting month of March. Semi-permanent migrants spend more time of the year away from home as compared to seasonal migrants and send periodic remittances at home (*ibid*). However, while a semi-permanent migrant remains a resident of the source region, permanent migrant shifts permanently to the destination region which becomes his new residence.

However, quantifying internal migrants in India have, over the years, proved to be a challenging task. It is primarily with the case of seasonal migrants, as they act as a floating population between their source and destination territory besides remaining invisible due to lack of documentation and record of work at the destination region

(Radhakrishnan, 2020). As a result, there are variations in data on the number of internal migrants in India as provided by different agencies. The United Nations Development Programme (UNDP), in a report in 2009, estimated around 714 million internal migrants globally, which is approximately four times the number of international migrants (Rajan and Sumeetha, 2020: 12).

Studies on internal migration of labourers in India have broadened in scope in recent years. While initial studies defined labour migration by either focusing on male migration or those migrating for economic reasons, more recent studies have attempted to fill the gaps by incorporating non-economic reasons involving female labour migrants who initially migrated due to marriage but are currently active in the labour market (Khan, 2020: 51). The latter studies demonstrated that the increase in the share of labour migrants in the labour force from 29% in 1983 to 30.50 in 2007-08 is primarily due to female labour migration alone (*ibid*: 53).

In 2007-08, there were 326 million internal migrants in India, which is around 1/3rd of the total population, of which 141 million were labour migrants (*ibid*: 51). As per the census data of 2011, in the year preceding the census, 8 million people moved to another district within the state and 4 million to another state (Imbert, 2020). Short term or seasonal migrants in current estimates range from 15 million to 100 million and are primarily rural to urban (Babu et al., 2020: 531). The Annual Economic Survey of India 2017 puts the number of seasonal migrants in the country to 139 million (Jeetendra, 2020). These short term or seasonal migrants affects roughly 5% of Indian households, most of which are poor or labour households (Tumbe, 2014: 4). Over 35% of them work in the construction sector, 20% in agricultural activities and 16% in manufacturing activities – all such migrants mediated through labour contractors (*ibid*) - besides engaging in other activities such as domestic help, handyman and street vendors (Verma, 2020). Since 2000, interstate migration has witnessed a considerable growth rate of 4.5% per annum, double the rate of the previous decade, with 5-6 million people migrating per year (Babu et al., 2020: 532).

Effects of lockdown on Labour Migrants

The general condition of the migrant labour is vulnerable despite being the backbone of the urban economy. To escape from poverty at home (primarily villages), they migrate to the cities and engage in construction works, domestic help, delivery services, manufacturing sector, vending, landless agricultural labourers and other daily wage works. They often work in low-paying, hazardous and inhospitable conditions, live in congested urban unhealthy settings, with little social security and employment safety to ensure a basic standard of living for themselves. Their deplorable condition is irrespective of being integral to the mostly unorganised and informal Indian economy, primarily the micro, small and medium enterprises (MSME's) which employs migrant labour the most and contribute around 45% of overall exports from India (Radhakrishnan, 2020).

Dispersed across the country and in a constant state of mobility, the migrant workers, especially the seasonal ones, are often unable to exercise their voting rights. Consequently, most are left without a political voice and finds excluded from the vote-bank dynamics of the destination states. In a heterogeneous country like India, inter-state labour migrant, in particular, experience language and cultural barriers in the destination state along with other implicit and explicit hurdles to formal social protection programmes that are biased towards the sedentary population (Ahmed, 2020: 720). National and international safeguards on human rights and working conditions of labour, including specific provisions such as Inter-State Migration Workers Act 1979, while provided on paper, is hardly enforced in practice to improve the conditions of the migrant labour. Such a situation renders the migrant labour extremely vulnerable and invisible as they rarely form part of the imaginations of development narrative in India (Venkataramakrishnan, 2020).

If the general condition of the migrant labour in India is vulnerable, the lockdown imposed due to Covid-19 has further degraded their condition to one of the worst off in the society. As workplaces were shut down, lakhs of migrant labourers lost jobs overnight. Employees and contractors who used to pay the labourers vanished. A survey by Stranded Workers Action Network (SWAN) of about 11,000 stranded workers found out that 89% of the labourers from their sample did not receive pay, 44% of them had ration left for less than one day, with several cases of people in the brink of starvation (Stranded Workers

Action Network, 2020: 9,16). With no source of income and no transport service, the migrant labour had no choice but to head home in an arduous foot journey. This started massive chains of reverse migration from cities to rural areas across the country, a scale reminiscent of the refugee exodus after partition in 1947 that displaced around 15 million people (Biswas, 2020b). The effects of Covid-19 may be much worse, as the World Bank in its report stated that the lockdown has an impact on 40 million internal migrant labourers with around 50,000 – 60,000 involved in the reverse migration process till April 2020 (World Bank, 2020: 32). Many bore the brunt of strict policing security personnel used force to keep the streets empty. Inter-state borders were closed, as a result of which many labourers could not reach their destination. Thousand slept on the street without food while the more fortunate ones took shelter at the relief camps set up by the state governments who scrambled to find a short term solution to the humanitarian crisis. Till April, 22,567 relief camps were set up across the country, most in Kerala (15,541) followed by Uttar Pradesh (2230), Maharashtra (1135) and Tamil Nadu (175) (Verma, 2020).

The government initially responded by arranging transport for the labourers to keep them away from the streets. This turned into a logistical nightmare as thousands of migrant labourers pressed against each other at bus terminals at major cities (Biswas, 2020b). The lack of coordination among states on logistical responsibilities, especially concerning train fare, only worsened the condition of labourers. The most unfortunate ones lost their lives on their way back home, the most tragic being that of 16 migrant labourers run over by a goods train in Aurangabad while they were sleeping on the railway track exhausted after walking 40 km from Jhalna Maharashtra towards their destination in Madhya Pradesh (Bannerjee and Mahale, 2000). A total of 198 workers lost their lives, most in Uttar Pradesh (94), followed by Madhya Pradesh (38), Bihar (16), Telangana (11), and Maharashtra (9) (Save Life Foundation, 2020: 2). Migrants who reached home had no respite either, as they had to follow quarantine rules for 14 days at centres many of which lacked basic amenities. The plight of migrant labourers also brought to the fore the differential effects of state intervention for different societal classes. While the affluent could afford to stay at home, the migrant labourers were fighting for sustenance. Also, the management of the internal migrant crisis stood in stark contrast to the government's approach to bringing back Indian migrants stranded abroad. While the internal migrants struggled in the streets, reports of a much better managed *Vande Bharat* mission to bring back thousands of international migrants to the country, created a sense of discriminatory treatment to the internal migrant labourers of the country.

Health and Human Rights Implications on Labour Migration

Reverse migration of labour at a scale witnessed in India after the lockdown also derailed the very rationale of implementing the lockdown – concern for public health. The World Bank, while highlighting the health implications of the reverse migration in India, stated that the containment measures might have actually contributed to the spread of the epidemic (Economic Times 2020a). In another report, the World Bank noted that 'high outmigration areas are more likely to have Covid-19 cases' as the flow of migrant workers could easily become vectors carrying the coronavirus back to other states and villages (Economic Times, 2020b). Even the government, on its part, justified the decision to halt the exodus of migrants on the grounds of community health as they pointed out that almost a third of the migrants returning to their hometown could be infected posing a serious risk to rural India, which has till then remained mostly unaffected from the pandemic (Bindra and Sharma, 2020). The lethal combination of health, hunger, sanitation and trauma had led to a humanitarian crisis at a scale not witnessed in the country in a long time (Stranded Workers Action Network, 2020: 1).

The labour migration crisis also underscored the need to safeguard individual human rights even in a pandemic situation. The crisis brought to attention the importance of maintaining a crucial balance between protecting the human rights of the individuals, even as other individual liberties are curtailed for the benefit of the community. Safeguarding certain civil, political, economic, social and cultural rights, along with the right to health as a fundamental human right especially to the vulnerable sections of the society, are especially crucial as states fight the pandemic. While certain rights such as the right to freedom of movement under Article 13 of the Universal Declaration of Human

Rights (UDHR) may be restricted, it should not be done in a manner that compromise on the dignity and rights of the individual as prescribed in Article 1, and freedom from cruel, inhuman and degrading treatment under article 5 of UDHR (United Nations, 2015). Similarly, an adequate standard of living to the highest attainable standards of physical and mental health (Article 12) as provided in the International Covenant on Economic, Social and Cultural Rights (ICESCR) (United Nations, 1967); right to life (Article 9), the prohibition of cruel, inhuman and degrading treatment (Article 10), respect of honour and dignity and privacy (Article 14), equitable procedure of resource to migrant workers (Article 16-20) of the International Convention on the Protection of the Rights of All Migrant Workers and Members of their Families (ICMRW) (United Nations, 1990), needs to be ensured even while pursuing the goals of public health.

The right to health, defined as the right to the highest attainable standard of health, was first reflected in the WHO constitution of 1946 and then reiterated in the 1968 declaration of Alma Ata and the World Health Declaration adopted by the World Health Assembly in 1998 (WHO, 2002: 9). It endorses a right-based approach to health using human rights as a framework for health development and making human rights an integral dimension of the design, implementation, monitoring and evaluation of health-related politics and programmes (*ibid*: 16). Similarly, the Siracusa principle, widely recognised as a legal standard for measuring valid limitations on human rights, makes clear that even when the state acts for good reason, it must respect human dignity and freedom (WHO, 2008: v). The principle further states that restrictions must be reasonable, non-discriminatory, less restrictive and not arbitrary, and based on a legitimate objective strictly necessary in a democratic society (*ibid*). Thus, WHO emphasised on the need to balance community interest with individual rights stating that while public health measures such as isolation, quarantine, social distancing and border controls are essential and legitimate, the burden they place on individual requires careful and reasonable use of such measures (WHO, 2007: 9). It is in this regard that the United Nations Network of Migrants expressed concern over reverse migration in India pointing out that 'successfully tackling the pandemic cannot be achieved without upholding the human rights' (International Organisation for Migration,

2020). Similarly, WHO stated that nations like India should see that the concerns of daily wagers and migrant workers are taken care of while imposing blanket lockdowns (Kaur, 2020).

The magnitude of economic and health implications of Covid-19 in the country, especially to the vulnerable sections like the migrant labour community, means that the government faces a challenging task in the days ahead. After the initial logistical chaos due to reverse migration, the government streamlined the transport arrangements to ensure a more orderly return of the labourers. Till June 2020, 67 lakhs migrants have returned home in 116 districts of 6 major outmigration states of Bihar, Uttar Pradesh, Rajasthan, Madhya Pradesh, Odisha and Jharkhand (Mathew, 2020).

Among the welfare measures, the government unveiled a US$ 23 billion economic package in March 2020, estimated to cover 800 million people in the subsequent three months entailing 5 kg wheat/ rice per person every month, gas cylinder per month and cash subsidies (Jayaswal 2020). This was followed by Rs. 20 Lakh crore *Atmanirbhar Bharat Abhiyaan* scheme in May which includes free food grains to 80 million migrant families for two months, 5000 crores special credit facility for 5 million street vendors, 30,000 crores emergency working capital scheme for farmers, Rs. 70,000 crore boost to lower-middle-class housing, Rs. 2 lakhs crores concessional credit offer to 25 million farmers through *Kisan* credit cards (*ibid*).

While lockdown was necessary to control the spread of the virus, it is, without doubt, a short term solution as evident by the phased withdrawal of restriction through unlocking since May. The government now has to get on with a crucial balancing act – to reopen the economy while keeping a lid at the pandemic spread and, at the same time, ensure the means of sustenance in terms of food, financial assistance and employment generation for the migrant labourers affected by the pandemic. A proper monitoring mechanism is crucial to make sure that the benefits reach as many of the vulnerable sections as possible. Given the fact that many migrant labours could not avail the government emergency welfare schemes, an appropriate mechanism should be in place to ensure that they receive their basic needs and do not suffer from the loss of income which might deter them from self-isolating themselves if necessary to contain the pandemic spread. While cash subsidies are essential, in the medium to long term the Mahatma Gandhi National Rural Employment Guarantee Scheme (MGNREGS) should be expanded in scope to generate regular income to the jobless. Such benefits should be as inclusive as possible so that labourers not registered can also avail the benefits, as exclusion are likely to be very large due to lack of comprehensive record especially in schemes such as Public Distribution System and *Pradhan Mantri Jan Dhan Yojana* (PMJDY). A proactive approach of the state towards the migrant labourers in their moment of crisis will help alleviate their fears, give them confidence towards the welfare state as they go back to their workplace, failing which it will have a substantial negative impact on urban development.

Conclusion

The Covid-19 pandemic has once again brought into prominence the longstanding debates on individualism and communitarian values in the particular context of states' response to the Covid-19 pandemic. This chapter has provided an analysis of these debates with specific emphasis on the impact of the Indian state's pandemic response on the labour class. The chapter highlighted the social, economic and health implications of reverse migration of the migrant labour, a section of people that has been reduced to one of the worst-off position as a result of the pandemic. While highlighting the importance of safeguarding human rights even while initiating stringent community protection measures, the chapter noted the challenge in balancing these two aspects. While moving ahead in such challenging times, since labourers are one of the worst affected segments due to the pandemic, state's response should be a combination of short to medium-term remedies that should cater to the emergent needs of the vulnerable sections like the migrant labourers. Being the backbone of the Indian economic development, the well being of the labour migrants will be crucial towards the goal of inclusive the development of the nation.

References

Ahmed, Nabeela (2020). "Vulnerability and Social Protection Access", in Rajan, S. Irudaya and Sumeetha M. (eds.) *Handbook of Internal Migrants in India*, New Delhi: Sage Publications.

Babu, M. Suresh et al. (2020). "Adverse Migration and Sub-National Welfareism", in Rajan, S. Irudaya and Sumeetha M. (eds.) *Handbook of Internal Migrants in India*, New Delhi: Sage Publications.

Bannerjee and Mahale (2000). "16 migrant workers run over by goods train near Aurangabad in Maharashtra", *The Hindu*, 8 May 2020, [Online: Web] Accessed 23 June 2020, URL: https://www.thehindu.com/news/national/other-states/16-migrant-workers-run- over-by- goods-train-near-Aurangabad-in-maharashtra/article31531352.ece

Bindra, Japnam and Neetu Chandra Sharma (2020). "Coronavirus: Govt tells SC one-third of migrant workers could be infected", *Livemint*, 1 April 2020, [Online: Web] Accessed 24 June 2020, URL: https://www.livemint.com/news/india/covid-19-govt-tells-sc-one- third-of-migrant-workers-could-be-infected-11585643185390.html.

Biswas, Soutik (2020a). "Indian coronavirus: Why lock down 1.3 bn people?", *BBC* News, 24 March 2020, [Online: Web] Accessed 15 June 2020, URL: https://www.bbc.com/news/world-asia-india-52027745.

Biswas, Soutik (2020b). Coronavirus: India's pandemic lockdown turns into a human tragedy", *BBC News*, 30 March 2020, [Online: Web] Accessed 15 June 2020, URL:https://www.bbc.com/news/world-asia-india-52086274

Economic Times (2020a). "Lockdown in India has impacted 40 million internal migrants: World Bank", 23rd April 2020, [Online: Web] Accessed 14th July 2020, URL: https://economictimes.indiatimes.com/news/politics-and-nation/lockdown-in- india-has- impacted-40-million-internal-migrants-world- bank/articleshow/75311966.cms?from=mdr

Economic Times (2020b). "Migrant workers returning home could spread coronavirus in sub-continent: World Bank", 12th April 2020, [Online: Web] Accessed 14th July 2020, URL: https://economictimes.indiatimes.com/ news/politics-and- nation/migrant-workers- returning-home-could-spread-coronavirus-in-sub- continent-world- bank/articleshow/75104522.cms.

Government of India (1897). The Epidemic Diseases Act, 1897, [Online: Web] Accessed 12th April 2020, URL:https://www.indiacode.nic.in/bitstream/123456789/10469/1/the_epidemic_d iseases _act%2C_1897.pdf.

Hale, Thomas et.al. (2020). Oxford Covid-19 Government Response Tracker, Blavatnik School of Government. [Online: Web] Accessed 23 June 2020, URL: www.bsg.ox.ac.uk/covidtracker.

ILO (2020a). ILO Monitor: Covid-19 and the World of Work, Third Edition, 29 April 2020, [Online: Web] Accessed 22 June 2020, URL:https://www.ilo.org/wcmsp5/groups/public/—dgreports/— dcomm/documents/briefingnote/wcms_743146.pdf.

Imbert, Clement (2020). "Covid-19: Expected Migrant Movement as Lockdown Eases", Ideas for India, 1 May 2020, [Online: Web] Accessed 15 June 2020, URL: https://www.ideasforindia.in/topics/governance/covid-19-expected-migrant- movement- as-lockdown-eases.html.

International Organisation for Migration (2020). "Forced returns of migrants must be suspended in times of Covid-19", *Statement by the United Nations Network on Migration, 14th May 2020, [Online: Web] Accessed 12 July 2020, URL:* https://www.iom.int/news/forced-returns-migrants-must-be-suspended- times- covid-19.

Jayaswal, Rajeev (2020). "Ration for migrants, farm relief in 2nd tranche of govt stimulus", *Hindustan Times*, 15th May 2020, [Online: Web] Accessed 20th June 2020, URL: https://www.hindustantimes.com/india-news/ration-for- migrants-farm-relief-in-2nd- tranche-of-govt-stimulus/story-oaNkawFe554GNhAxhBuDxL.html

Jeetendra (2020). "Covid-19: What about India's Migrant Workers?", *Down to Earth*, 30th March 2020, [Online: Web] Accessed 15 July 2020, URL:https://www.downtoearth.org.in/news/governance/covid-19-what-about- india-s- migrant-workers—70082

Kaur, Banjot (2020). "Covid-19: WHO criticises countries for not ensuring the dignity of migrants during lockdowns", *Down to Earth*, 31 March 2020, [Online: Web] Accessed 21 June 2020, URL: https://www.downtoearth.org.in/news/health/covid-19-who- criticises- countries-for-not-ensuring-dignity-of-migrants-during-lockdowns-70103

Khan, M. Imran (2020). "Labour Migration: Trends and Characteristics", in Rajan, S. Irudaya and Sumeetha M. (eds.) *Handbook of Internal Migrants in India*, New Delhi: Sage Publications.

Mathew, Liz (2020). "67 lakh migrants return to 116 dists in 6 states", Indian Express, 11th June 2020, [Online: Web] Accessed 17th June 2020, URL: https://indianexpress.com/article/india/coronavirus-lockdown-67-lakh-migrants- return-to- 116-dists-in-6-states-6453084/

Radhakrishnan, Trinanjan (2020). "Covid-19 Reveals Deep Vulnerabilities in India's Labor", *OXFAM India*, 17 April 2020, [Online: Web] Accessed 13th July 2020, URL: https://www.oxfamindia.org/blog/covid-19-reveals-deep- vulnerabilities-indias-labour

Rajan, S. Irudaya and Sumeetha M. (2020). "Migrant Odysseys", in Rajan, S. Irudaya and Sumeetha M. (eds.) *Handbook of Internal Migrants in India*, New Delhi: Sage Publications.

Save Life Foundation (2020). "Road Crash Deaths during COVID Lockdown Tracker", June 2020, [Online: Web], Accessed 15 July 2020, URL:https://savelifefoundation.org/wp- content/uploads/2020/06/ROAD- CRASH-TRACKER-KEY-DATA-POINTS-SLF.pdf.

Stranded Workers Action Network (2020). "21 Days and Counting: Covid-19 Lockdown, Migrant Workers, and the Inadequacy of Welfare Measures in India", 15 April 2020, [Online: Web] Accessed 18 July 2020, URL: Lockdown-and-Distress_Report-by-Stranded-Workers-Action-Network.pdf.

Tumbe, Chinmay (2014). "Missing Men, Migration and Labour Markets: Evidence from India", June 2014, [Online: Web] Accessed 22 June 2020, URL: http://www.ihdindia.org/sarnet/module1/ TumbeMissingMenMigrationand LaborM arketsi nIndia.pdf

United Nations (1967), "International Covenant on Economic, Social and Cultural Rights", [Online: Web] Accessed 11 July 2020, URL: https:// treaties.un.org/doc/Treaties/1976/01/19760103%2009- 57%20PM/ Ch_IV_03.pdf.

United Nations (1990). "International Convention on the Protection of the Rights of All Migrant Workers and Members of their Families", [Online: Web] Accessed 11 July 2020, URL: https://treaties.un.org/doc/Treaties/1990/ 12/19901218%2008- 12%20AM/Ch_IV_13p.pdf

United Nations (2015). "Universal Declaration of Human Rights", [Online: Web] Accessed 11th July 2020, URL:https://www.un.org/en/udhrbook/pdf/ udhr_booklet_en_web.pdf

Venkataramakrishnan, Rohan (2020). "India's seasonal migrants have been invisible for too long. This crisis should be a wake-up call", Scroll, 31 March 2020, [Online: Web] Accessed 17 July 2020, URL: https://scroll.in/ article/957742/indias-seasonal-migrants-have- been-invisible- for-too-long-this-crisis-should-be-a-wake-up-call

Verma, Anumeha (2020). "Covid-19 creates more uncertainty for migrant workers in India", *Global Voices*, 23 April 2020, [Online: Web] Accessed 17 July 2020, URL: https://globalvoices.org/2020/04/23/covid-19-creates-more-uncertainty- for-migrant- workers-in-india/#

WHO (2020a). Refugee and Migrant Health, [Online: Web] Accessed 12 June 2020, URL: https://www.who.int/migrants/en/.

WHO (2002). "25 Questions and Answers on Health and Human Rights", Health & Human Rights Publication Series, Issue No.1 [Online: Web] Accessed 12th July 2020, URL: https://www.who.int/hhr/information/25% 20Questions%20and%20Answers%20o n%20H ealth%20and%20 Human%20Rights.pdf.

WHO (2007). "Ethical considerations in developing a public health response to pandemic influenza", [Online: Web] Accessed 15 July 2020, URL: https:/ /www.who.int/csr/resources/publications/WHO_CDS_EPR_GIP_ 2007_2c. pdf

WHO (2008). "Addressing ethical issues in pandemic influenza planning", Discussion Papers, [Online: Web] Accessed 12 July 2020, URL: https:// www.who.int/csr/resources/publications/cds_flu_ethics_5web.pdf

World Bank (2020). "Covid-19 Crisis Through a Migration Lens", Migration and Development Brief 32, April 2020, [Online: Web] Accessed 30th June 2020, URL: https://openknowledge.worldbank.org/bitstream/handle/ 10986/33634/Covid-19-Crisis-Through-a-Migration-Lens.pdf? sequence=5&isAllowed=y

9

Inter-state Transportation Amidst the Pandemic: Contemplating the Role of NORKA in Successfully Recalling the Migrant Keralites During the Lockdown

Aswathikrishnan U.R & Nidhin C

Abstract

The Covid-19 pandemic has frozen the human life as its impact was different on different people. In India, an inevitable nation-wide lock-down was declared by the Union government to prevent the spreading of the virus. Even after the initial 21 days of lock-down, the cases began to increase in high rate forcing the government to extend the lockdown. During the lock-down, many people were not at their home but were at the places they temporarily relocated for job, education and guest visits. These people faced several problems with the extension of lockdown and they urge to return back to their native places. The NORKA department of Kerala had been given the task by the state government to lead the mission to manage the transportation of the Keralites back from various parts of the country. The chapter will look into the procedures of transportation managed by NORKA department of Kerala in successfully and safely bringing back the Keralites amidst the pandemic situation.

Key Words: *Covid-19, Transportation, NORKA, Migration, Kerala, Lockdown.*

Introduction

Migration, in any perspective, is a complex process but the procedures may seem simple. Migration demands attention from scholars of different disciplines and other policy wonks as the process is supposed to have a wider sphere of influence including security, health and human existence. Considering the high mortality rate, low recovery rate, lack of vaccine and spreading pace of coronavirus all over the world, the lockdown process in India also halted movements for the migrant workers as well as other residents by March 2020. The sudden outbreak of the pandemic and the following lockdown resulted in pause and loss of jobs on a large scale. Also, there were people who stuck in the middle of their temporary visiting purposes. By the mid-March, a large number of Indian nationals stranded over different places, both inside and abroad, became conscious of the deadly pandemic and began approaching their respective state governments to avail the transportation services for their return. Dangers behind the interstate and international migration facilitated from there onwards were coupled with the vulnerability of weak citizens including old-aged people, pregnant women, children and people with symptoms of other respiratory and heart diseases.

The transnational characteristics of Covid-19 among other contested global issues have found its form in the contemporary discussions and the combat efforts are being made at all the three levels namely, individual level, national level and the international level. To combat a global pandemic, more serious and conscious efforts are necessary at the above mentioned three levels. The policy measures took in each minute sphere of influence at the individual level matters much more than anything. But the competence of human psychology in adopting and employing the containment measures against Covid-19 suggested by the medical officers earns some distrust, hence making efforts against Covid-19 at an individual level less promissory. A combined effort made at the national and international level could counter such possible discrepancies at the individual level. There comes the importance of governmental and nongovernmental organisations of both international and national level in combating the pandemic. These organisations exert maximum possible pressure on the individual level to restrain their proximity to coronavirus and other communicable diseases. This external push to make individuals comply with the regulations and guidelines related to Covid-19 was a critical task in the context of inter-state migration during nationwide lockdown period and NORKA is a governmental organisation tasked with such a function at the national level. Analysing the functioning of NORKA during the nationwide lockdown following the Covid-19 outbreak could substantiate the role played by and impact of decisions made at the national level in resisting the pandemic. This chapter aims to articulate the timely management of transportation services by the department of NORKA amidst the Covid-19 pandemic.The chapter offers two main arguments, NORKA has been able to avert the crisis of community spread of coronavirus as much as possible by facilitating (a) an end-to-end transportation service, (b) an efficient interface through which the security and health departments were able to conduct timely check-ups for the returnees; the institutional capacity of NORKA ROOTS has proven to be effective and efficient since the organisation is successful in fulfilling its objectives at right time such as reaching out to non-resident Keralites stranded over different States in India and protecting their social security when they are at disadvantage.

Methodology

Existing literature on or related to the topic will be used as the basic resource in this research. Several websites, blogs and articles related to the issue will also be referred. Even though the research is qualitative; it won't be objective. For a closer understanding of the subject, the paper will include interviews with NORKA officials. The paper won't be using any fixed questionnaire for the interview and is an ex-facto research.

Objectives

In light of the above background, the study aims to understand the role played by NORKA in recalling the Keralites who were stuck across the nation during the Covid-19 crisis. The sub-goals of the study are as follows:

- To analyse the role, function and schemes of NORKA
- To understand the difficulties faced by the Keralites

- To examine the interventions and interactions done by NORKA in the matters of the Malayali migrants.

Norka and its Structure

The recent upsurge in migration of non-resident Keralites back to Kerala certainly implies a set of socio-economic challenges to duel with. Approximately 10 to 11 percent of Kerala's total population work outside Kerala and a significant part of their earnings were remitted back into the Indian economy. Kerala has benefited immensely from the remittances and the State government assumes remittances as a significant revenue channel. It has been reported that the remittances of Kerala are sufficient to wipe out 60 percent of its public debt in a study conducted in 2012 (Rajan, 2012). Therefore, the government of Kerala perceives social security of non-resident Keralites and their families with greater concern. Consequences of burgeoning unemployment in Kerala were partially covered by job offers from outside Kerala. In the past, expatriate communities' vulnerability to various fraudulent behaviours from sponsors and recruiting agents used to go beyond any normal level by which the state government of Kerala realised the necessity to provide best services and secure social security for the expatriate community. Kerala government once initiated to identify major issues and concerns for securing the safety of the expatriate community in their back and forth movements and other living conditions. Shortly in 1996, this resulted in the establishment of the Department of NORKA. Since then, the department provides its extensive support for emigrants in matters such as ensuring safe transportation, dignified life, better living conditions and easing other certificate formalities.

Considering the huge macroeconomic implications of remittances for socio-economic stability of Kerala, the department of NORKA used to strengthen the relationship between non-resident Keralites and the government of Kerala since 1996 via facilitating proper grievance-redress mechanisms, designing innovative policies and welfare programmes. NORKA became the first single window agency for assisting the expatriate community in 1996 and it is the first one of its kind in India (Balaram, 2012). The department of NORKA discharged its duties for securing migrant needs through NORKA ROOTS, a separate implementation agency. NORKA ROOTS became an intermediate channel or an interface for communications took place at each level in the process of migrant-transportation and it was able to achieve wide recognition for its excellent institutional framework. Previously the organisation of NORKA ROOTS was registered as a company under section 25 of Companies Act 1956. Later the organisation underwent a restructuring process by which it was converted into a government company whose sole authority rests with the government of Kerala. Since 2011, the structure of the governing board of NORKA ROOTS has incorporated the chief minister of Kerala as its chairman with two vice chairman positions. Minister of the Department of NORKA and a NORKA ROOTS committee member constitute the two vice-chairman posts of the board of directors. A chief executive officer presides over the other staff members of NORKA ROOTS. With the three directors representing NORKA ROOTS and a secretary representing both NORKA and NORKA ROOTS simultaneously, the board of directors comprises a total of eight members. Head office and two non-resident Keralites development offices are situated in Thiruvananthapuram, New Delhi and Mumbai respectively. NORKA ROOTS has two regional centres in Ernakulam district and Kozhikode district in Kerala.

Welfare Schemes of NORKA

The department of NORKA was entrusted with many objectives and NORKA ROOTS acted as the implementation agency for those objectives on wellbeing and security of non-resident Keralites and ensuring safe migration could be seen as a prime objective among others. Services provided by the NORKA ROOTS are extended to facilitating required actions for return emigrants such as rehabilitation and reintegration, financial assistance to needy and sick people, capital subsidies to business ventures. Also, creating a database of emigrants, conducting skill up-gradation programmes, socio-economic engagements and non-resident Keralites gatherings for them and promoting philanthropic activities constitute a major part of objectives pursued by the NORKA ROOTS. The department also aims to secure gainful and legal employment abroad for emigrants. A job portal and a call centre were established in 2010 and 2011 respectively. Regional centres of NORKA ROOTS have initiated the Apostille attestation service. NORKA ROOTS used to intervene in corresponding policy matters of emigration and protection of migrant rights. The department conducts pre-departure orientation programme since 2006 for those who are vulnerable to visa cheating and use of other despicable means for migration such as undocumented transportation. The pre-departure orientation programme provides other information relating to emigration rules, employment contract and customs regulations. NORKA ROOTS avails ambulance services and other financial assistance in the repatriation of corpses from outside of Kerala under Karunya scheme and reasonable financial assistance under the scheme Santhwana as part of availing distress relief fund for returnees (NORKA ROOTS, 2020). The Pravasi identity card helps emigrants to access free insurance coverage of Rs 2 lakhs for those who are at disadvantage. Thus, NORKA made sufficient efforts to create a fine human resource pool out of emigrants via channelising their resources and expertise. In a nutshell, the emigrants are receiving a handful of services from NORKA ROOTS on behalf of the Department of NORKA in various ways. Execution of NORKA ROOTS services and policies usually demands reasonable time as its governance is strictly bound to clearance of certain procedures and other official formalities. But the organisation pursued a quick action within the available short timeframe for securing safe transportation for the majority of emigrants during nation-wide lockdown.

Lockdown and its Impact

Amidst the increasing number of Covid-19 cases, the Union Government of India decided to declare an instant but inevitable nationwide lockdown for the then 21 days starting from the midnight of 24th of March 2020. The unexpected lockdown which prohibited people from stepping out of the place where they were then living caused serious tensions among the population, especially among the ones who had temporarily relocated for job, education and guest visits. The corona crisis had hit this people hard as they faced several issues including job loss, health emergencies, quest for proper treatment, mental trauma, unavailability of food, separation from family and high economic burdens. The people who were stuck at different places had no other way but to wait until the day when the restrictions on lockdown would be lifted. But the things were not as easy as it was expected and the increase in the number of cases forced the government to declare the second phase of lockdown extending the current one to another 19 days. This made the people across the country more restless and they urge to go back home. The case of the non-resident Keralites were not any different as they also showed high anxiety to return home (*The New Indian Express*, 2020). This made both the union and state government to intervene in the issue of transportation.

Norka's Co-ordination in Transportation

The government of Kerala thus decided to bring back its people who were stranded in various parts of the country. But this was a crucial task for the concerned authority as a slight mismanagement in transportation could bring huge disaster and chaos. The main responsibility for transportation was given to the NORKA department and they formed a procedural framework which guaranteed the safe return of the people. As a first step, the NORKA website opened the registration process for the returnees on 29th of April 2020 by collecting their details in order to prioritise the category that needed immediate return (*The Hindu,* 2020). Keralites across the nation showed high ecstasy and rush to register in the newly opened portal for interstate travel. Few days after the starting of the registration process, on 4th May 2020, the state government opened its borders in six check points including Aryankavu, Kumily, Walayar, Manjeswarama, Muthenga and Inchivila. Entry across the border was given only on the basis of permit passes allotted by the NORKA department and this was coordinated in such a way such that around 500 people could be accommodated. The government agencies had setup 60 counters in the borders which had government employees including school teachers, policemen, health official and revenue officers monitoring and executing the covid protocol (*The Economic Times,* 2020). The high traffic in the NORKA portal forced the government to temporarily stop the registration process for a day and a new platform named Jagratha portal was introduced very soon to manage the registration process. According to the reports by The News Minute (2020), the interstate travelers who crossed the borders of Kerala in a single day by road was 12,509 in numbers.

The application process through Jagrathaportal was very much systematic as it managed every minute details of the user in the most beneficial way. The request application for interstate travel pass was submitted to the respected district collector of the applicant through the website. The basic requirement for applying in the Covid-19 Jagrathaportal included the mobile number and NORKA registration id of the applicant. Every traveler was instructed to provide the vehicle number and the group travelers going to different districts were advised to choose different vehicle to travel. Then the applicant had to select the date, check post and time slot in which they would be reaching the border. The district collector who scrutinised the application granted the permission on the basis of emergency and the pass was distributed through SMS and email id of the user. The applicant was then instructed to reach the opted check post on time and cross the border after a thorough health checkup. To ensure social distancing, there was limitation in the maximum number of travelers in each vehicle according to its seating capacity. A maximum of four people in a five-seater, five people in a seven-seater, ten people in a van and twenty-five people in a bus were the allotted quota for the vehicles (Jagratha, 2020). The other state vehicles which helped the Keralites to reach back were given return pass by the concerned district collector. Moreover, the state government through NORKA also gave pass to people who need to cross the border to bring back their children, parents or spouse stuck at other Indian states. Thus, the NORKA department have addressed almost every concern related to the returnees, that too in a scientific way.

According to the public relations officer of NORKA Roots, the purpose of registration was not just to distribute permit pass but it had other dynamic uses as well. In-between the submission of the application and the approval of the same, there were lot of bureaucratic procedures to ensure the safety of the returnees. Once the application is submitted to the district collector through the NORKA website, the collector's office contacted the respective local body authorities, police station and health center of the applicant. The local body authorities collected the details of the applicant's house to ensure whether it has the facility for room quarantine and if not, an alternative government system was provided to accommodate the returnee. During the 14-day room quarantine, the health department continuously checked the health status of the returnee and admitted the persons having corona symptoms to observation. The duty of the police officials was to ensure that the returnee was not breaking the quarantine leading to serious spread. The permit pass was distributed by the district collector only after getting the response from the local body (Mankuzhy, 2020). Hence, the successful method adopted by the Kerala state government using NORKA department for interstate transportation was by tracing, tracking and caring the returnees.

Conclusion

The impact of corona virus has literally terminated people's mobility due to its high spreading nature. An inevitable lockdown declared by the government to stop the spreading of the virus kept people inside their house. But there was a population who were not at home but had temporarily relocated to different places for various needs. The unexpected lockdown separated them from their family. NORKA department of Kerala during that time took a systematic step to bring back the Keralites who wished to return. The aim of this chapter was to understand the timely management of interstate transportation services provided by NORKA amidst the Covid-19 pandemic. The two main arguments raised in this chapter are that NORKA had been able to prevent the crisis of community spread of coronavirus during the interstate transportation by an efficient interface through which the security and health departments were able to conduct timely check-ups for the returnees; and also the institutional capacity of NORKA ROOTS was effective and efficient by successfully fulfilling the objectives at right time such as reaching out to non-resident Keralites stranded over different states in India and protecting their social security when they were at disadvantage. For this purpose the essay had highlighted the high migrant population of Kerala in and outside India, the structure and function of NORKA, various welfare schemes implemented by NORKA, impact of the unexpected lockdown on people, NORKA's transportation management, procedures to gain state permit pass and the hand in hand coordination done by various government departments to ensure the safe return of the Keralites from other Indian states. In conclusion, it can be stated that the timely intervention and action taken by the NORKA department with the help of other government authorities to bring back the stranded Keralites was effective and efficient.

References

Balaram, A. (2012). *Norka*. Retrieved from Arthapedia: http://www.arthapedia.in/index.php?title=NORKA

Jagratha. (2020). *guide lines 2*. Retrieved from covid-19 jagratha portal: https://covid19jagratha.kerala.nic.in/

Mankuzhy, S. (2020). NORKA and the covid crisis. (N. C, Interviewer)

NORKA ROOTS. (2020). *Welfare schemes*. Retrieved from NORKA: https://norkaroots.org/

Rajan, S. I. (2012). *Assessment of NORKA-ROOTS (an implementing agency of the Department of NORKA - Non-resident Keralites Affairs of the Government of Kerala) and the Applicability of a Similar Organisation to other States in India.* Philippines: Migrant Forum in Asia.

The Economic times. (2020). *Kerala opens border at six places to enable Keralites return from other states*. Retrieved from The Economic Times: https://economictimes.indiatimes.com/news/politics-and-nation/kerala-opens-border-at-six-places-to-enable-keralites-return-from-other-states/articleshow/75530004.cms

The Hindu. (2020). *Keralites stranded in other States can now register to return home*. Retrieved from The Hindu : https://www.thehindu.com/news/national/kerala/keralites-stranded-in-other-states-can-now-register-for-return-home/article31457937.ece

The New Indian Express. (2020). *Huge demand from non-resident Keralites wanting to return home.* Retrieved from New Indian express: https://www.newindianexpress.com/states/kerala/2020/apr/27/huge-demand-from-non-resident-keralites-wanting-to-return-home-2136139.html

10

Role of Awareness in Combating Anxiety and Depression amid Covid-19

Dr. Reena Malik

Abstract

The world is facing a very tough time due to spread of this deadly virus Covid-19. The virus has created a situation of panic and thus affecting us physically, emotionally, mentally and financially. It has created a fear in our minds deterioting our mental health and well being, which gives birth to various problems like depression, stress, anxiety, fear etc. The present study aims at exploring the role of awareness in dealing with anxiety and depression. Data have been collected from 150 respondents through online questionnaire (Google doc) by random sampling technique from various states of India. Descriptive statistics, reliability analysis, factor analysis, correlation, t-test and regression tools were used for analyzing the data. The result shows that level of awareness regarding Covid-19 influences positively and helps in managing anxiety and depression.

Keywords: *Awareness, Depression, Anxiety, Mental health, Stress, Covid-19, Well being.*

Introduction

The pandemic Covid-19 has spread all across the world. It is a virus that spread by coming in contact of an infected person. World Health

Organisation, 2020 has defined this disease a contagious disease which belongs to "Coronaviridae" family. The virus has started from Wuhan city of China and is now spreading like wildfire and causing millions of deaths. It is a respiratory disorder contaminating human and animals showing symptoms of fatigue, high fever, cold and dry cough. It has the ability to multiply in human body and thus affecting the respiratory system causing death. WHO (2020) has confirmed that this virus affects the most to elderly people or people suffering from prolonged diseases like diabetes, blood pressure etc. Due to increasing number of cases and virus spreading across the world, WHO has declared this disease as Pandemic on March 11, 2020, after the first corona positive case reported in Kerala, India. The Indian government came into action and as the cases rose to 500, the government has imposed a 21 days lockdown in the country and extended it further to contain the spread of this deadly virus. This was just the beginning for this long battle. Various further lockdowns was announced by the Indian government subsequently. This was a crucial situation for all of us; everybody was in shock as it was the first time especially in India when such lockdowns were introduced. People were anxious and full of fear due to this outbreak of deadly virus. They were asked to remain at home and can go out only for essential services. This was very challenging and full of stress. Dar (2017) explained that stress can lead to some mental disorder like anxiety and depression. The situation was so bad that it has an impact on mental health and well being of people. Sin (1978) defined well being as a global assessment of quality of life of a person which is based on his chosen criteria. Due to this pandemic people across the world are experiencing certain disorders, anxiety, stress and depression. Government of different countries are helping people to get out of this anxiety and stress by creating awareness on this issue via radio, banners, media etc. Measures to prevent from this pandemic are also being communicated to the public time to time in order to remind them for their safety. There is no medicinal vaccination is available till now for this deadly virus, people are still in the state of fear and anxiety which ultimately impacts their mental health. The present study thus aims at exploring the impact of awareness on the mental health of the people during this lockdown.

Research Methodology

In order to identify the role of awareness to maintain mental health, a questionnaire was designed and the responses were obtained through online questionnaire distributed on social media platforms via Google form in month of April (2020) and the data was collected from 150 respondents from different regions of India as it was not confined to nay geographical area (distributed through online platforms). The internal consistency of the instrument was checked and is shown in subsequent parts ahead. Tools such as Cronbach's alpha, Factor analysis, Correlation, Regression are used to analyze the recorded responses.

Objectives of study

1. To know the level of awareness among people during pandemic.
2. To understand the role of awareness in combating anxiety and depression.
3. To explore the impact of awareness on anxiety and depression.

Hypotheses Formulation

On the basis of the above literature the undermentioned hypotheses has been developed:

H1: There is no significant impact of awareness on anxiety and depression during lockdown.

H2: There is no significant difference on the basis of gender regarding anxiety and depression.

H3: There is no association between awareness, anxiety and depression.

Respondent's Profile

Data as collected with the help of online questionnaire of a total of 250 respondents from different states of India. The returned and complete questionnaire in all manners was scrutinised and it was found that the complete responses were recorded for only 200 respondents. Most of the respondents were male (54%) and rest (46%) were females. Most of the respondents were educated and 70% of the respondents were postgraduate and belong to the age group of 25-35 years and most of them were professionals and had an average income of 30,000 INR.

Data Analysis

Table 1: Descriptive Statistics

Statements	*Mean*	*Std. Deviation*
Anxiety		
I am very nervous person	3.35	.898
I am bothered by my nervousness	3.07	.776
I feel very tense during lockdown	4.90	.809
I feel anxious and restless during lockdown	3.95	1.303
I find it difficult to calm down myself	3.10	.921
I feel upset due to this pandemic	4.81	1.023
I am very impatient	2.56	.790
I keep on thinking ways to prevent myself from pandemic	2.43	.808
Depression		
I feel very downhearted during lockdown	4.71	.937
I feel like doing nothing during pandemic	3.12	.810
I find myself in some stress during this time	3.80	.943
I consider very low spirit nowadays	4.41	1.201
Most of the time I think of Covid-19	4.33	.951
Awareness		
I am aware of Covid-19	4.99	.960
I am aware of preventive measures for pandemic	4.67	.891
Continuous messages from govt reminds to be careful	4.39	.921
I take care of all preventive measures	3.72	.732
I feel secure knowing about do's and don'ts	4.09	.930
I can prevent myself and family from pandemic	3.97	1.230
I feel satisfying after knowing about pandemic	4.04	.972
I regularly update myself related to pandemic	4.31	1.905
Knowing about preventing pandemic I feel good	3.88	1.212
Knowledge about virus helps me relax	4.11	.968

Source: Primary Data.

Table 1 depicts the descriptive statistics like mean and standard deviation for all the constructs and most of the respondents agree with the statements. The highest mean recorded (4.90) for "I feel very tense during lockdown" and the lowest (3.07) for the statement "I am bothered by my nervousness."

Table 2: Factor Loadings

Items	*Factor Loading*	*Cronbach's Alpha*	*Variation Explained*
I am very nervous person	.624	.883	15.231
I am bothered by my nervousness	.590		
I feel very tense during lockdown	.632		
I feel anxious and restless during lockdown	.502		
I find it difficult to calm down myself	.530		
I feel upset due to this pandemic	.680		
I am very impatient	.601		
I keep on thinking ways to prevent myself from pandemic	.715		
I feel very downhearted during lockdown	.783	.771	17.002
I feel like doing nothing during pandemic	.637		
I find myself in some stress during this time	.613		
I consider very low spirit now a days	.540		
Most of the time I think of covid-19	.768		
I am aware of Covid-19	.792	.745	42.105
I am aware of preventive measures for pandemic	.765		
Continuous messages from govt reminds to be careful	.670		
I take care of all preventive measures	.690		
I feel secure knowing about do's and don'ts	.763		
I can prevent myself and family from pandemic	.579		
I feel satisfying after knowing about pandemic	.690		
I regularly update myself related to pandemic	.613		
Knowing about preventing pandemic I feel good	.741		
Knowledge about virus helps me relax	.662		

Source: Primary Data.

To determine the validity and reliability certain statistical procedures were used. To validate, factor analysis was run. This procedure helped in ensuring that the set of the various items being reduced were similar to modeled number. To verify dimensionality of the variables (dependent and independent) three factor analysis was run by using (Varimax) rotation. For measure of sample adequacy KMO test was done for all the factor analyses, were more than 0.5. The total variance explained is 74.338%, as if the independent variable is causing 74% of variation in dependent variables.

Testing Hypotheses

After fulfilling the conditions of internal consistency and validity, further regression analysis was done in order to test the hypotheses for checking the influence of awareness on anxiety and depression.

Table 3: Gender relation with depression and anxiety

	Gender	*N*	*Mean*	*Std. Deviation*	*t*
Depression	Male	108	23.678	4.452	.992
	Female	92	21.034	3.776	
Anxiety	Male	108	21.442	3.280	.802
	Female	92	19.301	5.992	

Table 3 revealed that there is no significant difference in level of awareness and anxiety of male and female respondents involved in the present study. The results indicate that the mean score is higher for males (M=23.678; SD= 4.452) reflecting more depression than females (M=21.034; SD= 3.776).Similarly, male respondents (M=21.442; SD= 3.280) scored higher in anxiety than female respondents (M=19.301; SD= 5.992). On the application of the t-test, this difference between the mean of male and female was found insignificant.

Table 4: Correlation Matrix

	Awareness	*Anxiety*	*Depression*
Awareness	1		
Anxiety	-.932*	1	
Depression	-.732*	.667*	1

*Correlation significant at 0.05 level

Table 4 depicts that there exists a strong negative correlation between awareness and anxiety and awareness and depression. A moderate strong relation was witnessed between anxiety and depression at a 5% level of significance.

Result and Discussion

The present study focused on the awareness and its impact on anxiety and depression during Covid -19 and its impact on gender especially of anxiety and depression. For this purpose various statements related to awareness, anxiety and depression were analyzed by using factor analysis after checking for reliability and correlation among the constructs were analyzed as shown in correlation matrix. The data analyzed showed that there exists a negative correlation between anxiety and awareness (-.932) which is quite robust negative correlation. Similarly, depression and awareness also exhibit a strong negative correlation of (-.732). But strong positive correlation was found between anxiety and depression, (.667) which can be considered as two elements of mental health. A t-test was run to check the impact of depression and anxiety on male and female participants. But there found no significant difference on male and females of anxiety and depression with (t= .802 and .992) respectively for males and females undertaken in this study. With this we can say that awareness has negative correlation with mental health constructs i.e. anxiety and depression. The reliability for all three constructs awareness (.745), anxiety (.883), and depression (.771). Awareness as independent variable causes a total variation of 74% on mental health constructs anxiety and depression.

Conclusion

Maintaining good mental health is prerequisite for all of us especially during this stage where Covid-19 is spreading like wildfire across the world, and still there is no success in inventing medicine for the same. It is common to have fear in the mind regarding this deadly virus everyone is tensed, fearful, anxious and depressed as this virus has kept us in our homes during lockdown, no socialising, we even cannot step out of our homes. This is having a massive effect on the well being of the people. Nobody knows what is going to happen but just to have discussion over it. There is no alternative to getting aware and informed about thus deadly virus spread, prevention till the time any vaccine comes in existence. Government of different countries, NGO's, medical staff, social workers, media leaves no stone unturned to give repeated information regarding its prevention (washing hands, drinking lukewarm water, wear mask, keep social distancing etc.). This study revealed that awareness has helped in combating anxiety and depression which leads to a better mental and physical health. As more and more we get aware about the methods of prevention of this deadly virus, we can prevent ourselves and our loved ones from this disease. Thus, this study urges to media houses print and online to keep reminding people and provide latest information about Covid-19.

References

Carlsson-Szlezak, P., Reeves, M. & Swartz, P. (2020). Understanding the economic shock of coronavirus. Harvard Business Review, March 27, 2020. https://hbr.org/2020/03/ understanding- the-economic-shock-of-coronavirus.

Kirton, D. (2020). Chinese public dial in for support as coronavirus takes mental toll. Reuters, February 13, 2020. https://www.reuters.com/article/us-china-health-mental/ chinese-public-dial-in-for-support-as-coronavirus-takesmental-toll-idUSKBN2070H2

Rehm, J. & Shield, K.D. (2019). Global burden of disease and the impact of mental and addictive disorders. Curr Psychiatry Rep 2019; 21:10.

World Health Organisation: Coronavirus disease (Covid-19) outbreak - technical guidance - EUROPE: mental health and Covid-19. 2020. http:// www.euro.who.int/en/ healthtopics/ health-emergencies/coronavirus-covid-19/ novel-coronavirus-2019-ncovtechnical- guidance/ coronavirus-disease-covid-19-outbreak-technicalguidanceeurope/ mental-health-and-covid-19.

https://en.wikipedia.org/wiki/2019%e2%80%9320_coronavirus_pandemic

11

Coverage of Migrant issues in Digital news format: A Content Analysis

Dr. Shourini Banerjee, Sumedha Chaudhuri & S. Balaganapathy

Abstract

The coverage of the pandemic mostly dealt with the plight the migrants suffered due to the sudden announcement of the lockdown across the country from 24 March 2020 onwards. People had very less time to move to their hometown and the situation was grim as the media- print, television and social media were flooded with the pictures and bytes of the migrants. This paper is a content analysis of the diverse news coverage of the digital versions of the leading news media of the country. It is apparent that during the lockdown, the digital news was used widely and the circulation of the print had considerably gone down. The study took in the news articles published online by leading media houses from 26 March to 26 May. The results indicate that the news were mostly about the hardships and soul wrecking images of them but amidst all the troubles, there was lack of any follow up or a positive streak of news on the migrants life.

Keywords: *Migration, Covid, India, News channels, Coverage, Media.*

Introduction

As Mukhra & Krishan (2020) mentioned, "The country witnessed a large scale migration after the partition in 1947". Covid-19 has created a widespread panic across the nation after a 21 days nationwide lockdown was announced by the Prime Minister.

The students had already escaped the ordeal as most of them had already departed for their hometown as schools and colleges were announced closed from 17 March 2020. The migratory population who wanted to return their homes due to the lockdown was worst affected. India stands 49th in the Global poverty index and most of the poor venture to the cities in search of a job. The Census (2011) stated that the majority of the migrants settle down in Maharashtra and Delhi. Due to the restricted lockdown opportunities, there was a phase of reverse migration. The migrants chose to walk back towards their home which implied traveling across the state border as transport facilities were not available. The migrants returning back consisted of children, old, pregnant, sick as well. This internal reverse migration has led to disastrous impact as the economy came down to an all time low. Most of the cities are inhabited by the migrant people whether it is labourers or the blue collared officials. In such a grim situation, where the government was completely unprepared to handle such a huge crisis which deemed more than the Covid-19 health scare. The media was abundantly flashing the heart breaking pictures of the migrants lying on the road, walking barefoot, without food, water and money. Few NGOs gave their helping hands and shelter homes were created by the government but that was not enough as most of them set afoot. The reportage by the media was kind of mixed with social media playing the role of a saviour as well as spreading fake news. The coverage not only highlighted the plight but also focused on how they were susceptible to spread the virus and lead to community transmission. As mentioned in BBC (2020), "When migrants flee from the city they not only lose their livelihood but they may carry the infections to their native places". It is needless to say that urban migrants are a significant part of the development of the urban and posh cities, yet they were highly vulnerable during the crisis. Apart from that the reverse migration is also a major setback for the economies to rise up. With almost 40 million migrant labourers suffering, this paper aims at finding out the coverage of the media regarding the same.

Research Objectives

The study has formulated the following objectives for the study:

- To analyse the News reports pertaining Migration during the pandemic.

- To understand the theme of the news reports and the perspective.

Methodology

This study has analysed the news reports available in the digital platforms from 26 March to 26 May. The news was qualitatively analysed understanding whether the news was in positive light or not. News consumption is more due to the interest, credibility, immediacy and also because it was trending. So apart from Uses and Gratifications Theory, it is the Agenda Setting Theory also which will come into the light. Therefore, a pluralistic perspective over any issue definitely brings in equality in the dissemination of news. Journalism according to the dominant view is the process of institutionalising news gathering and reporting. Therefore, critically evaluating the viewpoint and the social responsibility behind the news is important and has been identified.

Analysis of the news reports:

1. **Alternative career option for the migrants**

   https://www.chathamhouse.org/expert/comment/covid-19-hidden-majority-indias-migration-crisis#

   This news article describes the alternative career options the migrant labourers have opted for once they returned to their hometowns. The picture describes their inclination towards farming and this will motivate many people. The article has ably discussed the pros and cons of the lack of employment opportunities for the migrants even though it is a part of the unorganised sector. The article ends with a hope that the migrants rise up again and do not live in deprived conditions with security in both health and jobs in the near future.

2. **MGNREGA Scheme for the migrants**

   With the nationwide lockdown amid Covid-19 resulting in unemployment and panic, migrant workers started returning to their native places on foot due to unavailability of transportation. Those who could reach their place were either kept on 14 day quarantine in government health centers or at home.

However, after completing the precautionary phase, some had to go back to their workplace in a bus or private vehicle while others were noticed dealing with an economic crisis in search of a sustaining daily income source.

Taking suo moto cognizance over the increasing depression, the central and state governments amended the Mahatma Gandhi National Rural Employment Guarantee Act (MGNREGA) and National Rural Employment Guarantee Act (NREGA) so as to engage these labourers in job opportunities and in turn support financially.

In a news report https://thewire.in/government/jharkhand-mgnrega-migrant-workers, it is mentioned about the MGNREGA scheme being worked out to offer employment scopes to the migrant workers returning to Jharkhand. This news is shining light after

The Outlook's report https://www.outlookindia.com/newsscroll/jharkhand-govt-launches-3-schemes-to-spike-mandays-for-mgnrega-to-help-returnee-migrant-workers/1824905 highlights Jharkhand government's initiative to launch the MGNREGA in scheme-wise in order to benefit the migrant labourers step by step. The initiative by the state government towards the migrant labourers emanates a positive hope for the readers after a dismal and pathetic situation faced by the migrants.

In a news report of The Print https://theprint.in/india/governance/lockdown-sees-record-spike-in-nrega-jobs-but-1-7-crore-applicants-fail-to-get-one/460818/ the failure of NREGA for the sake of migrant labourers reflects the loopholes as well as communication gap in fulfilling the livelihood of these desperate job seekers. This too mentions that though the scheme is available yet several do not get the opportunity to avail it.

3. Policy framework for the labours

https://www.bloombergquint.com/coronavirus-outbreak/a-policy-framework-for-indias-covid-19-migration The news report discusses the opportunities for taking up new jobs once the migrants reach their village. The counselling of the labourer is essential is also mentioned in the news report with able support from the local governing bodies. The news report emphasised on the dignity and the reduction of the urban and rural divide which stigmatises the poorest of the poor who venture out of their hometown for a better livelihood.

4. **Spraying the migrants with disinfectants**

   https://www.ndtv.com/delhi-news/coronavirus-lockdown-migrants-sprayed-with-disinfectant-in-delhi-civic-body-says-a-mistake-2233741

   The very headline of the news report is sure to enrage many others as it just depicts the inhuman way in which migrants have been treated and victimised of being the carriers of the virus. The picture depicts the helplessness of the migrants ready to head towards their hometown and the callous attitude of the municipal corporation. The last line of the news report states that several workers are walking towards their hometown in the absence of any transport facilities.

5. **New ministry for the migrants**

   https://indianexpress.com/article/opinion/columns/migrant-labour-crisis-india-coronavirus-lockdown-modi-govt-adhir-ranjan-chowdhury-6421503/

   This article is penned down by Lok Sabha MP Adhir Ranjan Chowdhury who criticised the Government's take on the handling of the migrant crisis as well as unprepared lockdown which led to a messy situation. The article ends with the writer claiming to set up a separate ministry for dealing with migrant affairs which will ease the difficulties for them in the near future.

6. **Migrants carrier of coronavirus**

   https://www.india.com/news/india/uttar-pradesh-news-50-migrant-workers-from-maharashtra-test-positive-for-coronavirus-fears-coming-true-say-officials-4034279/

   This news depicts and creates a panic amongst the readers as it confirms the rumour which has been going on that the migrants may transmit virus to the village upon their return. The officials in the news report from Uttar Pradesh have expressed their concern and anxiety. This definitely creates a situation where the migrants feel dejected and stereotyped as they returned from Maharashtra which has recorded the most number of cases.

7. **Fake news leading to Migrants assembling in Bandra**

   https://indianexpress.com/article/cities/mumbai/mumbai-news-report-misleading-led-to-gathering-at-bandra-says-court-6370029/

   This news indicates the trouble and chaos created due to fake news circulation in the social media about transportation available for the migrants. The Mumbai police and the civic body was dumbfounded and did not know how to handle the situation. The fake news was circulated by a journalist from ABP Majha who was taken into custody owing to a fake news report. The diligence and social responsibility is the prime duty for the media has been stated explicitly.

8. https://www.hindustantimes.com/india-news/govt-forms-empowered-groups-task-force-to-deal-with-covid-19-outbreak/story-mq8y4SjvLgb74v07359WDJ.html

   The formation of a special task force to combat the issues emerging out of the Lockdown and migrant labour crisis have been discussed here. The task force comprises senior bureaucrats. This news discusses how the group will oversee the medical health facilities available as well as the condition of the quarantine centres. This news depicts the working of the government towards Covid-19 crisis.

9. **Low death rate for Covid-19**

   https://www.usnews.com/news/world/articles/2020-05-26/india-coronavirus-cases-rise-as-millions-return-home

   This news report discusses the death rate and the recovery rate of the coronavirus cases. This news is definitely positive amidst the crisis and reduces the tension that arose due to the coronavirus panic. The news is by top global news agencies and therefore, this has a huge impact upon its readers.

10. Migrants from Pakistan refuse to return

https://thelogicalindian.com/news/migrants-from-pakistan-refuse-to-go-back-21254

The news discusses the Pakistani migrants who do not want to return to their country as they prefer the facility given by the Indian government to them. The migrants stated in the news report that the condition of minorities in Pakistan is not suitable and they would prefer to live in India under the Citizenship Amendment Act 2019.

11. Tear gas to Labourers

https://www.businessoffashion.com/articles/news-analysis/migrant-workers-in-india-face-police-backlash-after-defying-covid-19-lockdown

This news was published during the initial days of the lockdown and the panic stricken migrant labourers assembled in order to return to their native. The Police in order to manage the crowd had sprayed tear gas which enraged the distressed people further. The news also mentioned that though the cases were less compared to other countries yet it is mandatory to manage any kind of influx or exodus as it will spread the virus further.

12. Death of the Migrants

https://thewire.in/rights/coronavirus-national-lockdown-migrant-workers-dead

This news article described the horrific death of the migrant labourers while on their way towards the hometown among which there were children. The image in the news is also painful as it shows a child gulping water from a bottle amidst scorching heat. The toll the sudden lockdown has caused among the migrant labourers who wanted to return to their hometown has been reported here. The news report also highlights the inefficiency of the central and the state governments over managing the migrants.

Conclusion

Media has a huge impact upon its audience. The story angle of a particular announcement or event or incident presented either by a newspaper, news channel or news agency or news portal varied even during the ongoing pandemic. The home bound returning of migrant workers had both positive as well as impact for the society in large. Not only the media fraternity, but the government, NGOs, corporate houses, political parties and individuals joined hands towards the emerging paradigm of development communication among these workers. The social identity of these underprivileged was questioned by showcasing their emotions, health, insecurity, family and livelihood.

Therefore, this study has analysed few of the news related to the corona pandemic during the period of study. All kinds of news portals were taken up for seeking different dimensions of the stories published pertaining to the migrant labours. More studies on the same can be conducted taking into account other media as well. This study primarily highlighted the several news of the migrant labourers who were completely distressed due to the health scare as well as the loss of their economic source, house as well as a stigma. This study can serve an idea to the people/institutions/NGO's on the coverage on migration during the pandemic.

References

1. Richa Mukhra, Kewal Krishan, Tanuj Kanchan (2020) Covid-19 Sets off Mass Migration in India, Archives of Medical Research, ISSN 0188-4409. https://doi.org/10.1016/j.arcmed.2020.06.003
2. Sirkeci, Ibrahim & Yücesahin, M. (2020). Coronavirus and Migration: Analysis of Human Mobility and the Spread of Covid-19. Migration Letters. 17. 379-398. 10.33182/ml.v17i2.935.
3. Bhagat, R. & Sahoo, Harihar & Archana, Sahoo & Roy, K & Govil, Dipti. (2020). The Covid-19, Migration and Livelihood in India A Background Paper for Policy Makers International Institute for Population Sciences, Mumbai The Covid-19, Migration and Livelihood in India.
4. World Bank. 2020. Covid-19 Crisis Through a Migration Lens. Migration and Development Brief, no. 32. World Bank, Washington, DC. World Bank. https://openknowledge.worldbank.org/handle/10986/33634 License: CC BY 3.0 IGO.
5. Jan Sahas, (2020). Voices of the Invisible Citizens: A Rapid Assessment on the Impact of Covid-19 Lockdown on Internal Migrant Workers. April, New Delhi.
6. https://www.mohfw.gov.in/pdf/RevisedPsychosocialissuesofmigrants Covid-19.pdf

7. https://www.iom.int/sites/default/files/our_work/ICP/MPR/migration_factsheet_6_covid-19_and_migrants.pdf
8. https://www.chathamhouse.org/2020/07/covid-19-hidden-majority-indias-migration-crisis
9. https://migrationdataportal.org/themes/migration-data-relevant-covid-19-pandemic
10. https://www.globalprotectioncluster.org/wp-content/uploads/sg_policy_brief_on_people_on_the_move.pdf
11. https://www.ejumpcut.org/archive/onlinessays/JC34folder/TheoriesofNews.html

12

Role Played by NGO's in the Support of Migrant Labourers during Covid-19: A Study across NGO's of Bengaluru City

Ms. Sophia Sharon

Abstract

Indian migrant workers faced numerous difficulties during the Covid-19 pandemic. With factories and workplaces shut down due to the country's shutdown, millions of migrant workers were forced to cope with income loss, food shortages, and confusion about their future. Thousands of them then started walking back home, without any means of transportation due to the lockdown. In response, the central and state governments took various measures to assist them, and later arranged transport for them. More than 300 migrant workers died as a result of the lockdown (Indian migrant workers during the Covid-19 pandemic - Wikipedia), with reasons ranging from hunger, suicide, exhaustion, road and rail accidents, police brutality and denial of timely medical care. With this background, the current study aims at Understanding the Role of NGO's in a Pandemic situation and their impact on the lives of the migrant labourers. The research objectives are accomplished with the help of primary data collected from 100 migrant workers who are beneficiaries across 10 NGO's in Bangalore. The statistical tools used under study are the SPSS software used for Descriptive Statistics and Exploratory Factor analysis. The AMOS software is used to carry out the confirmatory factor analysis for the study. The findings revealed that majority of migrants have monthly income less than 10,000 which press the need for financial help during the economic crisis caused to due pandemics. More than half of the respondents earn income in form of wages which means that when there is no work there is no income and due to the crisis the economy has slowed down bring a halt to business activities and hence badly affecting the Migrant workers. The current study succeeded in creating a model for the roles of the NGO's towards the migrant workers in any pandemic situation. The model classified the roles as – Primary roles, secondary roles and collaborative government roles. The data fit the model well and it can be suggested as a way for further researchers who want to know in depth the activities and roles of NGO's during disasters or Pandemics.

Keywords: *Migration, Migrants, Laborers, Pandemic, Covid-19, Non-Profit Organisations.*

Introduction

In an offer to combat the spread of the novel Covid-19 infection, Governments around the world have been scrambling to participate in mass testing, isolates, follow-up contacts and possible shutdowns. On March 24, Indian Prime Minister Narendra Modi made the drastic move of seeking the country's prompt three-week lockdown—with just a few hours notice ahead of time. (Suparna Chaudhry and Shubha Kamala Prasad, 2020) While this measure was fundamental and rational, it brought to India's forefront the reputation of inadequately executing choices affecting the nation as a whole, especially as it abandoned a large number of out of nowhere unemployed temporary workers and further placed underestimated networks at risk.

In the midst of the enormous disturbance caused by the pandemic, non-governmental associations (NGOs) have taken a step towards filling in the holes of correspondence and transmitting basic things to underserved communities. NGOs in India perform a wide variety of jobs including but not limited to promoting transportation, government funding works for network development, advancing voting-based system, human rights, even-handed administration and investment by citizens, and so on. Taking into account the restricted accessibility of the administration's financial space, its spending on the social sector remains severely deficient.

The effect of inadequate provisioning of social component is compounded by the disintegration of network-level security networks. There are two models of the absence of childcare plans for working ladies, especially those at low-pay gatherings, and the decline of old consideration in families across different salary bunches. In these situations, NGOs' dedication to clearly neglected areas of society takes noteworthiness. Returning to the emergency Covid-19, our response should be both quick and long-term. While the administration seems to welcome the ability of NGOs to pursue the lockdown's prompt repercussions, the need is to cultivate a correlative and community-oriented commitment that looks back a long way. Support in the expansion of facilities and capacity in the health sector, as well as cutting-edge specialist co-ops such as ASHA, ANM and AWW and so on, are clear areas of co-ordinated effort in the medium and have been running since long ago.

There are numerous more subtle but incredibly important circles in which NGOs may take on a job of improving the adequacy of the administration's response. For example, as the administration reorganizes its expenditure to address the financial impact of the emergency, the services and divisions for underestimated networks and social segments, such as women and children, social equity, ancestral government assistance, water and sanitation and training, and so on, will be best positioned to benefit from the NGOs' examination-based support for ensuring NGOs can also help spread the holes in security networks that affect transient workers, provincial and urban poor people, just like most underestimated networks such as sex workers and transgender people, and so on. The sneaking threat of an ecological catastrophe due to environmental change further requires the need for powerful and manageable coordinated effort between government and non-governmental organisations. Not only that, NGOs have the HR, aptitude and involvement with these areas, the re-prioritisation of worldwide donors for tending to the consequences of the emergency gives them the power to bring some extra assets into the country, which is the great need.

Although it is the government's duty to take care of migrant workers, the commitment and role of NGOs "deserves all appreciation" for coming forward to support them by providing food, water and transportation during the "difficult time" of the Covid-19 pandemic, the Supreme Court stated on Tuesday.

The Supreme Court also praised the individuals who helped and played an important role in helping migrants and said that the community, moved by their miseries and difficulties, showed its "passion and devotion."

Preparing for a pandemic is crucial. That sector will play its role in ensuring that at-risk populations are aware of it, and can take steps to prevent and reduce pandemic influenza. NGOs are a significant sector capable of bridging the gap between information and action. Governments, donors and the international community need to recognize the unique and important roles that NGOs, particularly at community level, can play in preparedness programmes. In short, there is an immense need — and now a rare opportunity — for all stakeholders to play their positions in preparation for a potentially widespread and catastrophic disaster yet to materialise.

Review of Literature

An examination of NGOs' commitments to advancement by looking at the Aga Khan Rural Support Programme (AKRSP) exhibition and the watershed administration of the executives programme was attempted by Anil C. Shah and Sudarshan in about 35 towns in the Bhavnagar area of Savarkundla taluk, Gujarat. This contextual review acknowledged the reality that NGOs, with adequate and knowledgeable sources of information and planning, could contribute to country advancement through the design of the work and its fair impact on the procedures; given power, capacity and energy, the watershed administration system couldn't do anything about an impact.

An inquiry on Samuel C. Models of intentional associations identified with the provincial turn of events was focused on Voluntary Agencies and Social Change. A wide range of willing association exercises have been recognised, for example, good cause, alleviation, administration, government assistance, recovery, improvement of financial, natural, and human viewpoints. The analysis further confirmed the five characteristics of deliberate activities: expenditure by individuals, approach focused on reputation, monetary and social turn of events, person and gathering activity and willing intervention of government assistance. It depicted the enormous commitments of willful activities to advance a populist and confident example of social and financial transformation. In addition to counting unmistakable highlights and striking achievements of the NGOs, this examination also conducted an inside and out investigation into the techniques, approaches and systems that NGOs have received.

Surendra, K review on Community Participation and the Roles of NGOs. In Tamil Nadu three NGOs broke down. The focal theory was that supporting the frail gatherings in dynamic procedures brings about decreasing political force contrasts between the more impressive gatherings and the feeble ones. It confirmed NGOs' fundamental position in engaging the poor. The result of the review was that NGOs' job of engaging poor people was persuasive and proportionate to poor people's degree of interest. The main restriction was the avoidance of social and sociological viewpoints on the creation of individuals.

For a very long time, advancement was considered unique as a financial turn of events, and was essentially estimated as an expansion of gross national pay. In the wake of dissecting various rustic advancement ventures in the Third World: Dirk B.W.M. unmistakably called attention to the financial, social, hierarchical, administrative and specialised conditions of ventures that underline the uniqueness of the circumstance of the undertaking. Expound review of rustic advancement ventures revealed how each task should actually embrace an undertaking cycle and system that would meet the neighbourhood needs of the neighbourhood network. NGOs' triple points of interest clarified in the investigations were: progressively compelling aid delivery, well-known cooperation being developed procedures, and speaking to denied mass premiums; and the apparent inconveniences of NGOs were: making separate aid associations, quality versus quantity, accessibility of assets, and executive issues. The role of governments and NGOs in the creation of countries was seen as equally relevant as one cannot neglect the other.

Objectives

The research goals are:

- To research demographic features of Migrant Workers in Bengaluru.

- Understanding the role of NGOs during the Pandemic and their effect on Migrant Workers lives.
- Create a model for NGO roles to create sustainability among Migration workers during Pandemics.

Research Methodology

4.1 Research Type: Exploratory study aimed at examining the current condition of Migrant workers in the city of Bengaluru as the entire world is affected by the pandemic and the role of NGOs in these circumstances.

4.2 Data collection technique: Interview process-Because Migrant labourers are mostly illiterate and are not very interested in research, it is necessary to meet people, and to persuade them to respond to the interview schedules.

4.3 Data collection Tool: Interview schedule consisting of Likert scale agreement items as this measure is most recommended for assessing respondents' views and perceptions. The interview schedule is structured to be short and to the point because of the Covid-19 consequences of Social Distance. Demographic questions and 16 issues are answered relating to the functions and activities of the NGO's.

4.4 Sampling design: The population of Bengaluru, as per the 2011 census was 96.2 lakh people. Of these, a staggering 44.3 lakh people are classified as migrants, based on migration data recently released by the Office of the Registrar General & Census Commissioner. Using Unknown Population's Cochran Formula, the sample size is 100 migrant workers at 40 percent error and 5 percent significance level.

The researcher has therefore decided to survey 10 NGO's across the city of Bengaluru and randomly take 10 people from each NGO who may be beneficiaries of the NGO's.

4.5 Questionnaire reliability: The reliability of the questionnaire is checked with the help of Cronbach's Alpha and 26 items in the current study have a reliability statistic of 0.813 which is a good measure. The questionnaire's material validity is carried out and the Cronbanch's Alpha for 16 Likert scale items stood at 0.899 and the composite reliability is 0.871 and the Average variance Described is 3.009. All the criteria for validity fall within acceptable range.

4.6 Research methods: The statistical instruments used in the study are the SPSS software for Descriptive Statistics and Exploratory Factor Analysis, and the AMOS software is used to conduct the study's confirmatory factor analysis.

4.7 Study limitations: The study is based on the migrant workers' responses and the sample size is small due to the social distancing effects of Covid-19. The study is limited only to migrant workers' perceptions and may not be sufficient to finalise NGO's role model during pandemics.

Findings and Suggestions

5.1 Demographic Profile

The respondents' demographic profile showed that majorities of 67.9 percent of respondents are male and the remainders are female. The age group of Migrant Workers under study shows that a majority of 52.8 percent of respondents are over 55 years old and this call for a need to create more security for Bengaluru City's migrant workers. A majority of 83 percent of the respondents are women, which suggests a high degree of obligation on their shoulders. 62.3 percent of migrant workers worked on building sites, 16 percent worked in private offices. A large majority of 73.6 percent of migrant workers is an alphabets and only 3 respondents have completed their graduation, indicating a need for awareness among them to avoid harsh pandemic health effects. A majority of 83 percent of migrant workers have less than 10,000 monthly incomes that press for financial assistance during the economic crisis caused by pandemics. 57.5 percent of respondents earn income in the form of wages, which means that, when there is no work, there is no income and because of the crisis, the economy has slowed down bringing business activity to a halt and has therefore had a serious impact on migrant workers. Most of 85 percent of respondents live in rented houses and major expenses that need to be helped every month, this burden also affect migrant workers' peace. Most of the members in the family work in a migration worker for small amounts that will run the family but due to the Covid-19 all respondents mostly felt the pinch of the pandemic, particularly the economic conditions in cities where living standards are very high.

5.2 Descriptive statistics

Descriptive statistics are discussed regarding the functions and activities NGOs made during the current pandemic as viewed by the slum dwellers. Likert agreement scale is used where 1= Strong Disagreement and 5= Strong Consensus. The mean answer score shows the level of consensus on the declarations. Providing food and ration kits had the highest mean ratings of 4.62, 4.76 and 4.89 respectively, providing transportation services and providing cooked meals. Also the standard deviation is very small showing no major difference in the responses. Creating awareness (4.42), collaborating with government organisations

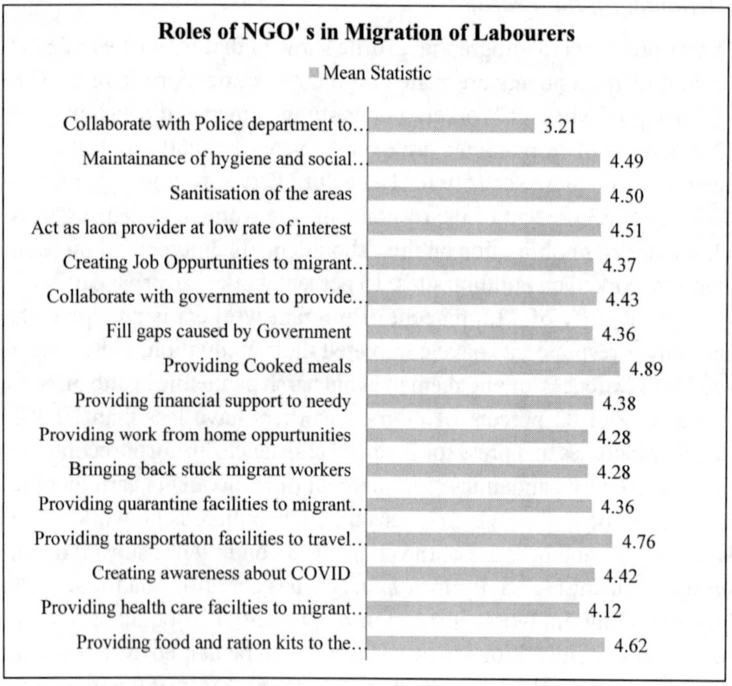

Source: Primary Source

Graph 1 : Role of NGO's in migration of Workers.

to provide adequate facilities (4.43), acting as loan providers at low interest rates (4.51) and sanitation of the surrounding migrant workers (4.50) have mean scores above 4 indicating agreement to a strong response range. The migrant workers often decide on the other positions, and the migrant workers' overall impression of performing NGO's positions during the unexpected conditions is strong. The minimum statistic shows the minimum answer value; not all respondents have chosen the choice of strong disagreement which is an accomplishment for the NGOs. The maximum statistics indicate that 5-strong agreement option-is preferred by the respondents. The skewness and kurtosis are within reasonable limits, and the data is said to be appropriate for further study.

5.3 Exploratory Factor Analysis

The KMO is a sampling adequacy measurement which compares the magnitudes of the observed correlation coefficients with the magnitudes of the partial correlation coefficients. The sampling adequacy measure Keyser-Meyer-Olkin is an index for comparing the magnitudes. It is found from the above table that the sampling adequacy KMO measure 0.837 and the sphericity test Barlett are statistically significant at 5 percent level. Bartlett test is 430.949 chi-square value with a significant value less than 0.05, indicating that the matrix of association is not an identity matrix and tends to be factorable. (Table 1)

Table 1

KMO and Bartlett's Test		
Kaiser-Meyer-Olkin Measure of Sampling Adequacy.		0.837
Bartlett's Test of Sphericity	Approx. Chi-Square	430.949
	df	45
	Sig.	0.000

Source: Calculated by SPSS Software using Primary data

Table 2

Total Variance Explained									
Component	*Initial Eigenvalues*			*Extraction Sums of Squared Loadings*			*Rotation Sums of Squared Loadings*		
	Total	*% of Variance*	*Cumulative %*	*Total*	*% of Variance*	*Cumulative %*	*Total*	*% of Variance*	*Cumulative %*
1.	2.244	22.436	22.436	2.244	42.436	42.436	2.013	40.126	40.126
2.	1.683	16.834	39.270	1.683	16.834	59.270	1.786	17.858	57.985
3.	1.215	12.152	51.422	1.215	22.152	71.422	1.344	23.437	71.422
4.	1.012	10.123	61.545						
5.	0.884	8.838	70.383						
6.	0.775	7.750	78.134						
7.	0.650	6.498	84.632						
8.	0.584	5.839	90.471						
9.	0.509	5.085	95.557						
10.	0.444	4.443	100.000	(No values only 3 Components extracted)					
Extraction Method: Principal Component Analysis.									

Source: Calculated by SPSS Software using Primary data.

From the above table it can be stated that the total variance of the set of inter-related items is extracted in order to define the underlying dimension in the data set by Maximum Likelihood Extraction Method with Varimax and Kaiser Normalisation for Factor Rotation. The total variance, extracted sums of square loads and the sums of rotation of square loads are shown. The average number of square loads removed is 71.422%. Three factors are identified using the Factor Analysis method mentioned

Table 3

Rotated Component Matrix[a]			
	Component		
	1	*2*	*3*
Role_NGO_12 Creating Job Opportunities to migrant workers	0.758		
Role_NGO_6 Bringing back stuck migrant workers	0.756		
Role_NGO_8 Providing financial support to needy	0.657		
Role_NGO_2 Providing health care facilties	0.623		
Role_NGO_11 Collaborate with government to provide facilities approved by government		0.779	
Role_NGO_10 Fill gaps caused by Government		0.688	

(Contd...)

Role_NGO_16 Collaborate with Police department to check COVID-19 related issues		0.625	
Role_NGO_4 Providing Transportation facilities for workers			0.692
Role_NGO_1 Providing food and ration kits to the Migrant Workers			0.642
Role_NGO_9 Providing Cooked meals			0.511
Extraction Method: Principal Component Analysis. Rotation Method: Varimax with Kaiser Normalization.			
a. Rotation converged in 4 iterations.			

Source: Calculated by SPSS Software using Primary data.

Table 4

Secondary Roles during the Pandemics	***Roles of collaboration with Government***	***Basic Roles during Pandemic***
Role_NGO_12 Creating Job Opportunities to migrant workers	Role_NGO_11 Collaborate with government to provide facilities approved by government	Role_NGO_4 Providing transportation Facilities for the Migrant Workers
Role_NGO_6 Bringing back stuck migrant workers	Role_NGO_10 Fill gaps caused by Government	Role_NGO_1 Providing food and ration kits to the slum dwellers
Role_NGO_8 Providing financial support to needy	Role_NGO_16 Collaborate with Police department to check COVID-19 related issues	Role_NGO_9 Providing Cooked meals
Role_NGO_2 Providing health care facilities		

Source: Calculated by SPSS Software using Primary data.

Due to lack of reliability and lack of validity, various items are omitted from the study after analyzing the performance of the explorative factor analysis. The initial number of items was 16 and the final number of items 10 is chosen and loaded in three variables (Table 3). The following table shows the variables and objects that were loaded under the same. (Table 4)

5.4 Confirmatory Factor Analysis

CFA is used to test the factor structure of Roles performed during pandemics by the NGO's. This is to determine if there is some association between these variables and the latent constructs they underlie. A path diagram was drawn which represents the interrelationships between these variables.

The diagram above shows the factor loading to the respective latent factor for each element. You can also see the things with error term and the ties between the latent factors. In the diagram Roles NGO during Pandemic, the CFA (Confirmatory Factor Analysis) model using AMOS is shown as the only exogenous latent factor and the remaining ones, namely primary roles, secondary roles and Collaborative Govt. are endogenous in the model shown in the route diagram. The things loading into the respective latent factor are more than 0.7 according to the CFA. The items therefore load significantly onto their respective latent factors.

Table 5

Model	*NPAR*	*CMIN*	*RMR*	*GFI*
Default model	34	447.156	0.0644	0.817

Source: Calculated by AMOS R Software using Primary data.

To validate the study scales, a three-factor measurement model was initiated, and confirmatory factor analysis (CFA) was performed to test the measurement model. The fit of the model was assessed on the basis of the fit indices, namely fitness index (GFI) and approximation of square error (RMSEA) means root. The model fits

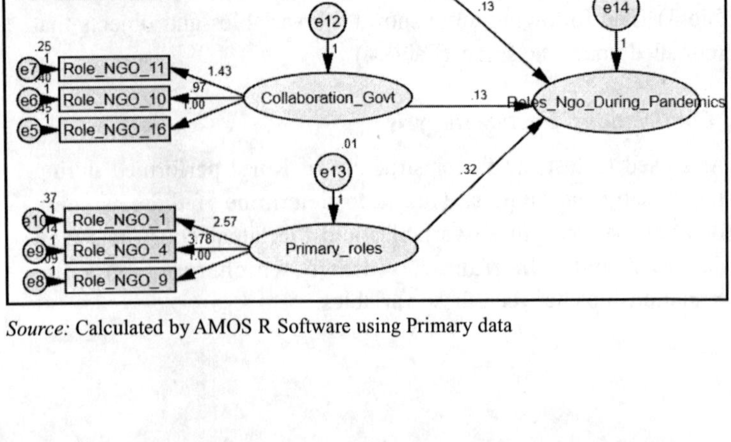

Source: Calculated by AMOS R Software using Primary data

the data well from the CFA output, because the Chi-Square value of 447.156 with 34 NPAR is statistically significant as the p value is 0.00. It Goodness of Fit Index (GFI) = 0.817 and approximation of Root Mean Square Error (RMSEA) = 0.0644.Figure: 2 Confirmatory Factor Analysis – Role of NGO's in pandemic

The structural relationship showed that Primary roles during pandemics have a greater impact as compared to the secondary and Collaboration with Government roles. As the Roles of the NGO increase in pandemics, 32% is contributed by fulfilling Primary roles. The secondary roles contribute to 13% each towards the role of NGO's during the Pandemics.

Future Role of NGO in India

From the findings of the study the following role is expected from the NGO's for management of post-pandemic situation:

- The NGO's should become indispensable lifelines and force multipliers for governments that will be struggling to deal with healthcare and essential commodities.
- The NGO's should likely be able to leverage their past actions and subsequent credibility to drive the message of social/ physical distancing to populations that may be unconvinced of government announcement.
- The NGO's should enable taking help from the wealthier sections of the society.
- By their actions and example, NGO's play a crucial role in creating alternate narratives of effective governance, holding government institutions to higher levels of performance and accountability.
- Finally, and perhaps most importantly, the form of civil society-state cooperation on display in Bengaluru and elsewhere throughout these extraordinary situation could provide the encouragement and the model for practical partnerships aimed not just at preparing for the next public health emergency but also for ameliorating the living conditions for Migrant workers in ordinary.

Suggestions

- Migrant workers' inclusion in national Covid-19 policy responses can help to ensure the realisation of equality and social justice.
- Bilateral and multilateral cooperation to migrant workers and their families can ensure their protection, safe return and effective reintegration into labour markets.
- Policies based upon social dialogue and full involvement of employers' and workers' organisations can foster inclusion of migrant workers in national responses.

Conclusions

The sudden crisis raised due to the Covid-19 pandemic has shaken the whole world, in such a situation; the plight of the undeserved communities or the slums is unimaginable. Luckily, along with the Government a number of NGO's are serving the communities right from the basic need of food to creating awareness on the pandemic and taking care of migrant workers. The current study created a model for the roles of the NGO's towards the Migrant Labourers in any pandemic situation. The model classified the roles as – Primary roles, secondary roles and collaborative government roles. The data fit the model well and it can be suggested as a way for further researchers who want to know in depth the activities and roles of NGO's during disasters or Pandemics.

References

George, C.E., Norman, G., Wadugodapitya, A. *et al.*, 2019. Health issues in a Bengaluru slum: findings from a household survey using a mobile screening toolkit in Devarajeevanahalli. *BMC Public Health* 19, 456 https://doi.org/10.1186/s12889-019-6756-7

https://www.academia.edu/23315329/Role_of_NGOs_In_Disaster_Management

Mathivaanan, Samuel C., (1 991). Voluntary Agencies and Social Change, Manas Publications, Delhi.

Shah, Anil C, and Sudarshan Iyengar, (19981. The Contribution of NGOs to Development: Some issues and a Case Study, in M.L. Dantwala, et a1 (ed), Social Change Through Voluntary Action, Sage Publications, New Delhi, pp. 92-112.

Van Dusseldorp, Dirk B.W.M., (1 992). Projects for Rural Development in the Third World: Preparation and Implementation, Wegeningen Agricultural University.

Vettivel, Surendra K., (1992). Community Participation - Empowering the poorest - Roles of NGOs, Vetri Publishers, New Delhi.

13

An Assessment of Social Interaction Anxiety among the Undergraduate and Postgraduate Students Facilitated Online Readiness Learning due to the Pandemic

Fariza Saidin, Tajbina Yasin

Abstract

The onset of corona virus has increased its alarming levels of spread and harshness during last couple of months. January 2020 is the month in which the deadly corona virus was certified as Pandemic by World Health Organisation (WHO). Considering the severity of these diseases the entire globe is facing a crisis wherein everyone is being held hostage inside four walls and fighting for it. The present study was carried out in Guwahati with an aim of investigation of readiness for online learning of university students during the outbreak of Covid-19. A total of students of both UG and PG programme were taken as sample (N-93) using convenient sampling. Findings indicated both UG and PG students had a positive correlation between online readiness learning and social interaction anxiety. Thus highlighting that the potential importance of online teaching learning process during crises to reduce to meet the academic challenges for both students and educators.

Key words: *Covid-19, Online learning, Student's Readiness.*

Introduction

Teaching learning is a continuous process and to continue its flow online learning can be used as a powerful weapon to overcome any crisis that can be encountered learners as well as educators specifically. But due to sudden outbreak of corona virus has undoubtly interrupt in the process. The onset of corona virus has increased its alarming levels of spread and harshness during last couple of months. January 2020 is the month in which the deadly corona virus was certified as Pandemic by World Health Organisation (WHO). Considering the severity of these diseases the entire globe is facing a crisis wherein everyone is being held hostage inside four walls and fighting for it. The pandemic of Covid-19 has affected almost every section of people and every aspects of life hence the teaching learning process. The outbreak of this disease has created anxiety; sever stress, disconnected, isolation, and hopelessness among people. During this contagion each and every spear and aspect of our daily life has been adversely affected to such an extent that life does not seem to be the same as before. In this time of crisis the education sector along with others has been hit in such a way that people all over the nation are forced to stay inside their home, borders are sealed, transportation services are shut down, market areas are deserted, office, educational institutions barred down. While this virus is unpredictable, precautionary measures are taken especially by education department to go for online classes. With changes of time technology has been widely used by everyone. The new generations of this digital era are more prone to use technology and are trying their best to extract from the changes that has taken place in every sector. Information and communication technology is regarded as one of the notable and supporting factor for the contribution of changes through providing digital platform where a new way of learning can be adopted and implemented. Hence the changes of technology thus help to enhance teaching learning process almost from everywhere (i.e. home, school). Various modes of online learning i.e. internet learning, tele-learning, video conference, sudio-video tape, computer assisted learning and many other have made it possible to access learning almost from anywhere and anytime and also added in making fruitful learning through various content available and experience for each learner (Karmakar & Nath, 2014). Without being in the class/ institutional premise one can avail e-learning and aid in learning process. Expansion of digital learning can be an effective tool in order to cater the need of higher education and meet the demand of the students and educators through various courses available. With the emergence of technology, the use of mobile phones, laptops, tablets and other digital sources, most of the students are availing online benefits. The alarming increase in the use of devices and sources in relation to education shows positive relation between the same. The role of education system in polishing individuals with the necessary skills for technology to maximise advantages can be overlooked (OECD, 2016). Technology can help us to gain the opportunity through which widening perception, comprehension, effective communication can be experienced and also to improve the relevance and quality of education (Rhema and Miliszewska, 2012).

Advancement of technology enables us to communicate with each other and share materials in different forms which in turn make us feel learning in a conventional classroom. The flexible nature of e-learning allows one to get tune in with their way of life and explore the subject matter. Hence the effectiveness of this platform cannot be ignored due to its widespread network to connect everyone and minimising geographical gaps.

Besides its connectivity, it multiplies the advantage for those who experience awkwardness being in crowd and have difficulties maintaining social relationship. In other words online teaching aids in establishing a better platform aids for individual with social interaction anxiety (Esfandiari et.al, 2013).

Social interaction anxiety characterised by an apprehension of unconstructive assessment and negative response by the individual in making connection to others. It is associated with weaken positive experiences and positive affect (Vassilopoulos & Banerjee, 2010). Social anxiety seems to affect learning performance too (Russel and Topham, 2012). Clarke & Fox 2017, reported negative belief and distress of students about themselves and perception by others which results in impairment in students activity due to social anxiety.

Studies claim that social anxiety found to be lower in students experiencing online communication (Yen et.al, 2012). A positive correlation was also observed between social interactional anxiety and readiness for online learning. Through online methods student can build comfortable environment which keep them away from face to face communication (Elnakeeb & Khalifa, 2016).

Hence an attempt is made through this piece of work to stress on the relationship between online readiness and higher social interaction anxiety among UG and PG students.

Related previous work

Rhema and Miliszewska (2012), carried out an investigation to re-built and re-develop its higher education system which was affected due to political crisis, the armed conflict, and the destruction through online learning to meet the demand of post crisis situation in Libya. They have highlighted the impact of the armed conflict on higher education and have suggested to used ICT and e-learning as an effective supportive tool for the affected learners.

Evidence collected supports the view that online learning is helpful for college students. Studies have attempted to compare online teaching with that of traditional teaching and revealed that the advantages of online teaching over traditional teaching as students are found to be better performer in online platform. It appears that combination of classroom learning with online learning results in best delivery method (Means et al., 2009; Friedman & Friedman, 2011).

An article by Mackey et. al (2012) discussed about online learning as a productive measure for attainment of academic resilience during crisis. A case study of immediate post-earthquake challenges of redesigning courses was provided to focus on different uses of online activities to meet the demand of teacher and students. Authors have recommended to proper uses of blended learning getting maximum benefits during emergency or unexpected circumstances.

Yen et.al (2015) attempted a comparative study between online and real-life interaction with sample of 2,348 college going students. Results indicated lower social anxiety with online interaction in comparison to offline interaction. Moreover subjects with high social anxiety also reported to have low social anxiety. The study suggested internet as substitute for reducing social anxiety.

Elnakeeb & Khalifa (2016) in their study discussed about the effectiveness of online learning that aids in effective educational transition and also in decreasing social interaction anxiety. They have used a descriptive cross-sectional correlation design with 404 nursing students keeping an aim of assessing the relationship between readiness in online learning and social interaction anxiety among nursing students. The finding of the study highlights a positive correlation between student's online readiness and social interaction anxiety.

Methodology: A survey method was applied to assess readiness for online learning of university students during the outbreak of Covid-19. Total no. of (N-60) students ranging from years participated in the study. Informed consent was taken from each participant before initiating the assessment. Convenient sampling was adopted which comprised total no. of UG students and PG students. This piece of work has used questionnaire which was distributed through online and well were returned. The questionnaire developed by McVay (2000, 2001), consisting 13 items to estimate a student orientation course towards online learning in a bachelor's degree within a university in the United States using 4-point likert scale.

Objectives

- To find out the correlation between SIAS and OLRS of UG students.
- To find out the correlation between SIAS and OLRS of PG students.
- To find out significant difference between UG and PG students in terms of SIAS.
- To find out significant difference between UG and PG students in terms of OLRS.

Hypothesis

- There will be no significant correlation between SIAS and OLRS of UG students.
- There will be no significant correlation between SIAS and OLRS of PG students.
- There will be no significant difference between UG and PG students in terms of SIAS.

There will be no significant difference between UG and PG students in terms of OLRS.

Tool for data collection: The datas were collected using two tools:

McVay's Readiness for online learning questionnaire was constructed as well as analysed for understanding the student's orientation towards online learning and is found to be useful. It was developed by Mc Vay. It is a readiness questionnaire and was published in 2001. It consists of 13 items rated on 4-point likert scale. The reliability of the questionnaire is considered to be satisfactory with the Cronbach Alpha of 0.83.

The Social Interaction Anxiety Scale was constructed by Mattick and Clarke to understand the social interaction anxiety among the individuals or classmates. It consists of 20 items rated on 5-point likert scale. In this scale there are three negatively rated items (5,9,11). The more the scores are scored higher the more higher the levels of social interaction anxiety. It also has a satisfactory internal consistency.

Sample size and method: The present study was a cross-sectional study, descriptive in nature. The total no. of participants consist of 93 from UG and PG programme. Convenience sampling method was used in selection of students from Guwahati metropolis.

Result

Table 1: Response rate of UG and PG students

Respondents	*Distributed*	*Received*
UG	50	49
PG	50	44

Table 2: Mean and Standard Deviation of UG and PG in Social Interaction Anxiety Scale

Variables	*Levels*	*Mean*	*SD*
SIAS	UG	59	18
	PG	38	17

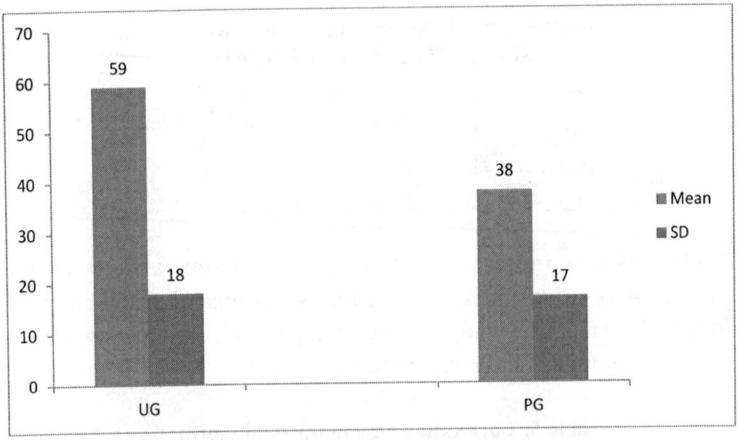

Figure 2: Mean and Standard Deviation of UG and PG in Social Interaction Anxiety Scale.

Table 3: Mean and Standard Deviation of UG and PG in Online Readiness Learning Scale

Variables	*Levels*	*Mean*	*SD*
OLRS	UG	34	11
	PG	27	11

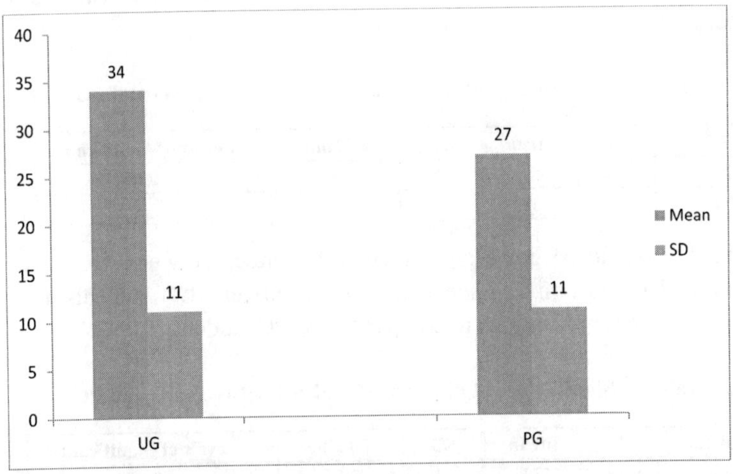

Figure 3: Mean and Standard Deviation of UG and PG in Online Readiness Learning Scale.

Table 4: Correlation among the total scores of SIAS and ORLS on the UG level

	SIAS	ORLS
SIAS	1	0.83
ORLS	0.83	1

*Correlation is positive and Significant at 0.05 level

The Table 4 indicated that social interaction anxiety was significantly positive with online readiness learning. Hence it can be said that students (UG) who are anxious about social interaction finds it easier to communicate in online mode.

Table 5: Correlation among the total scores of SIAS and ORLS on the PG level

	SIAS	ORLS
SIAS	1	0.92
ORLS	0.92	1

*Correlation is positive and Significant at 0.05 level

The Table 5 clearly indicating positive correlation between social interaction anxiety scale and the online learning. Students of PG showed significantly positive correlation with online readiness learning.

Table 6: Significance of difference in SIAS between UG and PG

SIAS	*N*	*Mean*	*SD*	*T Value*	*Levels of Significance*
UG	49	59	18	5.78	0.05
PG	44	38	17		

The Table 6 shows significant differences between UG and PG students in terms of social interaction anxiety. UG students are found to be more anxious in comparison to PG students.

Table 7: Significance of difference in OLRS between UG and PG

OLRS	N	Mean	SD	T Value	Levels of Significance
UG	49	34	11	3.07	0.05
PG	44	27	11		

Table 7 indicates differences in Online learning between the two group. UG students are found to have more readiness for online learning compared to PG students.

Discussion: From the Table 4, it can be inferred that the undergraduate students have a significant relationship between the two variables i.e., Social Interaction Anxiety Scale and Online Readiness Learning Scale with the r value of 0.83, indicating a 0.05 level of significance. This itself shows that undergraduates are inclined in accepting the online learning mode as their readiness have found to be high. It can also be stated that they have a high amount of Social Interaction Anxiety build within themselves as their experience to college environment is newer in comparison to other higher level students. It is often seen that students coming new to colleges or universities from a methodical school system, wish to explore their field of acquiring knowledge in different way. It also lighted on the aspect that some students find it easier to interact and excel through online medium because of their increasing social anxiety as the undergraduates come newly to this College environment. (Mayar Elnakeeb and Sabrein Mahmoud Ali Khalifa, 2016); (Wloodkowski, 2008).

However, this pandemic situation stood facilitating for them as they had aced in establishing a positive correlation between the two variables mentioned above. As some students found this period to be beneficial and as a whole they didn't let the crisis to overpower their learning enthusiasm. It is also seen that undergraduates can adapt themselves very well and being freshmen they can effectively use the online learning method. (Mayar Elnakeeb and Sabrein Mahmoud Ali Khalifa, 2016).

From the Table 5, it can be inferred that the Postgraduate students have a significant relationship between the two variables i.e., Social Interaction Anxiety Scale and Online Readiness Learning Scale with the r value of 0.92, indicating a 0.05 level of significance. Postgraduate students are more accustomed with the college environment or the traditional classroom learning method. (Mayar Elnakeeb and Sabrein Mahmoud Ali Khalifa, 2016). They also have the higher inclination of achieving something in their lives as they are about to closing up their academic career and step into work fields. In our study it is found that students have a higher Social Interaction Anxiety which also led to increase of Online Readiness Learning, thus establishing a positive correlation between the two variables. This can be supported by the above explanation and due to the increased tension because of the arisen pandemic crisis and it is heavily taking a toll on the mental health of the students, as rightly stated in an article Coronavirus and the Student Mental Health Crisis written by Anne Dennon. In another article from Psychology Today also supported the fact that Covid-19 is drastically increasing anxiety among college students which could also be the factor for their avoidance of socially interacting and preferring online learning to complete their existing enrolled course. Though contradictory studies suggest that higher level students does not show a significant relationship between the two variables mentioned but in our study the result have turned out to be different (Mayar Elnakeeb and Sabrein Mahmoud Ali Khalifa, 2016).

From the Table 6, it has been inferred that undergraduate students scored high compared to postgraduate students in terms of social interaction anxiety as evident from the mean scores. Since undergraduate students are new to the experience of college life which might bring changes in various aspects of their life including academic, personal, social and other that may create stress, anxiety within them. In college life there is a vast scope of meeting new friends coming from different places and cultural diversity which may restrict in their face to face interaction or in other words lead to social interaction anxiety among UG students. Social anxiety was found to be common among the age group of 18 and above and studies have confirmed that undergraduate are highly prone to social anxiety disorder (Kesseler et al, 2005; Hakami et al, 2018).

Table 7, highlights the inclination of undergraduate students towards online learning readiness than postgraduate students. Online activities are considered as one of the most attractive task especially for those who have just stepped in from traditional settings. Online platform gives ample opportunity to its consumer for getting engaged in various ways. Due to the flexibility of online learning students can get the most out of it by simultaneously doing other activities. Studies have claimed that undergraduate students shows interest in enrolling online courses which helps in applying different styles of learning (Rensburg, 2018; Artino & Stphens, 2009).

Conclusion: The aim of this paper was to investigate the correlation between Social Interaction anxiety and online readiness learning among UG and PG students. The findings stated that Social Interaction Anxiety and Online Readiness Learning had a positive correlation among both UG and PG students. Moreover PG students had a slight higher correlation factor than the UG students. This might be due to the impact of the Pandemic as it clearly mentions of its easily spread quality and also students wants to complete their course of academics which have been considered to be at stake. This crisis has not only impacted upon the lives of people and brought everything to a standstill; the education sector has very importantly faced a setback. But due to the transformation from offline to the online platform, to some extent it could be considered that the feeling of hopelessness and helplessness to overcome. Thus, this change to online platform also facilitated them as they could carry on with their studies without coming to actual contact of the physical world.

Hence to overcome this terrible pandemic and we will be back to normal schedule with the help of digital platform. Hence this piece of work will stress on effectiveness of online learning and students.

References

- Karmakar, A & Nath, A. (2014) E-Learning Methodologies, Strategies and Tools to implement lifetime education anywhere anytime, *International Journal of Innovative Research in Advanced Engineering*, Volume 1, Issue 4, 193-201.
- Artino, A. R. & Stephens, J. M. (2009). Academic motivation and self-regulation: A comparative analysis of undergraduate and graduate students learning online. *Internet & Higher Education*, 12(3/4), 146-151. doi: 10.1016/j.iheduc.2009.02.001
- Clarke, J., & Fox, J. (2017). The Impact of Social Anxiety on Occupational Participation in College Life. *Occupational Therapy in Mental Health, 33*, 31-46.
- Elnakeeb, M & Ali Khalifa, S.M. (2016). The Relationship Between Online Learning Readiness and Social Interaction Anxiety among Nursing Students in Alexandria University. *World Journal of Nursing Sciences* 2 (3): 140-152, DOI: 10.5829/idosi.wjns.2016.140.152

- El-Seoud, S.A., Taj-Eddin, I., Seddiek, N. & Mahmoud, M.(2014). E-Learning and Students' Motivation: A Research Study on the Effect of E-Learning on Higher Education. *International Journal of Emerging Technologies in Learing*. Vol. 9, no. 4.
- Esfandiari, N., Nouri, A., Golparvar, M., & Yarmohammadian, M. H. (2013). The relationship between social anxiety and online communication among adolescents in the city of Isfahan, Iran. *International Journal of Preventive Medicine*, *4*(4), 390–395.
- Friedman, H.H. & Friedman, L.W. (2011). Crises in Education: Online Learning as a Solution, *Scientific research*, Vol. 2, No. 3, 156-163.
- Hakami, R. M., Mahfouz, M. S., Adawi, A. M., Mahha, A. J., Athathi, A. J., Daghreeri, H. H., Najmi, H. H., & Areeshi, N. A. (2018). Social anxiety disorder and its impact in undergraduate students at Jazan University, Saudi Arabia. *Mental Illness*, *9*(2), 7274. https://doi.org/10.4081/mi.2017.7274
- Kessler, R. C., Chiu, W. T., Demler, O., Merikangas, K. R., & Walters, E. E. (2005). Prevalence, severity, and co-morbidity of 12-month DSM-IV disorders in the National Co-morbidity Survey Replication. *Archives of general psychiatry*, *62*(6), 617–627. https://doi.org/10.1001/archpsyc.62.6.617
- Means, B., Toyama, Y., Murphy, R., Bakia, M., & Jones, K. (2009). Evaluation of evidence-based practices in online learning: A meta analysis and review of online learning studies. U.S. Department of Education Office of Planning, Evaluation, and Policy Development, Policy and Program Studies Service https://www2.ed.gov/rschstat/eval/tech/evidence-based-practices/finalreport.pdf on 17th April 2020.
- OECD (2016). Innovating Education and Educating for Innovation: The Power of Digital Technologies and Skills, OECD Publishing, Paris. http://dx.doi.org/10.1787/9789264265097-en
- Rensburg, E.S.J. (2018). Effective online teaching and learning practices for undergraduate health sciences students: An integrative review. *International Journal of Africa Nursing Sciences*, Volume 9, 78-80.
- Rhema, A. & Miliszewska, I.(2012).The Potential of E-Learning in Assisting Post-Crisis Countries in Re-Building Their Higher Education Systems: The Case of Libya, *Issues in Informing Science and Information Technology*, Volume 9.
- Russel, G. and P. Topham, 2012. The impact of social anxiety on student learning and well-being in higher education. *Journal of Mental Health*, 21(4):375-385. DOI: 10.3109/09638237.2012.69450
- Tahir, R. & Arif, F.(2015). Mobile Technology in Children Education: Analyzing Parents' Attitude Towards Mobile Technology for Children. *Science and Information Conference*, 410-42.

- Vassilopoulos, S., & Banerjee, R. (2010). Social Interaction Anxiety and the Discounting of Positive Interpersonal Events. *Behavioral and Cognitive Psychotherapy*, 38(5), 597-609. doi:10.1017/S1352465810000433
- Yen, J. Y., Yen, C. F., Chen, C. S., Wang, P. W., Chang, Y. H., & Ko, C. H. (2012). Social anxiety in online and real-life interaction and their associated factors. *Cyber psychology, behavior and social networking*, *15*(1), 7–12. https://doi.org/10.1089/cyber.2011.0015

14

Migration and Women, Impact of Covid–19

Ms. S. Durga Devi

"Keep your Heels, Head and Standards High" – Coco Chanel

Human migration is nothing but permanent change of residence it can be by an individual or by a group. Migration excludes movements such as nomadism, migrant labour, commuting and tourism because all these are temporary in nature.

There are different kinds of migrations:

(1) Internal and International Migration:

When migration happens within a country you call it as internal. Movement can be by individuals and families from one place to another, for example: People from rural areas move to urban areas.

Migration happening from one country to another it is called as International migration.

(2) Voluntary or Forced Migration:

Voluntary migration takes place for better economic opportunities, like for the purpose of housing.

Forced migration happens due to various reasons such as during the time of war, the governments expel the people; forcibly people are transported as slaves or prisoners.

The Covid-19 outbreak has endangered the salary of migrant women especially household workers. Covid-19 has indeed affected the employment crisis as well.

Peril of Covid-19 for migrant women

The impact and implication of the Covid-19 coronavirus are completely different when we consider men and women. This has created great inequalities for people who are posed to vulnerable positions, such as migrants and women.

Specific risks that the pandemic has entailed

1. **Uncertainty of Job, victimisation and socio-economic consequences:** Women who are affected much are domestic workers. Many women have lost their jobs and some are forced not to continue their work till things get normal. Now the condition is as such that these domestic workers are facing job insecurity and are unsure of getting their jobs back and who are deprived of their source of income. Such conditions also increased sexual exploitation of women. Since there is no income over all it has severe impact on society and the basic needs of the people are not met. Economically the country also is affected severely.
2. **Preconception:** Presuming that migrants have Covid-19 just because they are migrants has affected severely and are targeted. Firstly, proper medical means are not available. The reason behind this is the number of cases increasing day by day and hospitals are not able to accommodate everyone. Moreover, people who are not affected are supposed to go on a quarantine of 14 days. Lack of quarantine hubs has once again caused a big problem. Women have deprived of legitimate and psychological aid due to gender-based vehemence.
3. **Considerably indecision averse towards disease:** Migrant women are not able to afford even the basic essential material to safeguard themselves against the virus. Face masks and hand sanitisers are indispensable which every person should

carry with themselves. Migrant women can be wearing the same mask for days together. These people are forced to be in over - crowded places and are prone to the virus. Sometimes these circumstances are unreliable and surprised to face the virus but also are not able to safeguard their families as well.

4. **Overworked of housework:** Women do double the work than man do. Women's work is not just limited to household work, she has several other responsibilities such as, cooking food for everyone at home, trying to complete her projects assigned by her workplace, taking care of the family members who are sick. All the members of the family are completely dependent on her for everything. If she is a married woman and having kids then she is literally overburdened, taking care of her in-laws needs, assisting her kids in handling the online classes and above all has very less time to take care of herself.
5. **Intensify gender-based violence:** Quarantine restrictions and mobility has forced many women to seclude themselves with their perverters. The violence on women has increased much more in such conditions. Earlier women had various organisations, NGOs who came to the rescue of women and fight for their rights. But now unfortunately there are no proper support networks for these isolated women. Most of these women have become silent victims of gender-based violence.

   These are some of the risks that pandemic has caused for women. For any problem there is a solution, we need to just apply it. Adequate implication of methods is very essential. More than solution, how do we handle the crisis is important. So, crisis management plays a vital role here.

Management of the crisis by migrant women

Many organisations have advised measures to overcome Covid - 19 situation, especially migrant women:

1. **Guarantee safe provisions:** UNDP recommended safe provisions, exceptionally at frontiers, can bring "the risk of contagion and situations of sexual and gender-based violence", this should be available to all the migrant population, even those with uneven positions.

2. **Furnish gratuity an exceptional amount:** Gratuity will be a great blessing to migrants and especially women such economic benefits will to a certain extent benefit the migrants.
3. **Provide protection equipment against Covid-19 in migrant assistance center:** The necessary stock such as face masks and hand sanitiser should be available to the migrants to safeguard their wellbeing. For expectant women, although "there is no evidence that they are at higher risk of severe illness than the general population", the WHO has cautioned probability of pulmonarydisorder during child-bearing.
4. **Expedite ingress to multi sector amenity:** Aptmeans are necessary to accord details on protection and relief centers to the migrant population and women, such as client service, fitness organisations, etc.
5. **Secure entrance to nursing home without differentiation:** Migrant women bear dual differentiation first, being women and second, for being migrants. It is mandatory that centers which provide assistance and care do not differentiate. Proper monitoring of such center can avoid sexual violence as well.
6. **Promote the distant functioning of facilities:** Practical apparatus and call endorsement are developed to meet the wants of migrant women. Those who are unable to access through other means can be helped through face to face options.

Predicament of Rural Women in India under migration chronicle

The rate of unemployment is high in rural areas, the agrarian section which is not so beneficial,on the whole it is the man and youth from destitute, farmer and socially disempowered groups who migrate to urban areas to take up job.

Now the Covid-19 pandemic week has led gigantic redundancy in India hundreds of thousands of men migrates are presently plunged in cities like Mumbai, Delhi and Surat. As the economy is at a halt and favourable occasion for salary employment are scorched, men are anticipated to return to their countryside residence.

It is inevitable that since there is less income and less job opportune occasion farmers and the family members of migrants either mortgage or sell their domestic animals some even go to the extent of taking credit from money lenders.

In September 2005 under UPA government the then prime minister Dr. Manmohan Singh, had passed an act of National Rural Employment Guarantee Act. The purpose of this act was to provide livelihood and security in rural areas for atleast 100 days wage employment. This was benefitting the women as their males were working in cities. Unfortunately as these men had to return to their homeland the rural women could not avail this opportunity.

Another aspect that effects the rural women is typically women are the last to eat and sometimes it may so happen that they will not get sufficient food to eat hence it leads to malnutrition and also are prone to various disease due to this.

Domestic violence is another factor which increases due to returning of the male members, Unemployment and less income in the family causes unnecessary conflicts in family, all the frustration is shown on the women. Otherwise women had the freedom to work, earn and meet her wants, Restrictions imposed on her was less but now it has increased she can't do anything without informing her husband. Savings whatever she did till now also might be utilised to run the family.

Covid-19 and the Impact on Women

> *"Any woman who understands the problems of running a home will be nearer to understand the problems of running a country."*
>
> ***- Margaret Thatcher***

In todays world we find women in every field and her contribution towards her family and society are commendable. NHS workforce in USA majority are women and in less developed countries the working women are less.

Economic Consequences of Covid-19 for Women

Women's participation in the labor market is often in the form of temporary employment in many countries. The representation of women across the world is less than 40% of total employment but if we include the women who are working part-time then it is 57%.Women's involvement in farms increases in those regions where there is lack of labor but now as the males have returned to their homes it deprives women in seeking job in the farms. In cities, since there are more number of nuclear families, loss of job and sick people at home has forced the women to stay at home and take care of them. If woman is a single parent who has lost her job due to the lay off during the pandemic, then it's going to have a lasting effect on her family. Millions of women are facing a great loss due to the pandemic situation. Already at least four in 10 women in India have lost their jobs during pandemic, according to the latest data from the center for monitoring, women have become jobless both in official and unofficial sector. Most of the women are employed in informal sector which is almost 94% of the total working women population. Women seek jobs in informal sector because it is easy to enter the sector. The barriers are very less in the sector. It also provides easy source of income to the unskilled illiterate women of a country. Due to the lack of education they continue to work in the same category of work permanently. They don't think of promotions or reaching greater heights in life. This support the family's livelihood with a little income which they earn. But this pandemic has closed doors for them to seek job anywhere else. Even after the lockdown is lifted, not all women will get back their jobs. Those who get jobs will have to compromise with lesser salaries for interior work. This will reduce the GDP of our country, as women workforce has been reduced. This is a great loss for the nation. As Swami Vivekananda quotes "the best thermometer to the progress of a nation is its treatment of its women". If women progress then automatically a nation will progress. By neglecting women, India is actually misplaced great opportunity to help its economy both recover from this pandemic and improve in the future. It's not possible for a bird to fly with one wing. If one wing is injured, then steps must be taken for its quick recovery, only then the nation can fly higher to greater heights.

Closure

Migration for positive reason is good which is for the betterment of man and improves the standard of living but forced migration is negative especially women in such critical situation which has increased her burden and put her life at risk. The only solution for these problems is pliable plans to inscribe women's concern as the effects of health crisis evolve over time. There is a very famous quote given by Dr. James Emmen Kwegyir Aggrey. "If you educate a man you educate an individual, but if you educate woman you educate a family". For the present situation we can tell that "If a man is health an individual is healthy but if a woman is healthy an entire family is healthy". That is the role played by women in the society.

15

A Social, Political and Economically Study of Changes in India after the Impact of Covid-19 Epidemic

Anil kumar, Dalip

Abstract

Coronavirus has affected every single class and every single region of the whole world. India has seen unwanted changes in every sector since March 24. As soon as the factories and companies were closed, the labourers had to flee to their regions and homes. Farmers had to contend with problems at the time of harvesting of crops in North India. The closure of schools, colleges and universities affected the education of students very much. A major issue of lack of health facilities came to the country. The people lost their jobs. The economy of the country has reached the trough. However, there are some changes that were not taking place even after a million human efforts, such as the movement of transport and the closure of industries have seen a historic change in the environment. But as soon as the lockdown began, many questions were raised in the country. For example, Can workers be brought back to industries? Can the economy be brought back on track? Will the lost employment be able to get back to the people again? How will health facilities be improved? How will the teaching process be corrected? All these questions have been placed at the centre of the study in this paper. The research paper has presented an analysis of the successes and failures of the efforts made by the Government during the lockdown. The main objective of this paper is to bring out the problems arising out of the epidemic, to uncover the hidden flaws within the system, to understand the failure of the government by lockdown without planning. The main objective of the research article is also to highlight the impact of corona epidemic on different sections and regions. To understand all these aspects, the system of protection and the experience gained directly has been used. To understand more and better, the various intellectuals have also been used to write the medicine. Suggestions have also been submitted at the end of the research.

Keyword: *Migrants, Agriculture, Covid-19, Capitalist economy, Education, Health.*

Introduction

There can be no doubt that the post-corona India will be much different from the pre-corona time. Whatever changes have come in the society at present or whatever changes will come further, nothing was predetermined. But we humans will have to play our roles in this change. Old structures break down, or become weak, at the time of disaster as we are witnessing this bitter truth in front of our eyes. So, new things will be created and few old ones will be transformed. In this context, the society also breaks down and restores itself in a new way. Everything that happened at time of the corona epidemic has happened before our eyes. Therefore, the shortcomings and qualities of the present system have come before us. That is where the people have had the opportunity to question and have been encouraged to commend them. People have returned to public life by exiting their private life. The rich or poor people who go to cities except villages have come back to rural life. The people have also tried to make this calamity an opportunity. Cutting across caste, religion, people have returned to collective life. Social organisations and social help groups have also openly helped the people everywhere in cities as well as in villages. Central government and state Governments have also extended their hands to help the most vulnerable people. Apart from all these things, we have a mess of questions, responsibilities and accountability regarding tackling such an epidemic. Anyhow, it has now become our responsibility to find various alternatives for smoothly running society.. **The biggest question is of the exodus of migrant labourers, who have faced the worst situations of life and death in the journey to their destinations for the first time after 1947**. The question is of the economy also where the employers are unable to pay the salaries to the employees and they are getting fired from their respective jobs. One question is from the system which has not even assured the poor that they could atleast get two time meal at the right time. Question is of those who only feed on daily earning and if there is no work it would be impossible for them to get a single piece of bread to their stomach. There are many more questions, whether it is related to farmers,to the politics, to domestic workers, to environment or related to the system of production and the consumption; after corona, all these things will not be the same as they were before.

Objective

(1) Attempting to understand the effects of corona epidemics.

(2) Presenting a picture of India after the change from the epidemic.

(3) Analyzing the success or failure of the lockdown.

(4) To analyse the efforts made by the Government.

(5) To understand the role of civil society and try to explain its responsibility towards society and the country as a responsibility.

(6) To strive to develop a new socio-economic and political outlook within the country.

Methodology

(1) Observation method has been used.

(2) Comparative method has been used.

(3) Articles written by intellectuals have been made the center of study.

(4) Some books also have been resorted to for general understanding.

(5) Covers their experience by informal interviews with farmers, labourers, students and teachers.

Observations

Migrant Lebours

Most of the labourers suffered due to the lockdown during the corona.

It was the same labourers who built houses all over the country, but they could not get the roof to hide the head. For many days without transport, there was a walk in sunshine, heat, rain. Employment was such that everyday earnings had a daily family belly. How many labourers would have been tired of walking on foot and may have completed life. It can be clearly said here that all this has happened because of the shortcomings and negligence of the government. The help of labourers has been made by social organisations and individually by the public. The exodus of labourers from states like Delhi, Haryana, Punjab was because the government could not provide them to dry ration. The central government definitely announced an assistance of Rs 1.70 lakh crore and once 20 lakh crore, but that announcement was only an announcement because it could not reach the workers. If help reaches, the labourers do not die at the bottom of the trains. After running 1000 kilometres, the labour girl does not die at a distance of just 14 kilometres from the house. If help reaches, the labourers from Delhi to Bihar do not go on bicycles and walk. The reason for the exodus of migrant labourers was also that the government was distributing ration to those who were ration card holders. There was some news from inside Kerala that the labourers did not leave the aid camps, otherwise about 12 crore labourers from all over the country were walking on the roads. There were incidents that the person walking on foot went to the house and succumbed to death. Now, the question stands that the labourers who came thousands of kilometres away from their homes went back for want of hunger and transport and those governments or people did not bother about their lives and families for whom they worked here. Now, bringing those labourers back to factories or companies at work will be a big challenge. If the labourers are not able to come back, it will be a very difficult task to bring the country's economy on track. Many labourers will not go back because they will be able to find a close job in their own territory. The labourers are less confident of governments anyway. The labourers will earn two paise less and fill their stomachs because they could not even earn where they had gone so far. Because after the lockdown was opened, when it was said to be compensation for the opposition workers, the government rejected the compensation saying that the government did not have any data on the death of the labourers. They would realise that after working so many days, they could not even add up so much that their family could fill the stomach for a month. This calamity has broken the labourers to such an extent that they have come to understand that the state is the state. So, we have to change the private life. The worker that works for us has to be respected, not ignoring the problems of it, standing with them. For the labourers, it has to be ensured that if the work is stopped for some reason, a few months can be arranged for him to eat and drink, to live. For this, we have to change the personal lifestyle. *The responsibility is especially to the government, because the government's option cannot be an NGO or a danvir person.*

Agriculture

India is an agrarian country. About 70% of the population of the country lives in villages. The population living in the village depends mainly on agriculture. It comes from big farmers, small farmers and agricultural labourers. When corona entered India, the time had come to ripening crops in the fields. Then, when the lockdown was imposed on 24th March, the crops had been cooked and the harvesting time had come. A large area of North India depends on migrant labourers. Due to the absence of labourers at the time of harvesting, many big farmers secretly brought their means to the labourers. Which increased their cost. But, still, about 80% of the farmers have worked with the agricultural labourers living in the village or the machinery was used more. This has brought out a number of things like sudden increase in the rate of wages, increase in machinery harvesting, delayed crop arrivals in mandis, closure of government and private industries, reduction in the earnings of the government, which led to the keeping of crops in the Mandis for several days and as well as the monsoon, which proved to be a huge loss for the farmers. Now, there was a problem here that the farmers with vegetables and fruits had to take a licence from the government to sell their crops. Now, whoever took the farmer's licence, the bureaucratic corruption was also clearly visible. But the fear of corona was so much that many vegetables and fruit farmers could not sell crops. Even if the sale was found, it looked at a very low price. The reason for these problems is that there is no storage of fruit vegetables in the village or in the Mandis so that the farmers can protect it a few days. The first day was consumed daily or went for business. But now it is not going to happen. Now, the government can ask the farmers to cover the scope of yield. One example is that the government has issued orders to the farmers not to put paddy inside Haryana at the time of sowing of paddy. There were other issues like doubling the cost of paddy tillage and sowing. The method of cultivation has to be changed due to not getting wages. It is going to have a direct bearing on yields. The delay in bank accounts after the sale of crops has also proved costly for the farmers. This has led to delay in crops and taking money on interest from moneylenders or agriculturists. Because in whichever village a single corona case came, the entire village was sealed. Due to which banks were also closed. Now, if you look at the changes that come thereafter, the government will try to buy the sale of crops under online registration. The government can also arrange for an open market system which will have a direct talk between farmers and traders. With three agricultural bills, one thing has proved to be true that now the MSP may think of eliminating the government. But the way the storage problem, the problem of labourers, the cost escalation and the increase in the debt burden on the farmers are giving rise to anger against the government in the farmers. Against the three agricultural bills, the farmers have also started showing their anger on the road. A big farmers' movement has been erected in the country. The government will have to solve the problems of the farmer now if it is not done now, then, when will it be done?

Health

During the corona, the hands of health facilities have been seen on the ground. The PPE kit has not yet become in the country, masks for doctors, shortage of gloves, loot by private hospitals, acute reduction in corona virus testing, shortage of doctors in the country. The situation had become even that the second and third year students also had to go on duty. The government also appealed to the public that in the world we are 112 in health facilities, so keep our attention. To be honest, the lack of high-level government facilities stopped the tongue of the governments. The closure of OPD has proved to be a huge setback for a large population of the country which is dependent only on government facilities. If I come to the statement of Minister Smriti Irani in the government, he said that we have given ration to 80 crores of people. Here, we can assume that 80 crores of people are dependent on government support. These are the people who cannot go to private hospitals. The government hospital is a place for them. When more than half of the country's population is dependent on government health, then the same means that there is a need to increase government health facilities. We take the corona as a specimen, because it can be followed by more major diseases. Therefore, there is a need for government facility of generic medicines in the country, increase in hospitals, bed facility, free treatment facility, very strict need to recruit doctors.

Education

We can understand the education sector by dividing it into two parts:

(1) School level education

(2) Higher education

1. School level primary and secondary education

Sitting on the bench at school prepares the reading environment by reading among the children and teaching on the Shyampattu by the front teacher. Reading for 6 to 8 hours continuously in school and playing among all children for half or 1 hour in between and inventing new games helps to increase the mental level of children. To prepare the children early in the morning to go to school and to make their own mind with them to please the children and to come back home from school and get the children to work in school. These are some of the things that are very small, but very important. From these things, the child learns and understands. Now, when children are not able to go to schools and all the work is being sent to mobile at home, it is a big loss. We all know the disadvantages of seeing mobile continuously, so I don't want to mention them. The sense of help of each other in the school will not be able to be from mobile studies. I have seen for the last six months that the focus on children is being reduced by parents. The school teachers were told that we are no longer able to teach the children in school. The education of children at home is also not being taken care of. So, some things will come into change and they should be used by the government. It would be advisable to open schools and study through technology. To maintain the collectivity of children, more and more education related programmes need to be promoted. Because of the economic crunch, it may not be that children have to be away from studies, which is already a very high number in our country. ***There is a great need at present to give more emphasis on government education and free education***. Because this is the time when the government needs the common citizens the most. There have also been reports from many places that teachers have been removed from the job. The government will have to stop such activities.

2. Higher Education

The students are facing a lot of hardships due to non-conduct of final year examinations and non-conduct of competitive examinations. The study has been completely halted due to the closure of children's books and hostels in colleges and universities on Holi. The library has been closed. Because of that, children are not able to get books or a good atmosphere. Students from the worst affected rural areas have been affected by this problem. Those who have neither a good phone to read in the village nor a good Internet facility. Now, there is a continuous pressure by the UGC to conduct the final year's examination at the earliest. Children studying in remote areas are not able to understand how they will be able to give exams without transport and without hostels. Libraries are also closed. The universities have started studying the second and final year in the first and second week of August through the Internet. There are also the same problems which have been seen in primary school education. No Internet facility, no laptop facility. After talking to many children, it was learnt that neither the teachers are able to read with concentration in reading online nor the children are able to read with concentration. Now, the government should think here that the children who have been studying for so many years, if they are sent forward without giving a semester test, what will be the problem. While the first and second year students have been sent forward without examination. The government report shows that the cases of self-murder of students have increased during the lockdown. The government should ensure that a certain time to open the library and come through certain departments. However, it has also been heard that the UGC is under pressure from big bureaucrats and capitalists. Because their children have to go to study abroad thereafter. Therefore, it is not valid to come abroad without examination. Here, the government should take the examination of the children who want to go out. If that is so, the government does not want to see the children with a large population of the country. This is not applicable only now, but will be applicable forever. ***We currently have another big good chance that the annual examination should be conducted by scrapping the semester system***. Because of the semester system, the June examinations had to be postponed. Now, it is slowly feeling that the December examinations have to be postponed. Now, there will be another concern that within six months, when the children are transported within the class for three to four months, how will they be able to make their entire syllabus? While at present, online studies have been started. It may not be said that the government should start to overcharge the responsibility.

Environment

We cannot understand the issue of international environment only in the context of India. To understand this, we have to bring the world environment into study ***'Kofi Annan'*** has said that ***"environmental problems come without passports"*** during corona period, the change within the environment has come within the whole world. The river Ganga could not be cleaned even with the campaign to clean the river Ganga of India, but the water of the Rivers Ganga and Yamuna was potable as soon as the industrial sector was closed during the corona. These days, the people of Delhi and Haryana have been seen taking a dip in the Yamuna. This means that the world's system of production has emerged before the world. As soon as the transport and industries were closed, clean air, clean water, clean environment was seen only in a few months. The speed at which carbon emissions have been taking place has ruined the lives of the people. ***According to the IPCC report, the earth's temperature is estimated to rise from 2.4 to 6.4 degrees Celsius by 2099 if it continues to produce at this pace***. In 1972, ***the Club of the Rome's report "Limited to Growth"*** showed that we would have to limit our economic growth. Because the natural resources on earth are limited. The ***Brandland Commission Report***, which was made in 1986, put forward the idea of sustainable development and said that we have to use natural resources in a way that meets our needs and also meets the needs of the future generation and they should also use them so that the needs of their later generation are also met. All these things will have to be considered by every country after the corona. If still not able to think, we will never be able to improve the environment. The world has a chance to rectify its mistakes. I am not talking about closing down industries, but using technical use in a right direction. We are so immersed in strength and profit that we have used technology for less and more for personal profits for the betterment of mankind. Which has a direct bearing on the environment. The time has come for governments to work together with a policy of cooperation. Every organism on this earth has the same right. So, for the right of all, we now have to protect rivers, drains, seas, glaciers, forests and mountains.

Economy

The economy of countries around the world has suffered a lot during corona period. The capitalist economy is dominated almost all over the world. The US, Russia, China, Britain, Italy, Japan, Germany, Australia, India, etc., half the world's major economies have succumbed during the corona, as international trade has seen a significant decline. India, if it talks, has **registered a decline of 23.9% in GDP in the last quarter**. Except in India's urban area, the rural sector has not seen much impact. Compared to the organised and unorganised sectors, the work of the unorganised sector has been affected, but not so much as the organised sector. Talking about the government and the private sector, both have seen a similar impact. Agriculture sector is an area in India which is on harvesting, meaning, once in about six months, the entire capital is received simultaneously. So, there is less impact here. We have to catch the pulse of this economy. It is not that only capitalist countries have harmed the environment, the socialist economies have also exploited the natural resources. Capitalism always thrives on the basis of profit. The most important is the profit. Apart from that, things do not matter much. That is why privatisation is growing rapidly, the capitalist system has influenced, not only affected but harmed everything for profit, individualism, privatisation, globalisation and liberalisation. Forests around the world destroyed in the name of development, contaminated rivers, nala, seas in the name of industrialisation, have broken the organised society in the name of personal profits. When India became independent,**Mahatma Gandhi said, "Don't adopt this European and Western model, it will never**

be right for the village of our country if we adopt it, we will first ruin our village" today we have come to that position. When capitalism came, it came talking about prosperity and employment. About 14 crore jobs of India have been snatched away during corona. It has a huge impact on unemployed youths. *(For example, the unemployed have also offered employment by clapping and ringing the plate from the government?)* During the unaccounted-to-produce economy, pedestrian workers did not have slippers to wear, no clothes to cover the body, while a lot of people in the country could get 20 - 20 pairs of clothes, many many pairs of shoes. A system which cannot give the need at the time of need cannot be said to be correct in any way. Then, whether it is a capitalist system, a socialist system or a democratic system. There is a need to think over it once again. Because the system which could not provide adequate quantities to employment, education, health needs to be considered once again. To understand the structure of Indian society, the culture of the village has to be understood in depth. The economy which could not feed the labourers of the country on the next day without working, the economy can never be right for India. The economy in which the Government of Haryana had to announce that it could not remove any job for the next 1 year and pay salaries to the employees. It becomes necessary to consider it once again. We have already studied in detail on different issues, so the economy has been tried to understand in the end. If India is to become self-reliant, we need to work on Mahatma Gandhi's Gram Swaraj, and decentralise the economy.

Politics

We speak many times that we are not interested in politics, but one thing should be understood that politics is very much interested in us. Something like that has crumbled in this lockdown and has come before us. Seeing the labourers on the streets, seeing the cramped condition of the farmers, looking at the declining session of education, seeing the minorities surrounded by the media and not showing things right through the media, a section of the society has become very agitated, which we call the intellectuals. Which includes artists, journalists, literators, historians, sociologists, economists and politicians. The interest of the above people has been very high. In this hour, these people have voiced a lot. Have questioned the power and the system. This corona virus has not only affected the deprived section, but the middle class has also been greatly affected. So, political people have had a good opportunity to keep their points. Non-profit organisations, social groups and political parties have tried their best to make these disadvantaged and affected in their favour. If you think that it will come under your flag, it will not happen, if you even think that your thoughts and old elections will come together, it is not going to happen on a large scale. It is the people who walk with the crowd and never come along with the crowd. In fact, the change of society will work as well as the thoughtful and the one who will come and hinge. After this corona virus, there is a political debate in every single section, and all have been compelled to understand the thinking. Therefore, whoever comes together will come together very thoughtfully. So, India's politics can see a drastic change. During the Kisan agitation in Haryana, the police personnel on police lathi charge themselves ignored the government's order and there have been many examples of farmers not providing platform to the political people. To raise only one farmer's point, the party's people themselves have separated from the party and participated in the Kisan agitation. The politics of religion have left people to retreat, the debate on Hindu-Muslim, India-Pakistan is no longer a long run. The way the youth have been tricked out of media and social media, the same youth has sat down in this corona period and has also raised the voice for employment. ***The Government will have to understand the opposition as to how the Prime Minister's Mann Ki Baat comes to 1 million unlike against 1 lakh likes on YouTube***. The way the IT cell of the parties is still being spread confusion has begun to understand the people. He may be with you now, but the lack of resources will quickly understand him.

Suggestion

(1) Migrant labour support centres should be constructed in every city of the country so that workers can be stopped and trusted in the same city if such an epidemic is encountered.

(2) Companies and factories can be approached to find out the lined workers during this epidemic. By financially assisting these labourers, the government can heal their wounds.

(3) The government should encourage farmers to store farmers' crops in the village. For which a large amount of subsidy should be given.

(4) Loans taken by farmers should now be waived off by the government by about 50%. Because the cost escalation and the prices of crops have come downd uring the lockdow. The loan waiver will enable balancing the income of the farmers.

(5) Mohalla clinics should be promoted within the country on the lines of the capital city of Delhi.

(6) A large number of doctors should be recruited in the country.

(7) The rights of panchayats should be enhanced.

(8) Panchayats should be given economic strength so that the problems of labourers can be solved in the village itself.

(9) Decision-making power should be strengthened in panchayats.

(10) Promote an agro-centric economy.

(11) The government needs to convene a special session of Parliament. During this Parliament session, developments during the Corona period should be discussed and special assistance funds should be created to help the affected class or region as the PM Cares Fund was prepared.

(12) Incentive programmes should be organised within schools to address the mental distress caused during lockdowns.

(13) In order to reduce the economic burden of parents, the government should waive off the fees of a few months of schools.

(14) The government should also take cognizance of the salary of teachers who could not be given in.

(15) A special fund should be created in each university to know the impact of corona through universities and colleges to the central government and the state government through universities and colleges and to conduct research on the epidemic.

(16) The manner in which the mainstream media has tried to create a communal atmosphere with false information should be dealt with by the government.

Conclusion

Now, after presenting an analysis on the main issues, ***we need a methodology that respects the diversity and the decentralised decision-making process*** to bring about this change. Only then can a better society and faster steps towards a better India be increased. We do not think that change will come slowly, change can come faster, as has come during corona, which we may not have imagined.

The corona epidemic has opened the drums of not only India but also the system of the whole world. Of course, we are not able to see those countries, but it is time to change. If still not, when will it happen? We have already made a lot of things. Now a strong desire is needed for this change. Now, the intellectual class has to come forward who can build consciousness, tell the difference between the right or wrong. It is not that it will be all easily. The roots of old issues are still in this land. The use of communalism which has happened during the lockdown will still stand in front. The increase in mental stress has led to an early increase in the cases of suicides of students. We have seen less change in the character of politics which is going to prove fatal to him. Because the people are being filled with anger by passing a number of bills in the hidden Parliament by locking them in the houses. If the common man is not organised and ready to fight for policies related to his surroundings, he will not be willing to fight for the problems of the people sitting away. ***During this lockdown, criminal incidents have gone down, but domestic violence has now been the same***. Within this change, we cannot achieve success only by involving farmers, labourers. We have to bring together small shopkeepers and small factories also. We have to understand that the assistance provided to the labourers was definitely commendable, but once we think that only filling the stomach is not enough. They should have also received food of their choice (pudding is not perfect). One of the most important thing is that we have to change our lifestyle. We face environmental problems. India will have to work on the way of sustainable development so that something can be saved for the time to come. We need to consider the path of Mahatma Gandhi. Except for a decentralised economy, India does not see another path of growth. We have to understand agriculture as an industry and work on positive policies for them to focus on cooperative agriculture. The great opportunity to once again handle the deteriorating education structure within the country has come into our hands. By removing attention from the policies of the global capitalist system, policy formulation has to be worked out according to the effectiveness of the country and the environment. It has become necessary to build an India like that.Where education, health, employment can be provided free to the people we have to change the luxury life. Unless we achieve economic, social and political strength, the country cannot grow. It will handle everything when every section of the country is accompanied by farmers, labourers, women, students, businessmen, shopkeepers, poor, rich and every sector, agriculture, industry, education, trade, medicine, employment. Leaving one will continue to be instability in the country. If we did not now, then when?

References

- Baylis, John, Smith, Steve, (2005). *The globalisation of world politics*, 3rd edition, Oxford : New Delhi.
- Roy, Arundhati, (2014). *katghare me loktantar,* Rajkamal : New Delhi.
- Kumar, Himanshu, *vikashadivasi or hinsa*, Notion Press : New Delhi.
- Priyadarshi, Neeraj, (11, Aug, 2020). *Corona:minimum doctors in Bihar but maximum death of doctors (hindi),* BBC HINDI: Online blogger.https:/ /www.bbc.com/hindi/india-53739076
- Joshi, Alok, (6, Aug, 2020). *Corona crisis: RBI's silence on GDP is intimidating (hindi)*, BBC HINDI : Online blogger. https://www.bbc.com/ hindi/india-53685144
- Kumar, Ravish, (24, July, 2020). *Private schools do not pay teacher's salary (hindi)*, facebook page ravish kumar.https://www.facebook.com/ 618840728314078/posts/1515096402021835/
- Choudhary, Rajender, (09, May, 2020). *Better society : now if not when? (hindi),*desh Haryana : online blogder.http://desharyana.in/archives/15756
- https://www.youtube.com/playlist?list=PL1BQkm1ZUCaXaugQIvoug Mf_6qxY6zLr7 (The Lallantop).

16

A Study on Work Related Stress caused by Covid-19 Pandemic

Ms. Shabnam Yesmin

Abstract

The outbreak of Covid-19 pandemic has affected all aspects of our lives without discriminating between the rich and poor or in case of nations whether a developed or an underdeveloped one. This paper tries to conduct a micro study on a small fraction of people of Guwahati city, Assam working in various sectors including MNC's. It is based on a survey of various employees, their feelings at the time of lockdown working remotely, their mental preparedness for returning to work during this pandemic without the availability of vaccines and how they are dealing with all the havoc created by the virus. This paper attempts to gauge the worries (related to job or other) which are generally crowding their minds due to the prevailing situation so that the policymakers dealing with such issues can tackle these problems effectively.

The methodology would be to conduct the survey through online mode using Google forms. Simple statistical tools will be used to present the findings, based on which suggestions would be made to tackle the problems adequately.

Introduction

Over the past few months, Covid-19 virus has spread all over infecting people in many countries around the world. Since its emergence in Wuhan city of China during the late 2019, the virus has spread within the world in a very short time. The overall number of global corona virus cases has crossed the 20 million mark -20, 001, 0019 to be specific and the death toll has reached 7,50,000 as on 12 Aug 2020. Due to nationwide lockdown its impact on socio-economic activities has come to a standstill affecting crores of people in India which has resulted in job loss and stress. With respect to continuity of business, companies have resorted to online mode of working amid this pandemic. Viruses have also affected in the past but the way digitalisation has been taking place is tremendous. But amid everything, it is important to understand the psychological well being of employees who are working remotely. Work related stress may occur if the employees feel that they are unheard by their supervisors for any issue faced while working from home during this challenging times. Also, they may find difficulty if not able to cope up with the workload which has increased due to lockdown. The corona virus pandemic is the greatest challenge we have been facing since World War II. It is much more than a health crisis. Millions of people have a threat to their jobs post-Covid-19 and thousands of people have already been laid off. In such a situation, this paper tries to understand the various worries running in the minds of the people because of the current situation and also tries to address the psychological issues faced in this pandemic before returning to normal due to the fear of contamination by the disease.

According to WHO, work related stress is the response people may have when presented with work demands and pressures that are not matched to their knowledge and abilities and which change their ability to cope. Stress occurs in a wide range of works circumstances but is often made worse when employees feel they have little support from supervisors and colleagues, as well as little control over work processes. There is often confusion between pressure or challenge and stress and sometimes it is used to excuse bad management practice.

Literature Review

Sharon Jayson (2010) his study shows that young adults experience negative emotions more frequently than those who are older. Negative emotions, such as stress and anger, are similar in that they consistently decline with age. After 50, things start dropping off dramatically in terms of worry and stress. That's the turning point in some ways, but it is not a magic number in terms of everything that is better. Stress is "constantly dropping, but the curve gets much steeper after age 50. Similar emotion research in which 184 people aged 18-94 were given beepers and asked to share their emotions at random times they were beeped during the day.

Chen and his collaborators (2009) during a study on the group of platform workers in an offshore oil company in South China, after controlling for age, educational level, marital status and years of offshore working, found that poor mental health is positively associated with occupational stress.

Elizabeth Scott, M.S. (2009) has stated that many people would expect those who hold higher-powered jobs to experience more stress to go with those jobs, but research from psychosomatic medicine and other research sources state that, it is those in lower socioeconomic levels experience greater levels of stress and experience more stress-related health problems as well. More often it is the higher-level workers who have more personal choices in their lifestyles and more resources at their disposal, leading to lower levels of stress. Those in higher socioeconomic levels make healthier choices: those of lower socioeconomic status tend to deal with stress by smoking. They are also more likely to skip breakfast, and have a less diverse social network. These factors are all correlated with poorer health outcomes. Higher socioeconomic status brings greater resources for health: those in lower levels of socioeconomic status tend to have poorer health outcomes because they are less able to take care of their health and even afford healthcare, among other things. This contributes to greater levels of stress.

Armstrong and Griffin, (2006) conducted a research that indicates that most stress for correctional staff comes from role stress, particularly in terms of role conflict, role ambiguity, role overload, perceived dangerousness of the job, and work-family conflict.

Stimulus (2006) identified in private sector that significantly more people experiences higher stress levels (22.6%) than in public sector (13.5%). The sectors showing the highest levels of stress are skilled trades (45% of workers), cleaning (36%), hotels, restaurants and catering, and retail (both 32.4%). In those sectors, two to three times many people experience high stress levels compared to other areas, such as manufacturing (13.1%), teaching (13.8%), the public sector (14.3%) or financial services (15.5%). A very low level of educational attainment is closely related to the experience of high stress levels. William Doyle (2006) found a graded association, where those with highest levels of income and education show the lowest levels of stress, those in the middle show higher levels, and those at the lowest end show the greatest levels.

Fotinatos-Ventouratos and Cooper (2005) revealed significant differences in terms of physical and psychological wellbeing amongst the male and female sample. Mohsin Aziz (2004) found that there was a difference in the level of stress between married and unmarried employees on several role stressors. However, level of education does not emerge as a significant differentiator of stressors. Sethi, King and Quick (2004) proposed that inadequate training, poor performance evaluations, lack of job security, working conditions, poor communication with other co-workers, fuzzy requirements and specifications, and lack of career development were the factors that make employees stressful.

Research Gap

The review of literature has shown various studies which have been conducted to identify work related stress and assess the psychological well being of employees. The research gap is found when it comes to study the factors causing stress caused by the pandemic because of returning to work without the availability of vaccines as unlock stages have started after almost 2 months of lockdown.

Objectives of the Study

- To understand the factors causing work related stress in this pandemic.
- To understand the mental preparedness of returning to work amid coronavirus pandemic.

Significance of the Study

The buzzword 'Corona Virus' has unfolded many challenges in every sector. Amid this ongoing pandemic, we are witnessing the change of work culture as social distancing measures have been implemented everywhere which has led employers to ponder how they can keep their people safe from the virus and continue their operations effectively. It is important to understand that it is a human crisis and hence having an empathetic, transparent and supportive approach towards employees is important. Fear and anxiety about this new disease and other emotions can be overwhelming, and workload can lead to burn out. As we are in the stage of unlock period announced by central government, we try to understand the mental state of people returning to work, their stress of being contaminated by the disease at the same time, their fear of being the carrier might also affect their family. Again, the stress that have gauged in the minds of the people because of the severe downfall in economic activity which will lead us to a stage which our country has never faced before is another major cause of stress in this pandemic. Hence how we cope with these emotions can affect our well-being as well as our family and community as a whole. During this pandemic, it is important to recognize what stress looks like, take necessary steps to build and learn to manage job stress.

Limitations of the Study

- The study is done on the basis of the data provided by the respondents which may affect the study if the data provided by them turns out to be wrong.
- The study is conducted on a small fraction of people whose results may not be generalised in the entire population.
- The questionnaire is designed based on our research objectives.

Research Methodology

The study is mainly based on primary data which is collected with the help of online circulated Google Form questionnaire and secondary data has been used from various sources, academic journals, paper presentations and websites. The time frame of collection of data is in the month of August, 2020 through structured questionnaire, which has fetched 100 responses of employees working in various corporate sectors. The respondents are the employees who are presently staying at home town due to lockdown and working from home. The study is descriptive in nature as it tries to state the factors which cause job related stress because of the prolonged lockdown to stop the spread of virus. It also tries to throw some light on their mental preparedness of employees for returning to work in the unlock stage and the worries faced by them for the havoc created by the virus. The statistical tool used for analyzing data is percentage analysis which is represented using pie charts.

Data Analysis and Interpretation

Analysis has been made on the opinion of the respondents:

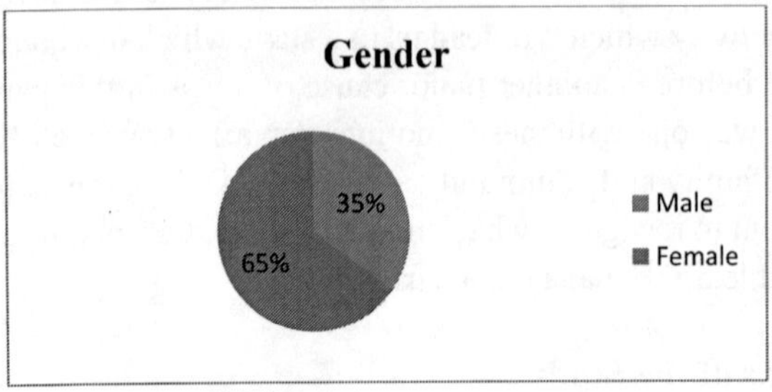

Source: Survey, 2020.

Chart 1: Gender of the respondents.

Interpretation: Among the respondents, it has been seen that there were 35% male respondents and 65% female respondents.

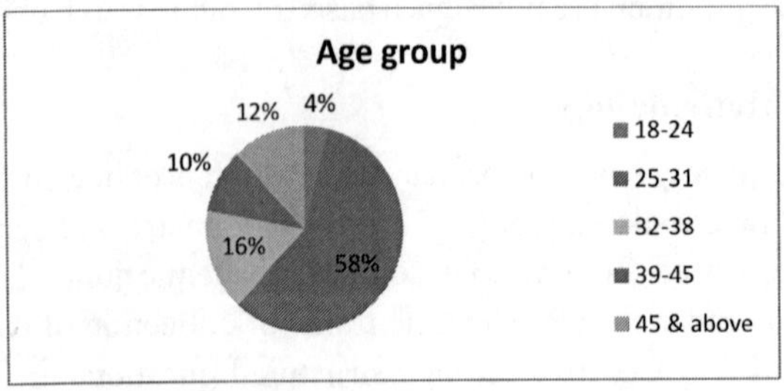

Source: Survey, 2020.

Chart 2: Age of the respondents.

Interpretation: Among the respondents, it has been seen that 4% belong to the age group of 18-24, 58% belong to the age group of 25-31, 16% belongs to 32-38, 10% belongs to 39-45 and the remaining 12% of my respondents belongs to the age group of 45 years and above.

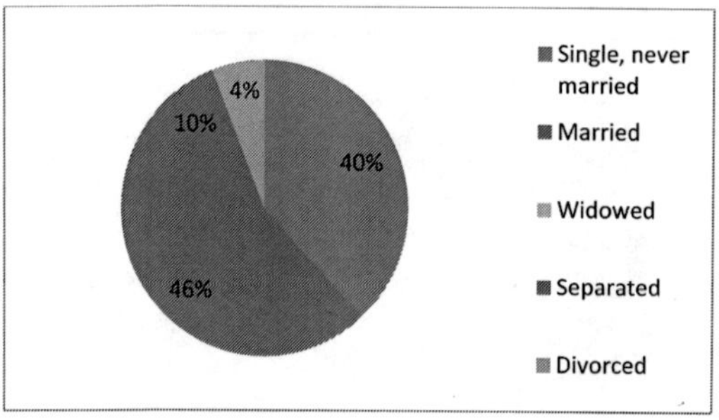

Source: Survey, 2020.

Chart 3: Marital status of the respondents.

Interpretation: The chart shows the respondents marital status, it has been seen that 40% of my respondents are single i.e. never married, 46% are married, 10% are separated and 4% are divorced.

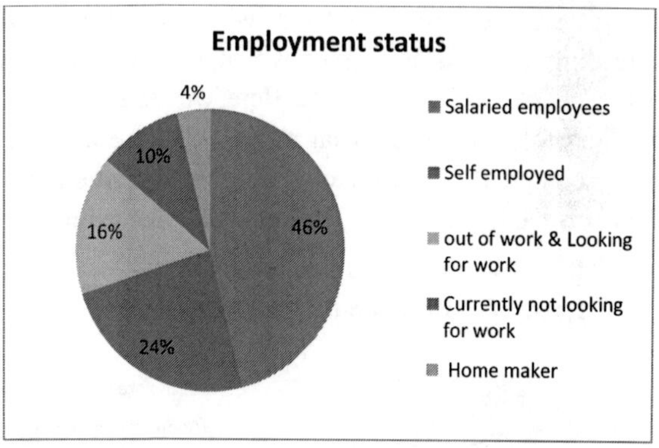

Source: Survey, 2020.

Chart 4: Employment status of the respondents.

Interpretation: It has been found that 46% of my respondents are salaried employees, 24% are self-employed, 16% are looking for vacancies, 10% are currently not looking for work due to the Covid-19 situation and the remaining 4% are home makers.

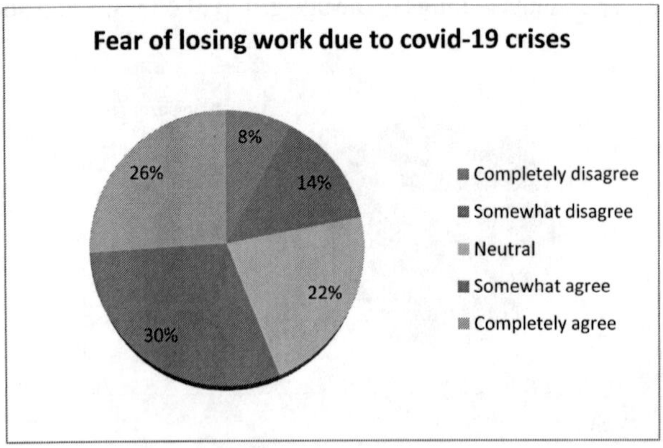

Source: Survey, 2020.

Chart 5: Fear of losing work in the short or long term due to Covid-19 crises.

Interpretation: From the survey, it has been found that majority of the respondent's fear of losing their work due to coronavirus crises which is a high cause of stress in this pandemic. The fear is mainly because of downturn in economic activity which will highly impact every sector; leading to recession or even worse, the virus hits business demands, causing people lose their jobs etc. Here, we see 26% completely agree to the statement, 30% somewhat agree, 22% are neutral, 14% somewhat disagree and 8% completely disagree which shows their confidence level on the job skills they hold for the near future.

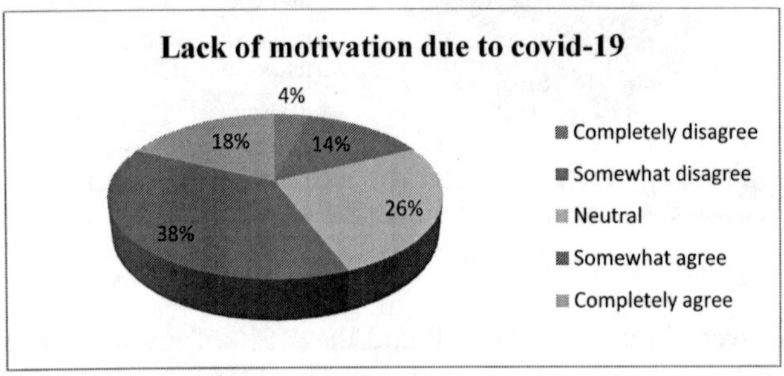

Source: Survey, 2020.

Chart 6: Corona crises have a negative impact on my personal motivation.

Interpretation: The coronavirus has impacted our lives in every way, from freedom of movement to the way we work. Thus, stress caused by the disease has however impacted on personal motivation. From the study, it has been found that 18% of people completely agree that they are having lack of motivation in work or anything they do and this is because of the covid crises, 38% somewhat agree that covid has negatively affected their level of motivation, however, 26% are neutral of the opinion, 14% somewhat disagree and the remaining 4% completely disagree on this regard.

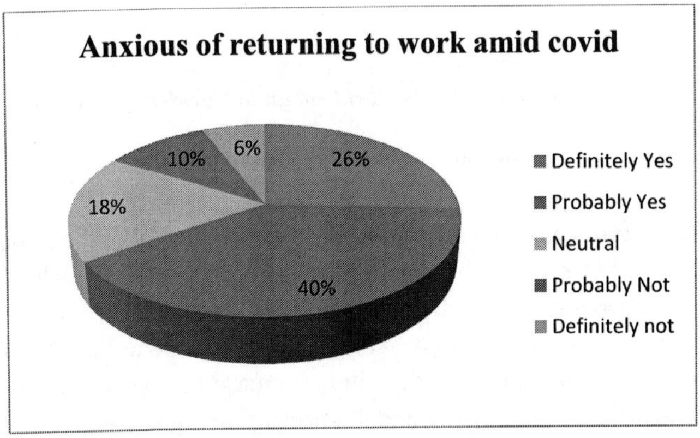

Source: Survey, 2020.

Chart 7: Feeling anxious of returning to work amid this global pandemic.

Interpretation: People are worried about themselves and their loved ones catching the virus and the future of the world or their jobs. Amid all these, as our country is in the unlock stage after almost 2 months of nationwide lockdown, people seem to have anxiety on the thought of returning to work, as we see majority of the respondents have said that they are worried to travel from their residence to the workplace. 26% of the respondents have said they definitely feel anxious on the thought of returning to work, 40% have said probably yes, 18% are neutral of the opinion, 10% have said they are probably not anxious of returning to their workplace and the remaining 6% are of the opinion that they are definitely not having any such worries for returning to workplace.

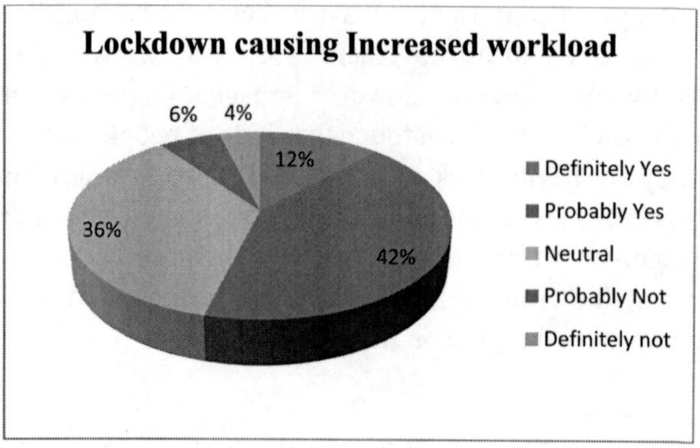

Source: Survey, 2020.

Chart 8: Increase in workload amid Covid-19 pandemic

Interpretation: Increase in workload is an important factor causing stress, work pressure has increased as targets were not able to meet amid lockdown. From the survey, it is found that 12% of the respondents strongly believe that their work pressure has increased, unable to meet targets because of lockdown which has negatively impacted their job causing stress, 42% say probably yes because due to lockdown works have piled up which has definitely increased in work pressure, 36% are neutral, remaining 6% and 4% are not facing any such issue due to Covid 19 lockdown.

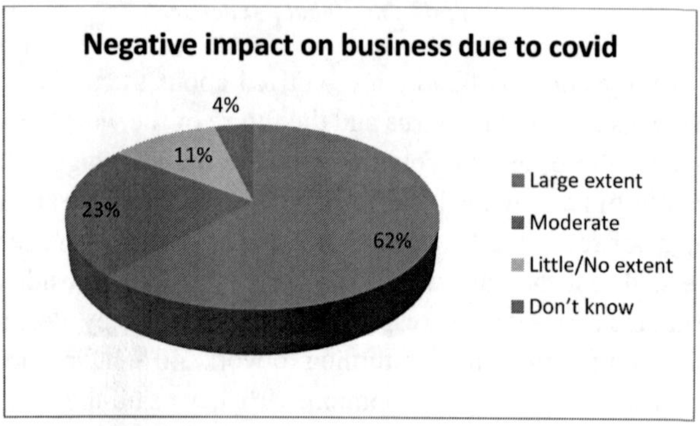

Source: Survey, 2020.

Chart 9: Negative impact on Business / Increments due to covid-19.

Interpretation: 62% of respondents belonging to self-employed category/ salaried employees have indicated that they have tremendously been facing a high negative impact on their business / Increments to a large extent due to Covid-19 crises, start ups and small business is the most affected sector, another 23% have indicated their opinion towards a moderate effect, 11% says little/no effect and remaining 4% are unaware of the situation.

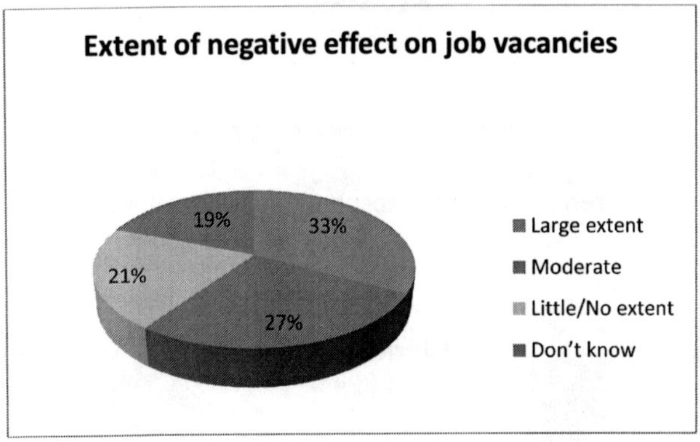

Source: Survey, 2020.

Chart 10: Extent of negative effect on interested job vacancies.

Interpretation: Unemployment rates are increasing and because of the ongoing pandemic, most of the companies have either postponed their recruitment or have cut down posts, even the joining dates for MBA graduates have been postponed leading to which so many MBA graduates or other academicians future are at risk. Hence we see 33% of respondents say that Covid crises has negatively affected their job vacancies to a large extent, 27% have indicated a moderate extent towards the effect, 21% said it might have little/ no extent towards their interest of job vacancy and the remaining 19% holds no opinion regarding this aspect.

Interpretation: The world is experiencing a vast pandemic in this century. Hence we see majority of respondents i.e. 61% say that they are feeling stressed during the pandemic. The stress could be for many reasons related to work or other. Another, 12% respondent indicated

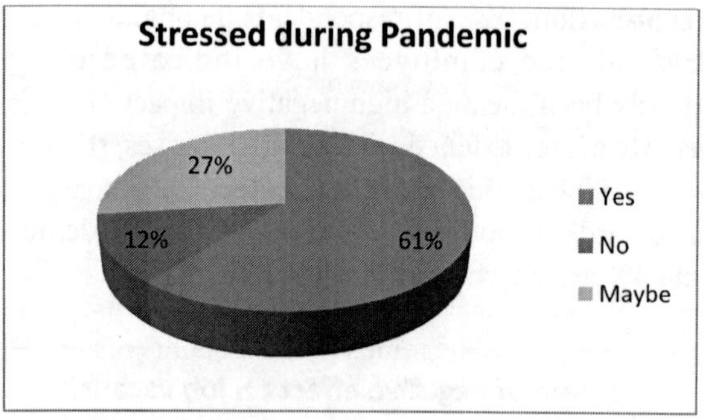

Source: Survey, 2020.

Chart 11: Stressed during pandemic.

no and the remaining 27% respondents are not very sure towards the feeling.

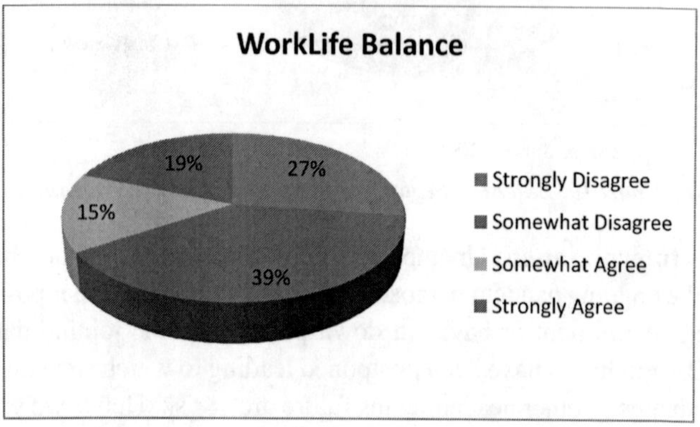

Source: Survey, 2020.

Chart 12: Work Life Balance maintained amid Covid-19 pandemic

Interpretation: Work Life Balance is considered to be important in every aspect of life. Work pressure or stress caused by any factor can impact work life balance. Here we see 27% of respondents strongly disagree that they are able to maintain work life balance, 39% somewhat disagree on the statement, 15% somewhat agree that they are able to maintain the work life balance and the remaining 19% strongly agrees that they are able to achieve work life balance.

Major Findings

- Stress, anxiety and depression will cause a serious damage to public mental health post-Covid-19 because of the havoc created by the virus.
- Majority of the respondents have a fear of losing their job because of the prevailing situations created by corona virus which may lead to recession or even worse. This sense of job insecurity in the minds of the respondents is a major factor of stress caused by the pandemic.
- Most of the respondents have reported increase in workload because of the prolonged lockdown which has highly caused stress in the minds of the respondents, coping with the workload is now a major challenge in every sector.
- Unemployment has always been an issue in our nation, and now with the wake of corona virus impacting all sectors of the economy, organisations are likely to reduce jobs post-covid-19, another major cause of stress in the minds of people.
- Most of the respondents have reported lack of motivation to work which will ultimately result in lower productivity, poor performance. The lack of motivation can be reduced by putting a limit to news consumption, regular updates are fine but constantly keeping up with the corona virus cycle leads to anxiety and nervousness.
- Majority of the respondents have indicated being anxious in returning to work as no vaccine has been yet developed. Hence, organisations need to strictly monitor hygiene in the workplace and safety protocol measures, providing mask and sanitiser's kit to every employee to stay safe from the virus.

Conclusion

Covid-19 has caused distress around the globe. It's not a health hazard anymore, it's a socio-cultural calamity and the impact created by the virus has significantly affected the minds of people. Thus, the research study tries to understand the anxiety, stress in the minds of the people of Assam who are not only affected by the virus in this pandemic but also had seen major floods which makes them loose millions of crops, villages gets displaced and even basic infrastructure gets destroyed. This creates a trauma in the region every year but this time due to the corona virus pandemic, the livelihoods of people of Assam is under threat. Small start up's, new ventures faces unprecedented uncertainty amid Covid-19 virus. Thus, the present study focuses on the anxiety, stress level in the minds of people of Assam because of the havoc created by the virus. Hence, the policymakers need to take care for its people and effective health management can be planned for a better future post-Covid-19.

References

Hawryluck, L, Gold W, Robinson S, Pogorski S, Galea S, Styra R. SARS control and psychological effects of quarantine, Toronto, Canada. Emerging Infectious Diseases. 2004;10(7):1206–1212. doi: 10.3201/eid1007.030703. [PMC free article] [PubMed] [CrossRef] [Google Scholar]

Holland, K. (2018, May 24). Anxiety: Causes, symptoms, treatment, and more. Retrieved 24 from https://www.healthline.com/health/anxiety.

Kumar, A, Nayar KR. Covid-19 and its mental health consequences. Journal of Mental Health. 2020 doi: 10.1080/09638237.2020.1757052. [PubMed] [CrossRef] [Google Scholar

Roy, D, Tripathy S, Kar S, Sharma N, Verma S, Kaushal V. Study of knowledge, attitude, anxiety & perceived mental healthcare need in Indian population during Covid-19 pandemic. Asian Journal of Psychiatry. 2020;51:102083. doi: 10.1016/j.ajp.2020.102083. [PMC free article] [PubMed] [CrossRef] [Google Scholar]

Usama Rehman, Mohammad G Shahnawaz, Neda H Khan, Korsi d khasrring, Masrat Khursheed, Kaveri Gupta, Dhristi Kashyap and Ritika Uniyal. Depression, anxiety and stress among Indians in times of covid-19 lockdown. Community of mental health, 2020 June 23. https://www.ncbi.nlm.nih.gov/pubmed/?term=Rehman%20U%5BAuthor%5D&cauthor=true&cauthor_uid=32577997

WHO. (2020). *Mental health and psychosocial considerations during the Covid-19 outbreak* [Ebook]. Retrieved from https://www.who.int/docs/default-source/coronaviruse/mental-health-considerations.pdf.

Xiang, Y, Yang Y, Li W, Zhang L, Zhang Q, Cheung T, Ng C. Timely mental health care for the 2019 novel coronavirus outbreak is urgently needed. The Lancet Psychiatry. 2020;7(3):228–229. doi: 10.1016/s2215-0366(20)30046-8. [PMC free article] [PubMed] [CrossRef] [Google Scholar]

17

Impact of the Covid-19 Pandemic on Migrant Workers in India

Neelofer Habib, Dr. Salima Jan

Abstract

Due to Coronavirus (Covid-19) pandemic the unprecedented situation has led to destruction of life on a wide scale. India is dealing with a pandemic situation that occurs due to corona and not only India;in fact, the whole world is facing such situation. Due to which all the sectors are badly affected and the pandemic has shaken us from our comfort zone.Covid-19 pandemic has affected all walks of life. In December 2019,the Covid-19 pandemic begins in China and spread to Europe, the United States and India in subsequent weeks, prompting governments to implement lockdown in their respective countries. With the coronavirus outbreak declared to be a pandemic by the WHO, people are facing a major challenge across the globe. Covid-19 pandemic has breakdown the entire world's health, the social and economic structure. Covid-19 pandemic is one of the worst happening in the history of mankind. Each country's Government is trying to control the pandemic by imposing several measures, including lockdown and discipline of social distancing. In India, because of the diversified population, different income groups, and social habits of people, the extended lockdown has made a severe impact on the lifestyle. Migrant jobs are the extreme sufferers of daily wage earners. Extended lockdown leads them to exhaust their handful of savings forcing them to begin their journey home. Struggling for daily bread and butter, the unavailability of transport facilities worsens their journey. This chapter highlights the issues of migrant workers related to health, economic, and social during the prolonged lockdowns.

Keywords: *Covid-19 Pandemic, Impact, Migrant workers.*

Introduction

The coronavirus pandemic (Covid-19), which originated in the city of Wuhan, and has spread rapidly around the globe. The World Health Organisation (WHO) in March 2020, declared the Coronavirus a pandemic disease which means that the deadly virus is circulating beyond control measures in most countries around the world. Coronavirus signs included fever, cough, tiredness, and breathing difficulties.

The individual initially shows mild symptoms and people treat this mostly as a mild flu. As it is a respiratory disease, it can spread via the inhalation of droplets in the air. It can also spread by touching the infected person. Coronavirus affects the social life of the individual, as many schools, colleges, universities and so on are closed. Many festivals, religious and social events were abruptly negated (Singh & Singh, 2020). This pandemic has begun in a world meticulously associated by both local and international population alterations and many people move for many reasons like employment, education, family, tourism and survival (Skeldon, 2018).

WHO reports that one in every thirty people worldwide is a migrant? An estimated 73 million migrant live in the European Regions. As the cycle of migration leads migrants to an accumulation of disadvantages during their life course. Deficient jobs and resources, and shut down of public transport, hundreds of thousands of migrants were forced to walk hundreds of miles back to their homelands with some dying along the way. This pandemic brought migrant workers and their livelihood at the doorstep of the government. Although they have built cities and the nation, their rights and entitlements were not recognised in policies and programmes. Migration places individuals in circumstances which may affect their physical and mental wellbeing. Conditions affecting the migration process will increase the susceptibility to illness. This is particularly correct for those people who migrate involuntarily, evading natural or man-made disasters. The process of migration also cuts across economic and social policies, human rights and justice issues, development goals, and social norms all of which are relevant to migration health.

During the Covid-19 pandemic, and the constraints imposed on everyday activities as part of social distancing norms to prevent the disease from spreading, most of the migrant workers prefer to migrate back to their hometowns. These migrant workers used all accessible means to return their endpoints during the prevailing Covid-19 pandemic. Nonetheless, many of them are stuck at borders, like state, district and national border areas. These are the most deprived sections of the society who depend on the daily wages for their survival, and in times of such distress require social support and sympathy. Immediate issues facing these migrant workers include food, housing, and healthcare, fear of getting infected, loss of employment, family concerns and distress. Migrants suffer from double burden of being poor and migrants. Many programmes intended for the disadvantaged groups do not reach them because of distinctiveness and proof of residence. The lack of fulfilment of the economic, social and political rights of migrants is a serious problem even though they are formal citizens; their substantive citizenship rights are not fulfilled. The Migration Working Group (2017) formed by the Ministry of Urban Housing and Poverty alleviation looked into the plight of migrant workers in the country and submitted its report to the Central Government and action of the report is still awaited. Meanwhile, the abrupt eruption of the migration crisis resulting from the outbreak of Covid-19 again reminds us the urgency of the matter.

Methodology of the Study

The present study was conducted to know the impact of the Covid-19 pandemic on migrant workers in India. The data of this study were collected by using secondary sources like research papers, reports, books. The themes included challenges related of healthcare service access, issues related to social and economic problems during the prolonged lockdown.

Literature Review

Ahmad et al., 2020 conducted a study on preparedness and impact of Covid-19 on Migrant workers in India. The study found out that the migrant workers are the severe suffers. It has been found out that the extended lockdown lead to exhaust their handful savings forcing them to start their journey to hometown and the unavailability of transport facilities worsens their journey.

Jane, 2016 conducted a study on the internal migrant labour issues and policies. This study has collected all the data from the secondary sources. The study found out that the challenges faced by the migrant labourers are more complex. This study examined that though the migrant labourers contribute more to India's economy but still they are not in a protective and affluent zone.

Singh, 2020 conducted a study on mental health of migrant labourers in Covid-19 pandemic and lockdown: Challenges ahead. In this study researcher stated that the Covid-19 outbreak and consequent nationwide lockdown have resulted in a significant deterioration in all the social determinants of health. Loss of income and jobs, insecurities, and social isolation are increasing and are likely to deteriorate the mental health of migrant population which may worsen in post lockdown periods. There are high chances of increase in suicide considering the poor utilisation of health services in general and mental health services in particular. In India, migrant labour is all pervasive but invisible. As a significant component, migrants play an important role in the labour market and India's growth story. They keep our cities running, but their existence is hardly acknowledged.

Challenges faced by the Migrant Workers

Migrant workers in India faced numerous difficulties due to Covid-19. All the workplaces and factories shut down due to the country's lockdown, millions of migrant workers faced income losses, food shortages and are insecure about their future (Slater & Masih, 2020; Kanika, 2020). By following these guidelines most of them and their families went hungry (Abi-Habib & Yasir, 2020). Because of the lockdown thousands of migrants then started to go back home, with some means of transportation. As a result of this lockdown, more than 300 migrant workers died, with explanations ranging from hunger, suicides, tiredness, road and rail accidents, police cruelty and the abjuration of timely medical care.

Migrants may be predominantly susceptible to the direct and indirect impacts of Covid-19 pandemic. Migrants are also at the intersection of gender, race and status with particular patterns of vulnerability: migrants are over-represented in less-income and marginalised sections, and face complex groups of difficulties associated with their dearth of access to well-being care, barring from welfare services, and distress of stigma. Although the shortage of perfect data makes it problematic to measure the detailed bearings they experience, in other locations certain proof of inexplicably impacted migrants has been identified.

Access to health services

Migrants in many countries do not relish equal entree to healthcare facilities as residents, particularly when they are in an unbalanced situation or on short-term visas and cannot be protected for Covid-19 treatment. There may also be inadequate access to healthcare where they have the right to specific services and limited awareness of the host context or the prioritisation of the person. Migrants are less likely to have access to general practitioners, and thus therefore have insufficient access to preventive care and that is both more complicated and more costly because emergency infrastructure ear drenched with Covid-19 patients. In addition, irregular migrants may afraid that immigration authorities maybe reported and expel them if they seek assistance that may weaken their ability to come forward for screening, testing, contact tracing or treatment.

Dearth of attention to local preventive methods, over-reliance on informal modes of communication, or adherence to culture-specific customs and adopting and practices may lead to behaviours that place migrants and their groups at increased jeopardy of diffusion (Arfaat, 2020). In combination with amplified opportunity to be affected by respiratory ailments related to their living circumstances, these factors make certain migrants highly susceptible to the direct well being influences of Covid-19 pandemic (Holguin et al., 2017).

Impact of the Covid-19 on Migrant Workers

Due to Covid-19, migrant workers are the most at risk in India. Government shutdown means economic difficulties who are mainly daily wage labourers, in addition to the apparent health risk. Calcutta Research Group is collecting a collection of news articles from various sources that highlight the misery of migrant workers at the time of the global pandemic. According to the Labour Rights organisation Aajiveeka, India has around 120 million migrant labourers. These workers face various dangers, from losing income to leaving for home in a rush to confronting police brutality. The World Economic Forum estimates that 139 million migrants are in the country (Sharma, 2017). The International Labour Organisation (ILO) estimated that about 400 million workers will be poverty-stricken due to the pandemic and lockdown. In India, most of the migrants originate from Uttar Pradesh and Bihar, followed by Rajasthan and Madhya Pradesh. The Mumbai and Delhi cities fascinate the maximum number of migrants. Although most men migrate for jobs, whereas women migrate because of marriage. Over 300 deaths were reported because of the lockdown until 5 May, reasons ranging from hunger, suicides (Elsa, 2020), overtiredness, (The Economic Times, 2020), road and rail accidents, (Gettleman, et al., 2020) police brutality (Mohanty, 2020) and abjuration of suitable medicinal care. Among the deaths informed were most of the downgraded migrants and labourers (Vij, 2020; Agarwal, 2020) 80 died on the Shramik Special trains while roaming back home, in one month since their launch (Elsa, 2020).

On 8 May, 16 migrants were killed by a freight train that had stopped to rest on railway tracks near Aurangabad in Maharashtra and eight migrant workers were killed on 14 May and almost 55 injured when they were collided with a bus near Guna, Madhya Pradesh (The Indian Express, 2020). On 16 May 24 migrant workers were killed and many more were injured when a trailer carrying migrants (along with sacks of lime) rammed into a stationary truck carrying also migrants in the Uttar Pradesh district of Auraiya.

Migrants are most susceptible to urban disasters and outbreaks. The first case of Covid-19 surfaced in India on January 30, 2020, and after the out-break the lockdown in the entire country was declared on 24th March for a period of 21 days. Borders have been locked, trade has been halted, factories, shops and all kinds of economic operations were shut down, with the exception of only the vital services. This proved to be a nightmare for hundreds of thousands of migrant workers who lost their livelihoods overnight and became homeless. Such immediate problems for migrant workers were related to food, shelter, loss of wages, fear of getting infected and anxiety. As a result, some of them started leaving from various cities to their homelands. Most migrants on the way have either lost their lives due to hardship, hunger, accident and some have even committed suicide. Sudden lockdown has also stranded many migrants in various cities across the country. Those who were roaming were stuck up at stations or state or district borders. Some were forced to walk hundreds of miles to reach their home towns where no public transportation was available. The very effort to stave off the pandemic has become one of most important Indian human tragedies in recent history.

Living conditions of Migrant workers

Due to Covid-19 pandemic, India is likely to face the job crisis. Migrant workers and informal sector workers are likely to suffer significantly (ILO, 2020). Migration in India is a livelihood strategy embraced by masses of people. Most of the migrant's labour and job migration is driven towards the urban areas. Migrant labourers are the foundation of the Indian economy. In India, out of 482 million workers nearly 194 millions are permanent and semi-permanent migrant workers. Additionally, there are about 15 million short-term migrant workers of temporary and circulatory nature (Keshri & Bhagat, 2012). Covid-19 pandemic has affected the most the latter following the all India lockdown. Immigration rates in general were higher in high-income states such as Delhi, Goa, Haryana, Punjab, Maharashtra, Gujarat and Karnataka, whereas low-income states such as Bihar, Uttar Pradesh, Jharkhand, Rajasthan and Odisha reported relatively higher rates of out-migration. The most vulnerable group would be those migrant workers who are working in the informal sector, those who have no job security or any social security. They will be badly affected by the coronavirus outbreak and following lockdown is going to affect them badly leading to their further impoverishment due to loss of livelihood. It may also significantly influence their food and nutritional intake, access to healthcare and education of children. Migrants often live in overcrowded conditions across the world without access to hygiene products, where it is difficult to accept social distancing and other basic prevention practices. In the absence of systematic screening, the risk of the disease spreading rapidly in and around these sites. Closure of the workplace can also lead to irregularities in countries where the employment status is linked to the employer and job of a worker. Irregularity, in effect, further decrease said entitlements and accessibility of welfare choices, while at the same time increasing the risks associated with and not linked to Covid-19 (Nyein, 2020).

Conclusion

To sum up, the national lockdown of India amid the Covid-19 pandemic has disrupted its migrant population critically. Hundreds of thousands of migrants were forced to walk hundreds of miles back to their hometowns with some dying along the way, losing employment and resources, and shutting down public transportation. By the economic impact of the Covid-19 outbreak, India's migrant workers are amongst the worst-hit. The pandemic of Covid-19 continues to have widespread effects on the world's workforces; migrant workers are among those with the brunt of the pandemic, migrant workers are overwhelmingly at risk from the impact of the pandemic due to unsafe and crowded living conditions, lockdowns and harsh containment measures, limited access to healthcare and basic facilities, precarious working conditions and exploitative labour systems.

References

Abi-Habib, M., & Yasir, S. (2020). India's Coronavirus Lockdown Leaves Vast Numbers Stranded and Hungry. T*he New York Times.* Retrieved 13 May 2020.

Agarwal, K.(2020). *N*ot Just the Aurangabad Accident, 383 People Have Died Due to the Punitive Lockdown". *The Wire*. Retrieved 10 May 2020.

Ahmad, M.S., Ahmad, R. & Ahmad, R.K. (2020). Preparedness and impact of Covid-19 on migrant workers in India. *International Migration*.

Arfaat, M. (2020). Rohingya refugees need a coronavirus lifeline, not an internet ban. *The New Humanitarian.* Retrieved 24 March 2020.

Elsa, E. (2020). "Coronavirus in India: 80 migrant workers have died on Shramik Special trains, Indian tweeps furious. *Gulf News*. Retrieved 31 May 2020.

Gettleman, J., Raj, S., & Kumar, H. (2020). As India Reopens, Deadly Accidents Break Out. *The New York Times*. Retrieved 13 May 2020.

Holguin, F., Moughrabieh, M. A., Ojeda, V., Patel, S. R., Peyrani, P., Pinedo, M., & Roman, J. (2017). Respiratory health in migrant populations: a crisis overlooked. *Annals of the American Thoracic Society*, *14*(2), 153-159.

International Labour Organisation (2020). Almost 25 million jobs could be lost worldwide as a result of Covid-19, says ILO. *News,* ILO, 18 March.

Jane, C.A.(2016). A study on the internal migrant labour issues and policies. *Indian Journal of Applied Research*. 6(4):81-83.

Keshri, K., & Bhagat, R. B. (2012). Temporary and seasonal migration: Regional pattern, characteristics and associated factors. *Economic and Political Weekly*, 81-88.

Mohanty, D. (2020). 56-year-old migrant dies on road to home, another dies after police lathi charge. *Hindustan Times.*

Nyein, N. (2020). Thai border closures over Covid-19 spark Myanmar migrants return, health concerns. The Irrawaddy, 23 March.

Sharma, K. (2017). India has 139 million internal migrants. They must not be forgotten. *World Economic Forum*. Retrieved 13 May 2020.

Singh, J. & Singh, J. (2020). Covid-19 and Its Impact on Society. *Electronic Research Journal of Social Sciences and Humanities.*2 (1):168-172.

Singh, O.P. (2020). Mental health of migrant laborers in Covid-19 pandemic and lockdown: Challenges ahead. *Indian Journal of Psychiatry.* 62(3): 233-234.

Skeldon, R. (2017). International Migration, internal migration, mobility and urbanisation: towards more integrated approaches. *Population Division, Department of Economic and Social Affairs, United Nations*.

Slater, J., & Masih, N. (2020). In India, the world's biggest lockdown has forced migrants to walk hundreds of miles home. *The Washington Post.* Mar, 28.

The Economic Times. (2020). 'Suicide leading cause for over 300 lockdown deaths in India, says study". Retrieved 13 May 2020.

The Indian Express (2020). Coronavirus lockdown: So far, over 130 migrants killed in accidents en route to their home states. Retrieved 8 June 2020.

Vij, S. (2020). "More than 300 Indians have died of the coronavirus and nearly 200 of the lockdown". *The Print*. Retrieved 13 May 2020.

18

Impact of Covid-19 on Migration and Women

Prantik Basak

Abstract

Covid-19 has shaken the very core of our reality. What started out in Wuhan in China has now turned into a global pandemic affecting every corner of the world. Area-wise quarantines have now turned into nationwide lockdowns. Places of work have been shut down abruptly with migrant workers being forced to return home thousands of miles away on feet. Like in every other discourse where women are invisible, so is the case in migration during Covid-19. The trauma of women migrants are surprisingly not so apparently portrayed by media. Images of migrant workers walking thousands of miles home and hundreds cooped up in inter-state buses and trains during the pandemic when contracting the virus was at its heights is an image that will not be forgotten easily. Migrant women workers have had it the hardest. Not only did they lose their jobs but also has the additional burden of taking care of their old and the children during these trying times.

Keywords: *Covid-19; job loss; migrant women; pandemic; lockdown.*

Introduction

Covid-19 has shaken the very core of our reality. What started out in Wuhan in China has now turned into a global pandemic affecting every corner of the world. Area-wise quarantines have now turned into nationwide lockdowns. Places of work have been shut down abruptly with migrant workers being forced to return home thousands of miles away on feet. Schools and colleges have been shut down; students are now studying in online classes. Life as we know it has transformed totally. Nobody knows when things will go back to normal, and many fear this new reality to be the new normal.

Like in every other discourse where women are invisible, so is the case in migration during Covid-19. The trauma of women migrants are surprisingly not so apparently portrayed by media. It needs to be understood that in India, both men and women migrate in large numbers to different parts of India in search for low-wage jobs. Women migrate in family units that work together. Single women work as live-in domestic help in metropolitan cities of Delhi, Mumbai, Chennai (Sapra, 2020). Women work as cook, as house help, in construction sites. Women are the silent other in an arena that is dominated by men. We have seen such women being captured on camera along with their husbands and children in the early months of the corona virus pandemic when they were forced to walk back hundreds of miles home by feet.

Review of literature

The Covid-19 has been here for about five months only. Most of the resources on Covid-19 and its impact on social life were available only on newspapers. Newspaper reporting was the main source of information on the topic. However, this work has been heavily influenced by the research paper titled '*Covid-19 and Women Migrant Workers: Impacts and Implications*' published by the International Organisation for Migration and authored by Laura Foley and Nicola Piper. The paper highlights how women have been in the frontlines battling the Covid-19 pandemic, how the pandemic has affected the migrant women workers and why there is a need for equity and an inclusive approach in terms of government policies responding to the pandemic crisis. A startling revelation brought forward by the paper is how irrespective of different countries and governments, the needs of women, especially those of migrant women, have not been fulfilled by policies. Data for South America and South-East Asia have been presented in the paper, and the conditions prevailing in India at a general level seem to reflect the truthfulness of the data presented. The global job loss and how job losses have affected the migrant workers differently have been put forward. Drawing from the facts presented in this paper and adding to it from national newspaper reporting, I have aimed to create a picture of the situation of migrant women workers in India.

Objectives

The objective of this paper has been manifold. The global pandemic has hit every aspect of daily life but it has affected different sections of the society differently. The main objective of the paper is to address the impact on the pandemic especially on the migrant women workers in India. The secondary objectives include the effects of job loss on migrant women, the effect of an abrupt announcement of lockdown on the migrant workers and the effects of lack of essentials for migrant workers returning home.

Methodology

The research method of secondary data analysis has been approached in order to carry out the following research. Newspaper reporting and research papers have been the main source of information. Due to nationwide lockdown, it was impossible to travel and conduct personal interviews and put forward survey reports. Also, online surveys were not possible as migrant workers were mostly not a citizen of the internet world. The sources of data are authentic and verified. Each report has been double-checked with other sources to verify the authenticity of the facts.

Discussion

We need to look at why the migration of women for work has increased, which is the rise of the middle class in India. Globalisation has led to a growth in the service sector which has created jobs for both men and women. Nuclear families with both the father and the mother working have led to rise of a lot of demands in the family. These demands are taken care of by the lower sections of the society. When educated middle-class women work in a professional space, after a 9 to 5 job it becomes impossible for them to carry out their traditional tasks like house chores and even child-rearing. This vacuum has been filled by migrant women workers.

Migrant women with basic education work as sales girls, as beauticians or as waitresses. There are some women who migrate to cities with their husband and search for low wage jobs. No matter what, all migrant women have to go through the same struggles. They are forced to live in unhealthy conditions, they face discrimination. Young women are also vulnerable to sexual violence (Sharma, 2020). Racial discrimination has also shown its face in this pandemic. Not just migrant workers but people from all walks of life from the north-east living in various parts of India have been spat on or called 'Corona' because of their looks.

It is roughly estimated that global unemployment figures could rise by almost 25 million as a result of Covid-19. Women migrant workers are bearing a major brunt of it since they are generally employed in the informal sectors with no job security. Loss in business during lockdown will force the hand of employers to fire their employees. Images and videos of women and their families walking home hundreds of miles in cruel summer conditions have been heart-wrenching. A halt in work means a halt in pay until work resumes. With all the pressure of not bringing in money home, migrant workers had to withstand the burden of walking back home as there were no transports available since the abrupt announcement of nationwide lockdown. Unable to pay rent, they had to leave for home. Even after lockdown had been lifted in some areas, many migrant workers were unable to go back to work either due to shortage of finances or due to lockdown in their area of residence, thus leading to a loss of work.

Women working as housemaids or house help often live in unsanitary slums lacking the privileges of clean water and sanitary essentials. Keeping the accompanying risks in mind, their employment has either been discontinued or in some cases suspended without pay. Unavailability of proper protective measures is a reason for concern too. Filter and non-filter N95 masks may range from 300 to 450 rupees, while proper gloves might cost a little less. For a daily wage earner experiencing a sudden loss in employment, this amount of money is huge, and buying it for a family of 4 or 5 is impossible. Poor and uneducated workers might go for cheaper fake protective gear, leaving themselves and the ones around them vulnerable.

Women tend to migrate to foreign lands too in search of work, as conditions in foreign soil might be better than their homeland. Foreign countries might provide more freedom and liberty to working women and equality in terms of payment. Migrant women are mostly working at the bottom ranks typically involving tasks that might be seen as menial. The gender wage gap is wide and apparent and the migrant women work in more precarious, insecure and informal employment that receives low pay (Piper, 2019). Not only do migrant women workers face violence in workplace but also have troubles accessing sexual and reproductive healthcare.

The Covid-19 pandemic has issued a global lockdown to curb the virus which has led to almost all major sectors coming to an abrupt halt. Only essential services like healthcare, social care and production and distribution of food have been allowed. Migrant women work in all these sectors, and are mostly represented among medical and low-wage service providers. If it was not apparent already, it is visibly clear now that it is largely women's labour that keeps global health and social care systems running (Piper, 2019). Not only are women vulnerable to the virus but also the responsibility of taking care of the sick fall on women, both migrant and non-migrant. Many also work as cleaners in within hospitals. Women generally take up the role of a nurse and therefore are in constant contact with sick patients. This makes them the most vulnerable to contracting the virus and spreading it after returning home, where they play the role of the house keeper.

The medical infrastructures of all the States in the world have been overwhelmed by the pressure of the corona virus pandemic. There is a shortage of protective equipment and skilled medical staff. There is an increased pressure on the nurses. Right now, over 20 lakh people have been affected by the virus in India alone. It is the nurses who have to deal with the concerned patients and their family members and this takes a toll on their mental health. There is no mechanism in place that will help them to deal with this overwhelming stress. They are forced to work extra hours and are not even paid more for it.

Women migrant workers in healthcare are facing an additional problem as women which exposes them to greater risk of contracting Covid-19, as personal protective equipments are not exactly unisexual in nature but are mostly made to fit men's bodies (Piper, 2019). These do not fit the women properly, leaving them at risk. In a country like India, there are not enough protective equipment available for the lakhs of medical workers who are working day and night to curb the corona virus. There were images of healthcare staff wearing raincoats as protective gear, which just makes it apparent, how grim the reality is.

Women migrant workers in the medical field have to work extra hours in light of this pandemic. This has become an extra burden for women workers with children. Due to closure of schools and unavailability of childcare services, additional caring and educational responsibilities have fallen on these women. We cannot also ignore the fact that without adequate protective equipment at work, children and elderly at home are being put at a risk, as it is children and the aged who are the most prone to getting affected by the corona virus.

As per the reports of the International Labour Organisation in 2015, there are an estimated 67 million domestic workers in the world, 80 percent of whom are women and 11.5 million of whom are migrants. Women constitute a major proportion of migrant workers generally involved in domestic work. Their chores range from cooking to cleaning to taking care of children. These workers were already unprotected and marginalised before the pandemic hit. Right now, they are at their vulnerable most position. With both national and state borders being closed, women who have been dismissed from their jobs lose their accommodation unable to return home. The situation is however not exactly better for women migrant workers in the domestic sector who have managed to continue with their employment. Due to lockdown, women working as domestic help are not able to go out for refreshments. Away from their own family, they need a time out for themselves after a day of hard work that would include various house chores. Due to fear of coming in contact with the virus, women migrant workers are forced to stay indoors.

When it comes to migrant women who do house chores in for multiple households, the problems are a bit different. Employers might ask them to stop working for other families, as travelling from one place of work to the other would increase the risk of contracting the virus. This is always an unacceptable choice for the workers as this would cause a major blow to their total income which is not enough to begin with. Besides this, women workers have to face a lot of difficulties while travelling from one place of work to the other. India was in complete lockdown from March to June with most major sectors being closed. Only essential services were operational. Women workers employed in households for domestic chores, however, in most cases had to continue with their work even during lockdown. This meant that they had to travel illegally during lockdown and often face police brutality when caught.

Many migrant women work as sex workers. The corona virus pandemic has left them jobless and has forced them to return to their homes or look for alternative sources of income. For example, sex workers in Delhi's GB road are unable to find new jobs due to their local address. The stigma of being a sex worker immediately destroys all possibilities of a new source of employment. Rations are available but it is not enough, as there are expenses for other essential utilities. NGOs are not involved in raising funds for sex workers due to the myth that sex workers earn a lot (Agarwal, 2020).

Recommendations

Evidence suggests that the world is on the eve of far greater international mobility largely due to work force decline and population ageing, coupled with low birth rates in many industrialised countries. Migrants will be even more essential to address labour market needs and the sustainability of economic development in many countries (Kariyawasam, 2017). Today, this is as true as it can get. Also, a big chunk of migrant workers are women, who mostly migrate for finances and in search for empowerment. Therefore, policymakers need to make gender-sensitive labour migration laws.

Indian Finance Minister Nirmala Sitharaman acknowledged the significance of MGNREGS in providing jobs to returning workers in rural areas (Ramani, 2020). However, in reality, MGNREGS provide for jobs that include hard manual labour which would be okay for male workers but might not be possible for female workers. Therefore, the government needs to provide for alternative sources of work for the returning migrant women workers.

The Labour Union Model rights-based approach and works for better implementation of labour laws and regulation of labour flows. Such can be implemented in the case of migrant workers in India.

Amid growing distress among migrant labour during the ongoing lockdown, the National Commission for Women had set off a review of legal provisions in law related to Inter-State women migrant workers (Pandit, 2020). Sexual violence against poor women is prevalent and migrant women workers on road returning home were the most vulnerable in these regards. Laws need to be put up to protect migrant women workers.

In Singapore, foreign migrant workers cannot work without valid permits while in Malaysia the inflow and outflow of migrant workers is regulated (Sakdapolrak, 2002). In quite a similar fashion, agencies need to be set up that can track migrant women workers employed in different sectors and report this to higher governmental bodies in charge of allocating and distributing resources. Such resources can be provided to the list of migrant women workers in times of emergencies such as this current pandemic.

Conclusion

Covid-19 has punched humanity in the gut. While the world suffers, it is the poorest of the poor who suffer the most. The life conditions of migrant workers were difficult to begin with. Images of migrant workers walking thousands of miles home and hundreds cooped up in inter-state buses and trains during the pandemic when contracting the virus was at its heights is an image that will not be forgotten easily. Migrant women workers have had it the hardest. Not only did they lose their jobs but also has the additional burden of taking care of their old and the children during these trying times. Migrant women workers in the informal sectors are not protected by any laws and are always at the mercy of their employers. Often they are subjected to sexual violence. They might also have to provide sexual favour to their employers to loan some money during these trying times. The world governments need to take a stand for these migrant workers. The lockdown was abruptly announced in India, giving zero time to the migrant workers to at least pack up and leave for home. There was shortage of transportation and what we saw was bus stations flooded with thousands of migrant workers fighting for a seat to home. At a time when social distancing was a necessity, an abrupt lockdown had forced people to ignore distancing and just fight for a way home. We can only wonder if the government even cared about the consequences of the abrupt lockdown on the migrant workers, especially the women.

References

Agarwal, P. (2020, July 14). *'Who Will Give Us Jobs?': Delhi's Sex Workers Hit Hard By Covid-19*. Retrieved August 14, 2020, from The Quint: https://www.thequint.com/news/india/coronavirus-covid-19-hit-sex-workers-jobs

Kariyawasam, P. (2017, January 28). *Protecting the Rights of Women Migrant Workers*. Retrieved 10 1, 2020, from The Wire: https://thewire.in/women/migrant-women-workers

Pandit, A. (2020, May 14). *NCW sets off review of laws related to migrant women workers*. Retrieved September 29, 2020, from Times of India: https://timesofindia.indiatimes.com/india/ncw-sets-off-review-of-laws-related-to-migrant-women-workers/articleshow/75745050.cms

Piper, L. F. (2019). *Covid-19 AND WOMEN:Impacts and implications*. Retrieved August 12, 2020, from IOM Online Bookstore: https://publications.iom.int/system/files/pdf/the-gender-dimensions-of-the-labour-migration.pdf

Ramani, S. (2020). *Coronavirus package | Will migrant workers benefit from the Centre's measures?* Retrieved 10 1, 2020, from The Hindu: https://www.thehindu.com/news/national/coronavirus-package-will-migrant-workers-benefit-from-the-centres-measures/article31603590.ece

Sakdapolrak, P. (2002, December). *Protection of Women Migrant Workers*. Retrieved October 1, 2020, from The World Bank: http://documents1.worldbank.org/curated/en/366911468170040936/pdf/512560v10WP0Bo1UBLIC10ProtectionWMW.pdf

Sapra, I. (2020, April 25). *Why don't we see the women? The untold story of Covid-19 migration*. Retrieved August 4, 2020, from The Indian Express: https://indianexpress.com/article/opinion/why-dont-we-see-the-women-the-untold-story-of-covid-19-migration-6378557/

Sharma, K. (2020, May 22). *Even in the Covid-19 migrant narrative Women don't count*. Retrieved August 4, 2020, from Mathrubhumi: https://english.mathrubhumi.com/features/specials/even-in-the-covid-19-migrant-narrative-women-don-t-count-1.4777812

19

Role of Migration and Urbanisation in the Transmission of Novel Coronavirus in India

Alka Rani, Abhishek Gupta

Abstract

Novel coronavirus epidemic surfaced in Wuhan, Hubei province, China and spread globally. India was also not spared and recorded large number of cases. Although this virus has affected all classes but the migrants were the worst affected. India having development activities in all states due to urbanisation have to and fro movement of migratory population. Thus, the role of urbanisation, affluence, migrants in the transmission of Covid-19 was studied in this chapter. Data for Covid-19 cases were obtained from Covid-19 tracker website of Indian Council of Medical Research (ICMR), New Delhi, for affluence from National Family Health Survey (NFHS) of 2015-16 and for individual cases and travel history details from Kaggle.com. The data showed population movement possessing major role in transmission of Covid-19 disease in India. Pearson's correlation analysis showed urbanisation i.e. urban population (r=0.41) and population density (r=0.27) having positive role while presence of migratory population (-0.34 to -0.37 in urban and rural respectively) having negative role in spreading coronavirus disease in Delhi. Urbanisation i.e. Urban residence, population growth, population density and migration (migratory population) strongly influence number of corona cases with medium to high (r=0.34 to 0.75) impact on this disease in Uttar Pradesh. Living conditions of migratory population i.e. overcrowding and lack of basic hygiene are further aggravating the problem as social distancing and hand washing becomes difficult to implement. Further attention towards urban areas especially slums and migrants which lives in unhygienic conditions and overcrowding is essential.

Keywords: *Migration, urbanisation, Covid-19, affluence, population movement, transmission.*

Introduction

Role of migrant population in the spread of infectious disease is recognised since earlier times. They can introduce infection or can enhance the potential of a disease to transmit it locally. For example, HIV was introduced into naïve populations and potential of transmission in local for tuberculosis (TB) reinforced by population movement (Barnett and Walker, 2008). Stephen S. Morse defined emerging infectious diseases as "infections that have newly appeared in a population or have existed but are rapidly increasing in incidence or geographic range" (Bhagat et al. 2020).Covid-19 emerged as a global pandemic causing a considerable amount of cases. This outbreak started from China by the new-year as per Chinese lunar calendar when about 5 million people left capital city of Hubei province i.e. Wuhan and spread this disease worldwide. The migration played a significant role in transmission of SARS-CoV-2 to other countries from China and within countries when this disease reached a country (Jiang and Luo, 2020; Yuan, 2020). The first case of Covid -19 surfaced on January 30, 2020, and rose subsequently leading to lockdown imposed on 24th March 2020 (Adhikari et al., 2020). With the closure of all types of economic activities a large number of migrants lost their livelihood. Out of fear and anxiety with no source of income, no food and shelter reverse migration evidenced. Many deaths were also reported among them due to hunger, suicide, walking a long distance when met with an accident and also coronavirus infection (Bhagat et al., 2020). As per UNDESA about 26.2 per 100,000 population were migrants with Covid-19 confirmed cases in India (UNDESA, 2019). The only methods to fight the coronavirus disease suggested to be social distancing and quarantine for the infected individuals (Chowdhury et al., 2020; Smith and Freedman, 2020). This study is an attempt to examine the role of urbanisation, and migration in the transmission of Covid-19 in India.

Review of literature

SARS-CoV-2 has caused large number of cases and deaths all over the world. In India, the numbers of cases were 6,310,267 with 98,708 deaths on 30th September 2020. Worst affected states were Maharashtra, Andhra Pradesh, Karnataka, Tamil Nadu, Uttar Pradesh and Delhi (ICMR, 2020). Coronavirus family has been reported of causing respiratory disease earlier too. In November 2002, SARS Coronavirus (SARS-CoV) i.e. Severe Acute Respiratory Syndrome infected human for the first time in the Guangdong province of southern China and was responsible for more than 8000 cases in 26 countries. As per WHO, perhaps bats were the reservoir spreading this virus to other animals (civet cats) and then to humans. Again in 2012, another disease from this family i.e. Middle East Respiratory Syndrome coronavirus (MERS-CoV) was first identified in Saudi Arabia. Scientific evidence suggests that dromedary camels are a major reservoir host for MERS-CoV through which this virus transmitted to humans. MERS-CoV affected 27 countries of which Saudi Arabia contributed 80% of the cases (WHO, 2003, 2012). Corona virus new strain which belongs to same family of Coronaviridae has appeared in December 2019. This new strain was named as a novel coronavirus on January 7, by WHO. Later renamed as severe acute respiratory syndrome coronavirus 2 (SARS-CoV-2) (Harapan et al., 2020).

Coronavirus is reported in humans as well as in animals in the earlier studies too. In children of India it caused fever, cough, sore throat and shortness of breath (Malhotra et al., 2016). In animals, this virus was reported in dogs (Deka et al., 2013), cattles (Hansa et al., 2012), and mithuns (Rajkhowa et al., 2007). Therefore, coronavirus is evolving continuously from SARS to MERS to current fatal disease. India was largely insulated from both the diseases with SARS-CoV having less than 15 cases (3 probable cases of which one developed pneumonia and 10 suspected cases) and no cases from MERS-CoV at all (WHO, 2002, 2012). But SARS-CoV-2 has also affected India causing large number of cases and deaths and threat to economy.

Objectives

The objective of this paper is to study the role of migration and urbanisation in transmission of Covid-19. Two states i.e. Delhi (urbanised with migrated population from other states) and Uttar Pradesh (urbanising with movement of migrants inside and outside the state) are compared in their districts to further explore the role of urbanisation and migration.

Methodology

Data on individual level Covid-19 cases in India from 30th January 2020 till 26th April 2020 were obtained from Kaggle (https://www.kaggle.com/sudalairajkumar/covid19-in-india). Data on affluence in selected districts of Delhi and Uttar Pradesh was created using compute from transform tool in SPSS version 21. Correlation and regression analysis was done using MS excel. Information on parameters like electricity, cooking using clean fuel, health, literacy, population etc. in case of Delhi and anaemia, vaccination (all), contraceptive use, registered births and delivery in case of UP was obtained from National Family Health Survey (NFHS) for the year 2015-16. Information on Data for Covid-19 cases as on 24th June 2020 for comparing with districts of Delhi and Covid-19 cases as on 25th June 2020 for comparing affluence of all districts was obtained from Indian Council of Medical Research (ICMR) Covid-19 tracker (https://www.covid19india.org/demographics). Data on deaths of migrants during lockdown is available from the datasets of SaveLife foundation (https://savelifefoundation.org/covidtracker/).

Districts of Delhi and Uttar Pradesh state are under study. The total number of people infected with coronavirus on 15 August 2020 reported to be 1,50,652 (deaths=4,178) and in Uttar Pradesh 1,45,287 (deaths=2,335)(Government of India, 2020). Delhi has more than 90% urban population in all districts. As per 2011 census, about 97.58 % migrants in districts of Delhi were living in urban (Census, 2011). It had reported of first case of Covid-19 pandemic on March 2, 2020. It has become one of the hotspot after Maharashtra and Tamil Nadu on 15th August, 2020. High income states like Delhi, Maharashtra, Goa, Punjab, Gujarat, Haryana and Karnataka has in-migration from low income states such as Bihar, Uttar Pradesh, Jharkhand, Rajasthan and Odisha. Uttar Pradesh is the most populous state in India, divided into 75 districts. Its population has increased by over 26% in 20 years i.e. 1991 to 2001. Its population density is 828/people/Km^2 (Census, 2011).

First case of Covid-19 pandemic was reported from Ghaziabad on March, 4, 2020. It has reported highest number of returnee migrants (Gaur, 2020).

Observations and Discussion

Role of travel in Covid-19 cases in India

Travel history of population since the appearance of first Covid-19 case on 30th January 2020 till 26th April 2020 is presented in figure 1. The countries of return were arranged as Asian (Malaysia, Thailand, Sri Lanka, Indonesia and others), European (Italy, London, UK, France and others), American (US and South America), Arabian (Dubai, Abu Dhabi, Iran, and others) and others include Australian and African travellers. The travellers within India presented in the same period with Covid-19 cases were Delhi, Maharashtra, and other Indian states such as Kerala, Tamil Nadu, Madhya Pradesh, West Bengal, Gujarat, and Uttar Pradesh. Delhi and Mumbai has the largest number of travellers followed by those travelled to Dubai, UAE, Iran, and Abu Dhabi taken together as Arab countries. Next to these were European

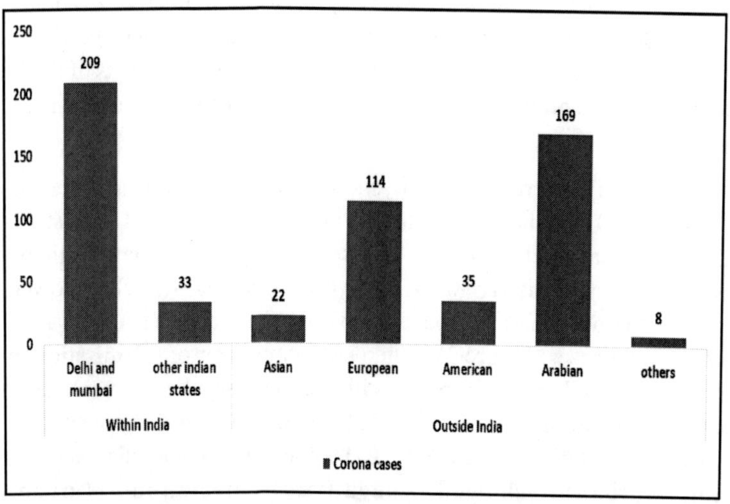

Figure 1: Travel history within and outside India of population with primary novel coronavirus infection (Arabian: Middle East, North Africa, and Greater Arabia, American: North, Central and South America).

countries with a maximum number of cases travelled to Italy. Hence, from Wuhan Coronavirus spread to several countries from where it reached India through population movement. The metropolitan cities like Delhi and Mumbai well connected to other countries by Air travel had Coronavirus as a result of population mobility to Delhi and Mumbai along with Bengaluru, Chennai etc. and spread it all over India. By 26th April 2020, only 5.18% cases had travelled outside India and others were either having a travel history within India or are close contact of the infected travellers. Hence, population movement possesses a major role in the progress of Covid-19 disease within and across countries.

Association of coronavirus cases with migration and urbanisation

Urbanisation has also been recognised as a key factor in transmission of Covid-19. Once this virus entered a country, population density played its role in its transmission. Influence of affluence on Covid-19 is also found as more affluent cities were the red zones, i.e. they were the hotspots of Covid-19 cases. District-wise data of affluence showed another influence of urbanisation on Covid-19 transmission. More affluent districts of India were having a larger number of Covid-19 cases (Bhatia et al., 2020). Role of migration has not been studied so far. Here we associated urbanisation and migration in districts of Delhi and UP with coronavirus disease (using cases) to find any existing relationship.

Pearson's correlation analysis showed a medium association ($r=0.49$, $p=0.160$) between affluence and corona cases (till August 14, 2020) in Uttar Pradesh. Figure 2 presents this positive relationship by Regression analysis ($R^2=0.24$). However, districts of Delhi showed negative association ($r=-0.363$, $p=0.337$, $R^2=0.13$) between urbanisation and corona cases (Figure 3). When each parameter of urbanisation in districts of Delhi was compared with corona cases then percentage of urban population ($r=0.41$, $R^2=0.17$) and population density showed positive correlation ($r=0.27$, $R^2=0.07$) while migratory population (rural and urban) showed negative correlation (urban, $r=-0.34$, $R^2=0.13$, rural$=-0.37$, $R^2=0.14$). Thus, urbanisation i.e. urban population and population density has positive role while presence of migratory population has negative role in spreading coronavirus in

Delhi (Table 1, Figure 4). Urbanisation and migration in Uttar Pradesh strongly influence number of corona cases. Urban residence, population, population density, migratory population all have medium to high impact on this disease (Table 1). It is evidenced from the correlation coefficient values given in Table 1. Figure 5 presented districts of UP with corona cases. Most affluent district influenced by corona was Lucknow, followed by Ghaziabad and Allahabad. Similarly, in case of districts of Delhi West and North districts were the most urbanised districts having large number of corona cases (Figure 6).

Table 1: Urbanisation parameters and their association with corona virus cases using correlation and regression analysis

State	*Parameter*	*r values*	*R^2 values*	*Regression equation*
Delhi	Migratory population in urban	-0.345434347	0.13	y=-3613.6x+1E+06
	Migratory population in rural	-0.374585317	0.14	y=-225.75x+34692
	Percent Urban population	0.407215904	0.17	y=8.5597x-773.87
	Population density	0.270767712	0.07	y=0.0013x+46.1
Uttar Pradesh	Urban residence	0.75	0.56	y=30.312x+98859
	population	0.34	0.12	y=110.25x+3E+06
	Population density	0.48	0.235	y=0.107x+875.33
	Migratory population	0.62	0.38	y=81.478x+899240

Source: Census 2011, NFHS 2015-16.

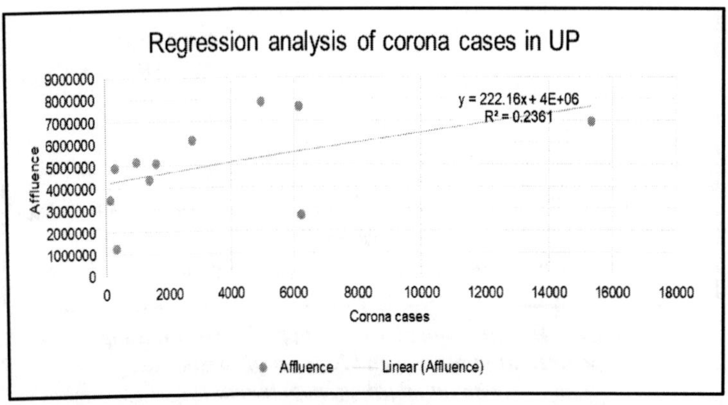

Figure 2: Regression plot showing positive relationship between affluence and corona cases in Uttar Pradesh.

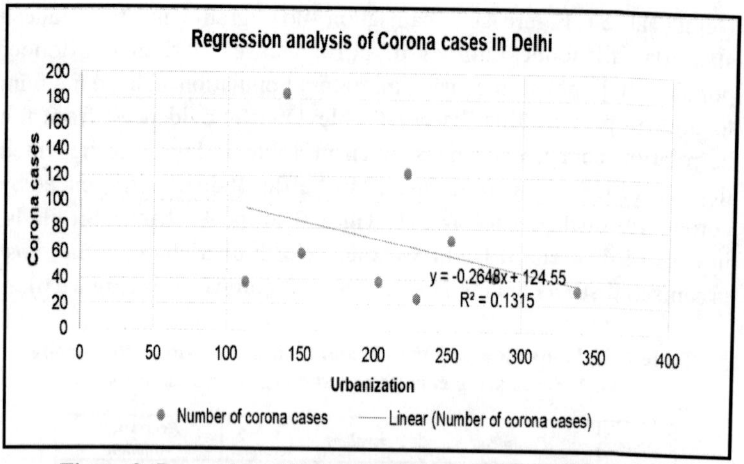

Figure 3: Regression plot showing negative relationship between urbanisation and corona cases using migratory population with urban population %, and population density in Delhi.

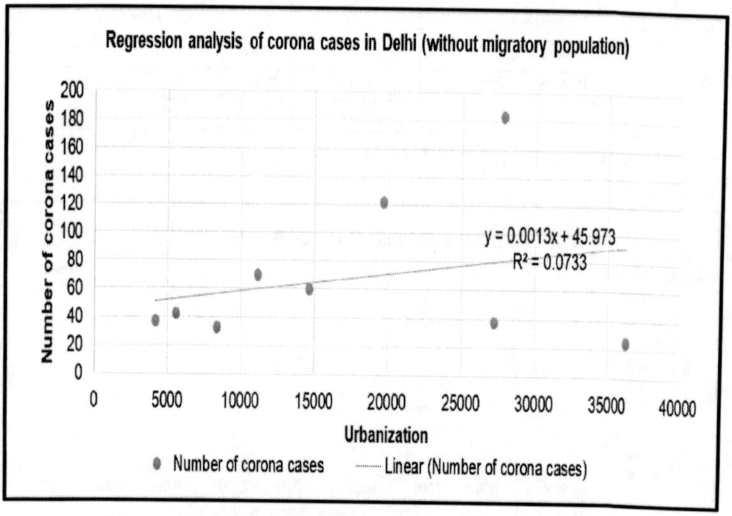

Figure 4: Regression plot showing positive relationship between urbanisation and Number of corona cases without migratory population.

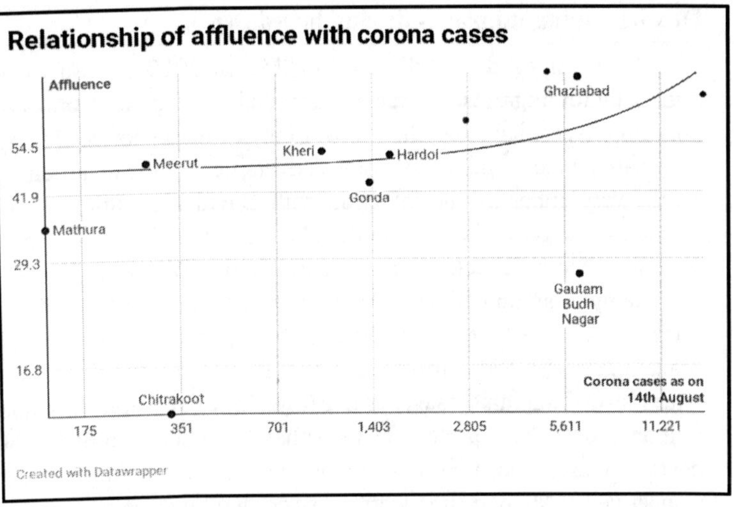

Source: Census 2011, NFHS 2015-16.

Figure 5: Relationship of Affluence of Districts in UP with Coronavirus (Affluence calculated from parameters like population, population density, urban residence, migratory population, contraceptive usage, all vaccination in children, anaemia in children and adults).

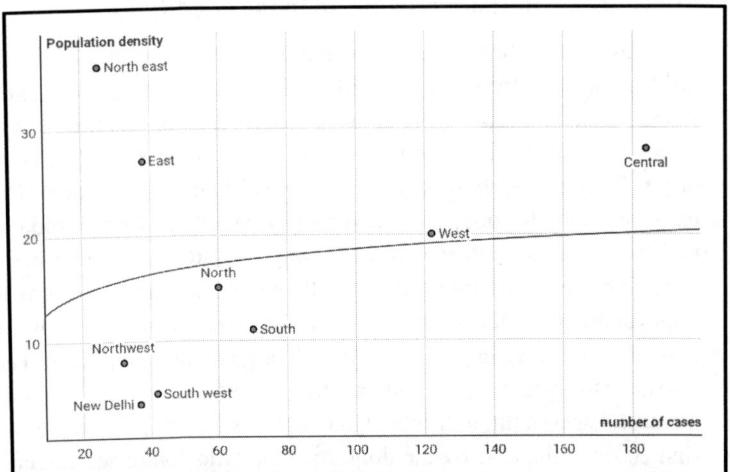

Source: Census 2011, NFHS 2015-16.

Figure 6: Relationship of urbanisation of Districts in Delhi with Coronavirus Urbanisation level calculated from parameters like urban population and population density.

Deaths among migrants during lockdown

Lockdown imposed in India on 25th March 2020 proved to be a nightmare for migrants. Migrants whether a low-wage workers or high post employees, have lost their jobs. Many of these started fleeing to their native places and faced various adversities. Some lost their lives on the way either by the infection with Covid-19, while others by accidents, hunger and even suicide. Those reached their native places were found to be infected with the coronavirus (Bhagat et al., 2020). For example, among Bihar migrants out of 4,273 cases, 3,079 were migrants i.e. 75 % (Kumar, 2020). In Uttar Pradesh, including Maharajganj (8), Siddharthanagar (11), Basti (16), Bareilly (4) and others several migrants tested positive (Shukla 2020). The deaths among migrants were also reported in which phase 3 lockdown only has 60% deaths (phases one, two and four witnessed 25, 17 and 38 deaths respectively). Many deaths were reported due to accidents on roads. For example, about 26.4% deaths among migrants were due to road crash deaths. Most of these were due to speeding, vehicle collision and vehicle overturn (Banakar, 2020).

Migrants are at more risk due to living conditions

In India, 37 % of the Country's population is internal migrants (Census 2011). Migrants are at high risk of contracting Covid-19 disease due to their living conditions. They live in overcrowded conditions, high density, lack of basic hygiene etc. Public health measures like social distancing, hand washing, self-isolation are difficult to implement. They have no access to food, water and money which has further added to their woes. Most of these are daily wage workers with poor health conditions. Whether infected or not they have no separate rooms for implementing social distancing. Due to non-availability of water source in their homes they have to share it with large number of people. They also have to share common toilets. Their homes are too small to remain inside. Dharavi slum of Mumbai, the most densely populated area had first coronavirus case by the domestic help who contracted infection from their US-returned employer (Ray, 2020). Later, large number of cases were reported in this area (Mahale, 2020). These migrants with lockdown are trying to reach their native villages. UP has reported of highest number of returnee migrants (about 2.25 lakhs) (Gaur, 2020).

Only 3% of them were found infected with coronavirus. If reached another problem will be the potential virus spread in these villages without proper health facilities. Thus, data on cases in migrants and on the districts which should be on high alert for as these workers return to their homes.

Recommendations

Based on finding, it is suggested that society and government have to work together in response to Covid-19. Social distancing, self-hygiene and increase in testing capacity are the only possible ways to control this disease until vaccine arrives. Migrants require attention as they are the worst affected population not only because of coronavirus but their worsening living conditions. Urban areas are at high risk and contracting more infection, and the situation in urban slums in worst. Those returning to their native rural areas bring with them the Covid-19 virus thus spreading to these areas where no health facilities are available. There is a need to devise tool for district level planning is also necessary. India due to large population, densely populated urban areas, and a large number of moving migrant worker has further become challenge requiring attention for stopping spread of Covid-19 outbreak. No data on migrants on their jobs, their losses or coronavirus cases is available so far. Thus, no assessment of their situation can be done, which is necessary.

Conclusions

The role of migration and urbanisation; and the risk of coronavirus on migrants is presented through this study. Early cases in India were through the migration of population throughout from Wuhan to which Arab countries like Dubai, Italy and Abu Dhabi were the highest contributors. This infected population came in contact with the uninfected population in metro cities like Delhi, Mumbai, Chennai, and Bengaluru etc. when returned to their native places (Figure 1). Thus, most of the cases were those who travelled to Delhi and Mumbai. Districts in Delhi and UP were associated using correlation and regression analysis (Table 1). Affluent districts found to have larger number of Covid-19 cases which is due to higher population density and urban population. Delhi has more cases in districts with higher population density, and percentage of urban population, however, migratory population showed negative influence. Uttar Pradesh districts showed medium to high positive relationship with urbanisation as well as migration. Lucknow, Ghaziabad, Moradabad, Meerut and others among selected districts have displayed this positive relationship with coronavirus disease in UP. West and North districts of Delhi with high population density and urban population have positive relationship with coronavirus disease. Although this study has showed difference in relationship of urbanisation and migration in two states yet further study is required.

Movement of migrants to their rural native has also been warned of spread of virus to the rural areas from the current affluent districts. Migratory population usually stay in unhygienic living conditions with overcrowding and lack of basic hygiene hence social distancing, hand washing and other cleanliness measures are difficult to implement. Migrants are also facing death during lockdown not only due to infection with novel coronavirus but also due to hunger and accidents on their way back home. Urban areas particularly slums and migrants are thus at high risk of covid-19 disease and requires attention.

References

1. Adhikari, A., Narayanan, R., Dhorajiwala, S., &Mundoli, S. (2020). 21 days and counting: Covid-19 lockdown, migrant workers, and the inadequacy of welfare measures in India.
2. Banakar, P. (2020). "Most migrants died during Covid-19 lockdown 3.0: SaveLife Foundation."*Indian Express*. Available at: https://www.newindianexpress.com/nation/2020/jun/03/most-migrants-died-during-covid-19-lockdown-30-savelife-foundation-2151565. Updated on: accessed on: June 3, 2020, accessed on: August 10, 2020.
3. Barnett, E. D. & Walker, P. F. (2008). Role of immigrants and migrants in emerging infectious diseases. *Medical Clinics of North America,*92(6), 1447-1458.
4. Bhagat, R. B., Reshmi, R. S., Sahoo, H., Roy, A. K., & Govil, D. (2020). The Covid-19, Migration and Livelihood in India (No. id: 13054).
5. Bhatia, S., & Devulapalli, S.(2020). Mapped: The spread of coronavirus across India's districts. livemint, 2020.Available at: https://www.livemint.com/news/india/mapped-the-spread-of-coronavirus-across-india-s-districts-11587179250870. Updated on: April 19, 2020, accessed on: August 10, 2020.

6. Chowdhury, A., Kabir, K. A., & Tanimoto, J. (2020). How quarantine and social distancing policy can suppress the outbreak of novel coronavirus in developing or under poverty level countries: a mathematical and statistical analysis.
7. Deka, D., Phukan, A., & Sarma, D. (2013). Epidemiology of parvovirus and coronavirus infections in dogs in Assam. *Indian Vet. J,* 90(9), 49-51.
8. Gaur, V. (2020). Uttar Pradesh brings back highest number of migrants: Govt. Available at: https://economictimes.indiatimes.com/news/politics-and-nation/uttar-pradesh-brings-back-highest-number-of-migrants-govt/articleshow/75680285.cms#: updated on : May 11, 2020, accessed on August 15, 2020.
9. Hansa, A., Rai, R., Dhama, K., & Wani, M. (2012). ELISA and RT-PCR based detection of bovine coronavirus in Northern India. *Asian Journal of Animal and Veterinary Advances,* 7(11), 1120-1129.
10. Harapan, H., Itoh, N., Yufika, A., Winardi, W., Keam, S., Te, H., Megawati, D., Hayati, Z., Wagner, A.L. & Mudatsir, M. (2020). Coronavirus disease 2019 (Covid-19): A literature review. *Journal of Infection and Public Health.*
11. Jiang, J. & Luo, L. (2020). Influence of population mobility on the novel coronavirus disease (Covid-19) epidemic: based on panel data from Hubei, China. *Global Health Research and Policy,* 5, 1-10.
12. Kumar, M. (2020). 75% Coronavirus Patients In Bihar Are Migrants Who Returned Home. *NDTV Coronavirus full coverage*. Available at: https://www.ndtv.com/india-news/75-coronavirus-patients-in-bihar-are-migrants-who-returned-home-2240239. Updated on: June 3, 2020, accessed on: August 10, 2020.
13. Mahale, A. & Shelar, J. (2020). Coronavirus in Dharavi | When a virus finds space in India's largest slum.*The Hindu*. Available at: https://www.ndtv.com/india-news/75-coronavirus-patients-in-bihar-are-migrants-who-returned-home-2240239.Updated on: May, 9, 2020, accessed on: August 12, 2020.
14. Rajkhowa, S., Rajkhowa, C., & Hazarika, G. (2007). Serological evidence of coronavirus infection in mithuns (Bos frontalis) from India.
15. Ray, A. (2020). Mumbai: Dharavi shows how to fight Covid-19. Daily coronavirus count declines sharply. *Livemint*. Available at: https://www.livemint.com/news/india/mumbai-dharavi-shows-how-to-fight-covid-19-daily-coronavirus-count-in-falls-to-10-11591784810792.Updated on: June 10, 2020, accessed on: August 12, 2020.
16. Shukla, N. (2020). Eastern UP witnesses sudden rise in coronavirus cases as over 1,400 migrants test positive. *India Today*. Available at: https://www.indiatoday.in/india/story/eastern-uttar-pradesh-rise-in-coronavirus-cases-migrants-test-positive-1681190-2020-05-23. Updated on: May 23, 2020, accessed on: August 12, 2020.

17. Wilder-Smith, A. & Freedman D. (2020). Isolation, quarantine, social distancing and community containment: pivotal role for old-style public health measures in the novel coronavirus (2019-nCoV) outbreak. *Journal of travel medicine*, 27(2), taaa020.
18. Yuan, C. (2020). "A simple model to assess Wuhan lock-down effect and region efforts during Covid-19 epidemic in China Mainland." *medRxiv*.

20

Covid-19 and Re-thinking Problem of Migrant Workers in India: An Overview

Gayadhar Malik

Abstract

The recent turmoil of Covid-19 pandemic made us realise the problems of migrant worker all over India because the migrants are particularly lower paid jobs. The Covid-19 pandemic almost touched every country in the world and its impact on various sectors particularly on vulnerable groups who play an important role in country's economic development. Developing country like India has gained new engagement in mitigating the migrant problems especially during pandemic.Complete lockdown of India which created urgent demand for public transportation among workers scattered at different parts of India to send them to their native places. But it has witnessed that hundreds of migrant workers irrespective of gender they lost their life while returning back their home. The crisis of migrant workers has been a new challenging dimension at globally in general and India in particular. The problem of migrants during lockdown and their experiences need to highlight in a substantive manner.Though there is no real data available in official website this paper is purely based on secondary data available in internet, newspaper, reports, and articles. This paper investigates the issues of migrant workers due to Covid-19 and their struggle nationwide. The paper also highlights some of the measures taken by government and also argues that robust decisions were required to address the different issues faced by migrant workers and suggestions have been put to prevent workers problem.

Keywords: *Migrant Worker, Covid-19, Lockdown, Pandemic.*

Introduction

The recent surge of Covid-19 pandemic globally has taught us new lesson to understand the problems of marginalised sections particularly in Indian perspective. Let us first overlook the past epidemics in India in particular. The problem of migrant workers is not new but it has long experience. The past epidemics was hardly concerned with the problems of migrant workers in the best cities in India like Chennai (Madras), Kolkata (Calcutta), Mumbai (Bombay), and there are also many urban areas largely suffered from various epidemics like influenza, smallpox, plague, malaria and cholera (Davis, 1951; Banthia and Dyson, 1999; Hill, 2011). In 1896, Mumbai termed as most important figure in plague and in 1918 also influenza. These two diseases were seen in Mumbai and it spread India's north and east side. There were large numbers of people lost their live due to out-break of influenza and huge numbers of migrant workers were suffered (Hill, 2011). During the time, numbers of cases were reported where the excess fatality and problem of livelihood had reported. It was the time in 1994 the plague epidemic out-broke throughout the western part of India with base in Surat city (Gujarat). It has been witnessed that Surat city is largely industrial city and maximum migrant workers reside in the city as daily labourer. People go outside as migrant because of their better economic development, better education for their children and better livelihood. But sometimes the epidemics forced them to come back to their native places where they have no affordable wages to run their family.

In India, migrants are the sole contributor in economic growth, skill development, innovation and building of the nation. Migrants flee from the city not only they lose their livelihood but also they carry diseases to their native place (BBC, 2020). The history tells us whenever epidemic out-breaks, migrant workers and marginalised sections suffer extensively. However, in urban sector, the policies, programmes and planning for the urban development hardly initiated therefore they are not considered as a part of the urban community. It seems the achieving of the urban and rural development has been failed to recognize the migrant workers. It is the biggest mistake in achieving the realisation of good governance and sustainable development not only in India but also in every parts of the country as well. It needs to realise that migrants are not a victim but they are vulnerable in some extent. Migrants are engaged in many hazardous works, like 3D works (dirty, dangerous and demeaning) which mainly urban hate to do because they thought these jobs are only for marginalised sections and we will pay for it, no matter if the worker lose their life. Many cases have been reported that migrants are denied to access healthcare and social security programmes due to involvement in urban and rural society. Whenever migrants go outside for work they lose their political rights and they stay away at the time of election from their home constituency and are not able to cast their vote.

Review of Literature

This part deals with some literature relating to the topic. The literature on migrant workers and Covid-19 in recent years have witnessed that how India's migrant worker struggle against food, money, and job etc. Despite all, the literature highlights some factual assessment done by various scholars and their extensive work on migrant worker during this pandemic make us to think again to understand their problems.

Lahiri (1984) reported that the migration labourer originated from the unfavourable conditions where they reside. He highlights technological displacement, radical changes in share cropping systems drought and crop failures and various kinds of discrimination were the responsible for labourers to enter the migrant stream.

An article written by **Madhunika Lyer** (2020), on "*Migration in India and the impact of the lockdown on migrants*" highlights some of the issues on migrant worker during lockdown. She highlights how migrant workers are facing various problems during Covid-19 era and what are the major steps taken by government regarding migrant labour issues during the pandemic.

A study done by **Purusutham Chaudhari, Swati Rai, and A. Hanan** (2020) on Socio-Economic impact on Healthcare Professionals in India. The study has found there are number of issues emerged after Covid-19 pandemic especially in health sector such as economic recession, lack of logistic support, administrative chaos, lack of adequate manpower and ongoing spread of the infections. In the concluding remarks the authors suggested that government has to support and encourage healthcare professionals to combat this pandemic together.

A series carried out on Covid-19 and its impact on migrants livelihood in International Institute for Population Science, Mumbai by **B.R. Bhagat, Rashmi R.S., Harihar Sahoo, Archana K. Roy and Dipti Govil** (2020) highlight some theoretical explanations of migrant workers in India. The series discusses about various diseases like influenza, plague, malaria, smallpox and cholera and its impact on workers livelihood in India in different time period. But 2020 reminds the authors to rewrite on same issues on Covid-19 and its impact on migrant livelihood. The series discusses how Covid-19 pandemic impact on livelihood of downtrodden people of India. In concluding part it suggests various measures to be taken by the government.

Objectives

- To understand the migrant problems in India in terms of Covid-19 perspective.
- To analyse and discuss migrants livelihood and their rights in legal provision.
- To assess the living and working conditions of migrant workers.

Methodology and Data Sources

Migrant workers are facing wide range of problems throughout the world in general and India is particular. In this paper secondary data has been used to understand the whole scenario of migrant worker during the Covid-19 pandemic. Data has been analysed systematically and descriptive method has been used. For the explanation and analysis of data various migration characteristics have been used such as demographic characteristics, living conditions, nature of work, wages, income level, and remittances, etc. Secondary data have been collected through recent published research articles, journals, newspapers, and government reports.

Observations and Discussions

Migration basically a movement of people who away from their native place of residence, either within own country or other countries. In India, migrant workers have been scattered in different places like crosses one native place to other state for searching for better wages to run their family smoothly. Migrants also crosses the borders of own country to other countries.

In this point of view, we should remind our constitutional provisions which has been significant in protecting the workers' rights. Article 43 (a) of Indian constitution says '*participation of workers in management of industries.*' The State shall take necessary steps to secure the workers participation in the management of undertakings, establishment or other organisations engaged in any industry. Directive Principles of State Policy (DPSP) has taken major responsibility to secure the workers life and provide them opportunity in management and industrial sector. But the issues are always reminding us about workers problem particularly migrants in several fields.

The 2011 data census on migration says India had 45.6 crore migrants and compared to 31.5 crore migrants in 2001. It has been reported that between 2001 and 2011, while the population increased by 18%, at the same time the migrants also increased by 45%. As per 2011 census, 99% of total migration was internal and 1% immigrants. Therefore, we may classify the internal migrants on the basis of origin and their destination i.e., rural-rural, rural-urban, urban-rural, and urban-urban. These classifications can make us to understand the problem of migrant workers in a specific manner. And there is also another way of classification of migrant like intra-state and inter-state in this regard. As per 2011 census, inter-state movement accounted for almost 88% of all internal migration (39.6 crore persons). There are also variations across States in terms of inter-state migration flows. As per 2011 census, Uttar Pradesh and Bihar were the largest inter-state migrants while Delhi and Maharashtra were the largest receiver in this regard. In this complex situation it has been reported that around 83 lakh residents of Uttar Pradesh and 63 lakh residents of Bihar moved either temporarily or permanently to other States. Maharashtra has occupied around 60 lakh people from across India those have migrated. These are the basic themes of migrants of Indian States.

Problems faced by migrant workers

The above discussion makes us to realise what are the basic problems faced by migrant workers and what are the constitutional provisions to prevent them from some sort of problems. First of all, we need to understand what our Fundamental Rights says about this. Article 19 (1)(e) of the Indian constitution which guarantees all citizens have rights to reside and settle in any part of the country and subject to reasonable restrictions in the interest of the general public or protection of any Scheduled Tribe. The major problem or challenges faced by migrants are lack of social security and healthcare facilities and poor implementation of relating provisions, lack of registration of state-provided benefits especially in distribution of food through PDS and lack of affordable housing and basic amenities in both urban and rural areas respectively.

Covid-19 and Its Impact on Indian Migrant Workers

The recent spread of coronavirus throughout the world had identified for the first time in China's Wuhan city in the month of November 2019. The spread of coronavirus worldwide which created panic in every human beings mind. In fact the new virus named Covid-19 (Corona Virus Diseases-2019) as all might have known and later the World Health Organisation (WHO) declared this as a pandemic on March 11, 2020 which severely attack elderly and those how have pre-existing health conditions. At this juncture, the WHO warned almost every country in the world to stop the escalation of coronavirus which transmits from person to person. To stop the rapid out-break of Covid-19 major steps such as use face mask, maintaining social distance stay indoors, avoid crowded areas and always sanitise hand have been taking to break the chain of corona virus. In this context, India has also initiated different steps to control the spread of coronavirus from its rapid escalation.

In spite of all these, in India the coronavirus was first identified in the State of Kerala on 30th January, 2020. After that the virus gradually transmitted to person to person. To stop the rapid surge of virus throughout India the government decided complete lockdown in whole country to control the out-break of this novel coronavirus. Eventually on 24th March, 2020 government decided 21 days lockdown whole country without opinions of best intellectuals of India as well as opposition parties also. The hasty announcement of complete lockdown throughout India which made realise millions of migrant workers how to reach home, how to earn money, how to maintain family these are the major challenges in those days. No food and no work are also major challenges therein. The announcement of lockdown which created panic in every mind of Indian. This is the greatest tragedy India since partition as Historian Ramchandra Guha added. He also added that the migrant tragedy could have been averted if Prime Minister Narendra Modi had given a short notice to return home before the lockdown imposed. The sudden banning of train services, public transport and air travels, sealed of all borders no movement from one state to another to stalk the novel coronavirus war main purpose. But somewhat the decision was good but on the other hand millions of migrants throughout the India were suffering from different horrible situations now the situations have more or less come down due to certain relaxations has been imposed since April 2020.

Migrants Facing Problem during Covid-19 Lockdown some Factual Assessment

The real problem of migrant has not been solving since India's partition. Here, some of the factual insights that has been reported after imposition of lockdown in India in general migrants facing problem in particular. However, the hardship of migrants is not an ending process due to government's inability to provide maximus wages and larger opportunities in their respective states. The novel coronavirus which taught millions of migrants and poor people a new lesson that how our government is draconian in his decision. Let's move into India's new strategy in relation to migrant workers in this pandemic.

It has been reported that the novel coronavirus which have lowered all sectors such as economy, education and no physical contact but on the other hand the healthcare system of India more or less have improved. Social distance, always use face mask and no physical contact these are the measures taken by the Indian government to diminish the out-break of virus.In this context there are three dimensions such as healthcare, economy and society in which our country is striving till today. But it is pertinent to draw attention on present scenario of India's migrant workers livelihood and necessary measures that have been taken by central government. First of all, we shall look at the matter of after announcement of lockdown lakhs of migrants, including daily wage workers, hundreds of people cycled or hitchhiked to their native place and sometimes thousands of people walked away without food and money. It has been reported that hundreds of people lost their lives while walking on the road due to non-availability of food during their journey even 25 migrant workers died in road accident in Uttar Pradesh this is not the only case there are many cases took place during their journey. This image shocked the nation and made it global headlines where migrants were undermined by nationwide lockdown. There were also raising questions about the government's handling of the situation.

The total exclusion of such marginalised people from food, money and other benefits realise them to find out alternative solution to reach their home place. These alternative solutions were some used boat in the sea and some used truck and giving the owner high amount of money to reach their home. This situation not only to save their lives but also to save their family members as well. This situation might not have seen if Prime Minister given at least short notice to return home, Mr. Guha said. But they didn't know the consequences of a lockdown and they imposed direct responsibility to the workers which has unfolded yet. It is significant to say that when there were few infections of Covid-19 patients they might have safely reached their home and can re-integrated with their communities. But now, so many of them infected where they were staying without proper shelter and are carries disease to their native place. At this juncture, some of the migrants died either due to hardship on the way, hunger, accident and some even committed suicide. After so many hurdles all state governments decided to send migrant workers to their native place by buses or trains. During the bus travel some accident also took place due to some irregularities. While government allowed train travel specially for migrants the train got delayed with changing its routes which gave more pain to the migrants. These are the major problems faced by migrants during the first 21 days lockdown. A telephonic survey has done by Jan Sahas (2020) over 3000 migrants from north central India, the study shows that majority of the migrant workers were daily wage earners and at the time of lockdown, only 42% were left with no ration, one-third was stuck at destination city with no access of food, water and money, 94% don't have worker's identity card. The migrants who had reached their native places, were seen as carrying infection with themselves and were ill-treated by the police and native villagers. It has been reported that a group of returnees were sprayed with chemicals to disinfect them for which the local administration apologised (India Today, 2020). This is one of the biggest streams of mass return migration in the country. The barbaric treatment with returnees were first took place while they were facing various problems which has already been discussed in the earlier sections. This is a greatest human tragedy in Indian history.

Meanwhile, government had announced Rs. 1.70-lakh-crore package on 26th March 2020 under the Pradhan Mantri Gareeb Kalyan Yojona to mitigate the effect of the lockdown particularly on the vulnerable groups. The package was for health workers, farmers, MANREGA workers, economically weaker sections, especially women, elderly, and other sector workers, Jan Dhan account holders and Ujjawala beneficiaries. This scheme also added 5 kg of rice or wheat and one kg of preferred pulses every month to 80 crore beneficiaries for the next three months. At the same time central government also asked to the state governments to use Building and Construction Workers Welfare Fund of Rs. 52000 crores to provide relief to Construction Workers through direct benefit transfer (DBT). Later RBI also joined with a sharp cut of interest rate along with a series of alternative measures to lend to besieged businesses (Bloomberg Quint, 2020). The beneficiaries also received some services through PDS and there were also irregularities in their management of this public distribution system by local dealers.

The Ministry of Home Affairs (MHA) also directed house owners not to charge rent during this pandemic and employee should make the payment of wages of their workers without having any deduction. It is important to note that MHA also set-up a control room to monitor the crisis 24X7 to ensure that essential commodities to be provided. All state governments were allowed to provide special relief to the migrant workers from their State Disaster Relief Fund (SDRF) such as provide food, immediate accommodation and medical facilities for homeless particularly for migrant workers and special relief camps were set-up with provision of food, shelter and other basic amenities. It has been reported that till 31st March, 2020, there were as much as 21,604 relief camps were set-up for stranded workers. There were 23 lakhs more persons were also provided food (Kulkarni, 2020). Ministry of HomeAffairs ordered immediate health actions for migrant workers where they were staying called congregation of migrant workers and immediate health risk management. These are the measures taken by central government to control the migration crisis. Central Government has also permitted Non-governmental Organisations (NGOs) and other volunteers to paid their attention towards migrants. Now some more or less non-governmental organisations have involved in helping migrants with substantial effort have been made to feed people those were hungry. In Gurugram, many restaurants were also serving food to more than 75,000 people daily (Goel, 2020) and WIPRO is donating 40,000 food packets per day. But this is not the only one or two instances, there are many instances throughout India where thousands of volunteers and NGOs were also involved to save human lives. It is pertinent to say that these measures should have taken before announcement of lockdown though we had preventive options but unfortunately still we are suffering the same crisis. The situation has been worsening day by day, now India has become the third worsen Covid-19 infected countries in the world after USA and Brazil. Though government has relaxed in some factories and industries to re-open, the migrants who have suffered more troubles they might not interested to return to factories and cities in search for work. It seems until the situation is normalised they might be involved in their native work places despite low wages.

Violation of Labour Law in India during Covid-19

After lockdown migrant worker intended to return their native place due to several problems. During lockdown workers left their jobs and many stayed there with affordable facilities were providing by the company owners. With this duration, many State governments have increased working hours of labourers even without overtime payments. In this context, we should remind Karl Marx's idea about exploitation by one class over another those are weaker or working class. But India's figure in this regard has some anomalies in protecting workers rights as Dr. Babasaheb Ambedkar had mentioned workers' rights and social security are the prime concern of constitution to ensure protection of unorganised workers in their old age. At this point of view, Ambedkar was one of them who always stood for the Depressed Classes in the Round Table Conference and demanded freedom of peasant workers from the clutches of cruel landlords. The same situation also seen in India during Covid-19 pandemic. States like Gujarat, Goa, Madhya Pradesh, Maharashtra, Odisha, Punjab, Rajasthan and also Uttar Pradesh have changed their own labour laws by amending some provisions or suspending other laws.

Moreover, it was against the International Labour Organisation (ILO) convention which was signed by India on working hours. The signed was effectively done that workers should not be forced for more than their actual hours. But it is recent evident from the Indian States like Himachal Pradesh, Gujarat, Rajasthan and Uttar Pradesh these States can force the workers to work 72 hours a week, an increase of 24 hours which was earlier 48 hours. It has been reported that workers have been forced to work extra 12 hours in a day on six working days of a week now and earlier it was eight hours per day. It is significant to note that there are completely violations of labour laws as well as violations of ILO convention Law. Moreover, the migrant worker's justice still to be achieved in a constitutional procedure. Now they have become seeker of the justice which has not been properly utilised by State governments.

Suggestions

The result of this paper says it is an unprecedented humanitarian disaster that millions of poor migrants were facing lots of problems where it seems justice has died due to draconian and barbaric repression over weaker sections. In spite of all situations major suggestive steps need be taken into consideration. These are:

- The government should provide safety and security against low wages, physical, mental and sexual exploitation at work places.

- India should ratify all the relevant international conventions (ILO) that respect the dignity of labour and labour law should not be diminished. Freedom of workers association and protection of the rights should be taken into consideration.
- This is the prime responsibility of the States to protect migrant and other workers in the unorganised sector by International labour standards and there should be a separate ministry for migrants' affairs, dealing with domestic problems of migrants in India.
- Government should promote NGOs and volunteers to build an alternative strategy like workers movement for effective awareness programmes about their prerogative rights and stand against exploitation of migrants.

Conclusion

The above assessment of migrant workers has some shortcomings in some extend. Today, the migrant workers crisis has no certainty how long it will continue. The Covid-19 pandemic impact on migrants irrespective of religion, gender, and caste which made us to realise the real picture of migrants' workers during lockdown. The measures that had taken by Central Government somewhat acceptable though we had other options to stop the reescalation of Coronavirus. The paper also discussed about some factual assessments of problems faced by workers and discussed their way of life after announcement of lockdown. The argument could be drawn for and against to look after the migrations crisis in India where hundreds of people died and lakhs of people left their jobs. First argument is for, government has taken necessary steps to tackle or averted the situation and nationwide lockdown was necessary. Government had circulated largest package for vulnerable groups to engage them in their earning places. Second, is against, the government should have noticed to the workers before lockdown and necessary steps should have taken which announced later. In this point of view the migrant crisis we might not have seen today if Prime Minister had given a short notice to the workers before lockdown which they later infected in Coronavirus and carries diseases to their native place. It is significant here that government has completely failure to provide justice to the workers and at the same time they diminished the constitutional laws without critically analysing the labour crisis. It was unfortunate that many State governments collected fare from the migrant labourers while sending them home by trains and buses. Despite all this is necessary to understand the problem of migrant worker and we should explore the current situation of country in terms of Covid-19 pandemic.

In the democratic world, it is necessary to argue important dimensions of migrant workers standards and workers rights (Migrant Rights) and our major concern should on raise voice against inequalities following the process of Rule of Law.

References

Bhagat, R.B., Keshri, K and Imtiyaz Ali (2013). *Emigration and flow of remittances in India, Migration and Development,* Vol. 2, No. 1, 2013, pp. 93-105.

Census, 2011. Office of the Registrar General & Census Commissioner, Ministry of Home Affairs.

Constitution of India, Article 43 (a), Article 19.

Guha, Ramachandra (2020). *Migrant owes greatest mandate tragedy in India since partition*. The Hindu Newspaper 24th May.

Hill, Kenneth (2011). *Influenza in India 1918: excess mortality reassessed*, Genus, Vol. 67, No. 2, pp. 9-29.

International Organisation for Migration (2019) World Migration Report 2020, IOM, Geneva.

Meghwal, Arjun Ram (1 May 2020). *B R Ambedkar laid the foundation for workers' rights, social security in India.* The Indian Express.

Negi, Chitranjali (2020). *Human Rights Violations of Migrants workers in India during Covid-19 Pandemic.* The research paper has not been peer reviewed. Electronic copy available at: https//ssm.com/abstract=3629773.

21

A Study of Working Women Residing at PG's in Chennai City

Dr. K. Puspham, Dr. S.K. Ramani

Abstract

In India the tremendous development due to the technological advancement has promoted large scale migration of people irrespective of the gender. Both men and women are away from their family seeking employment opportunities in urban or city capitals. Participation of female labour force rates in low level in India. 48 percent of the Indian population of women are working actively under the age category of 15 years and older. In urban India women participation in work force is impressive. And among the working women who reside in urban areas employed mostly in private sectors are accommodated at private hostels and PG's. Working women face a double burden of taking care of family and balancing their job due to their working conditions and job opportunities face problems both at home and at work place. In this connection this paper describes the living conditions of working women residing in PG's and who are detached from their family members for employment. This study was analyzed using both primary and secondary data among working women and the study results suggest measures for overall livelihood and living conditions of working women in private residence.

Introduction

Women contribution has increased as work force that leads to a more equal disbursement of working hours across the world. Nature of

Women participation in different from employment Skills in Western European countries. Access to paying for occupation has remain unequal related to their workforce level.

20 percent of women only getting payment for their non-agricultural jobs in southeren Asia, Africa and western Asia. Paid employment rate of women grows outside of agriculture 4 percent by 2008. Women still contributes for agricultural work for developments of their communities and regions. The range of social, economic and cultural factors provided for the impact of gender distribution in different occupation, and a region or country. An average level of differences reflects by the United Nations for 2004 and 2007 statistics (totals may not add up to 100 percent due to rounding).

Significance of the Study

Woman status has changes in India. Majority of Indian working women are more independent and aware of their legal right such as right to work, equal treatment, maintenance of property, and remaining working women unaware of these rights. Working women age of marriage, extent of literacy, dual role family and work places that may affect their quality of life. India has the tremendous development due to the technological advancement and promoting large scale migration of people irrespective of the gender. Both men and women are away from their family seeking employment opportunities in urban or city capitals. 48 percent of the Indian population of women are working actively under the age category of 15 years and older. In urban India women participation in work force is impressive. And among the working women who reside in urban areas employed mostly in private sectors are accommodated at private hostels and PG's. Working women face a double burden of taking care of family and balancing their job due to their working conditions. In this connection this paper describes the living conditions of working women residing in PG's and who are detached from their family members for employment.

Review of the Study

Hate (1978) in her book pointed out that in Maharashtra with the advent of Independence has a positive changes in the status of political, economic and social conditions among working and non-working women. **Robinson and Skarie (1980)** in their study represents that stress relationship to locus controls, internally oriented to individuals show less perception of role overload and ambiguity among the working women.

Rose H Phelps Stokes (1906) has examined the study of the conditions of working women faced the hardship and consequences are duty-bound not merely to support their own families, and whether working women will or not, to the support of other families and live in idle expensiveness upon the passage of working people's toil. This study shows that recognition of working people of our country . Strikes and industrial disturbance leads to unwilling class hatred and craving for larger justice for the socialistic programme. This study found to be self and factory sisters working conditions are damaging to the health of body, mind and spirit to the working women. Also this study reveals that working women in a day maximum hours spent in the working places and monotonous repetition of purely mechanical actions, amid-ill ventilated and unsanitary surroundings destroys bodily due to our work. This inbuilt characters of potential and glad thought and actions are essential to higher type of personality development become paralytic.

Working women feels that excessive toil on her part and unnecessary burdens fairly distributed of production, and waste prevailed less widely. Working women meets economically no justice that requires of physical and spiritual exhaustion, absolved from the necessity of labour through the accident of birth or waste in idleness and luxuriousness production and the product fellows.

Working woman felt that languor and depression and weakness with existing industrial conditions, and they can feel no justice in an industrial system conditions creates the unfriendly to physical and mental health and practices. Excessive hours of toil and consequent craving for relaxation and refreshmen and seeking of gayety and recreation after the days works is done, and that conditions underlies alone gayety and recreation has an average working girl in our large cities are far from conducive to the highest standards of societal life.

The needs to be recreation and social enjoyment, and particularly so after hours of arduous toil, to seek recreation and refreshment. This is the social pleasures among every working man and woman. So, working girl may looked upon employer as friendly to coworkers but narrow sense friendship does not seem to fulfill the requirements of justice.

Objective of Study

To explore the problems of working women residing in PG's.

Method of the Study

The study was conducted only within the Chennai city PG's and the data was collected from 73 working women residing as Paying Guest (PG's) in Chennai city. This study has adopted both Primary and Secondary data's used for analysis. The primary data were collected among working women through the Interview Schedule.

Interpretation of the study

Occupational Status

Women said that grandmothers and mothers could only dream off their movement for the paid employment outside the home. Women are automotive and used to be done work by men. Working women have more choice and independence stayed at home in factories and sweatshops. This type of work contradiction shows that more women are working often still worse paid than men, in part-time jobs or in the huge informal employment sector provides with little protection and few rights. In many places, working women rate increased by the necessity of having double wages to made a satisfaction. Woman participated in different occupations which include about 61.6 percent of the respondents are working at IT sectors followed by medical professions (23 percent) and 10 percent of working women as professors and the remaining 5.4 percent working as storekeepers.

Problems Faced by Working Women Residing at PG's

Working women face health problems at a large scale level. Many women workers complain of frequent headaches, back pain, vascular system disorders, eye itching, tiredness, emotional and mental confusions. This study of the working women highlights that 87 percent of women suffer from health complications and only 13 percent of working women has not faced any kind of health complications like headache, depression, compactness problem etc. As a single working women face a lot of accommodation problem, they are working in a outside area they cannot transformation of families along with her. Working women face many problems in balancing their work and family life as residing away from family. They frequently met issues are travelling time and distance of work place which is not safety during late working hours which is a common problem for women employed in IT sectors, harassment at work place includes work load and completion of work in a target period etc., career opportunities does not balance with their level of education, unequal pay though legally eligible to set the equal earnings for the equal work.

Family Conditions of the Working Women

Empowering women jobs and business is a crucial step towards gender equality, working woman not just get a chance to venture out of their homes, but to excel in their careers and to achieve their potential. As an egalitarian society, our responsibility to give them the opportunity and the environment in which they are free to do so. Society change, when women go to the work the family organisation set to the new conditions will fare the best in financial conditions and they face the trouble of working conditions and issues of caring the family. As women being primary caretaker of young children, they play a vital role in facilitating or clogging changes in family life. As a working woman they missed the chance of caretaking of young children and elders of their entire family members.

Women traditionally have the major responsibility for socialisation their children, but in the present scenario as women in the workforce has increased, they are disturbed in their socialisation activities and are inclined to concentrate more on the working conditions. Women were left to take care of health and children. The involvement of women in workforce and the time spent in working places has reduced the caring of family members and their mental attitudes, their behaviours conditions. Mothers and working women's were more aware of the need to change their socialisation method than the family members without any negative impact of the cultures.

The study reveals that only 33 percent of the working women did not face any problems relating to social unit life and professional life and a majority, nearly 67 percent of working women respondents found to be difficult to manage family unit life and professional life as they have gone domestic place holidays and take care of the family, attend to their children needs and manage all their family related matters. The working women try to balance the family life and work life with great difficulties and adopt coping strategies to carry all the work-load and take care of their private life. The present study highlights the ways in which the working conditions of women have improved over the years and at the same time they have lost the assistance and help of husband's family and sisters-in-laws. Women have suffered at the hands of their professional management in the form of pay gap, poor maternity leaves and not able to be fully qualified for top management positions. Working women should feel empowered when both at work and at home and her commitment to both should not be a hindrance to her development to professional and family commitments. In general, working women position that people respect them in their work place and outside give more respects for their occupational status. Also, they are more interested in the community and societal levels activities, compared to those who are not participated as a member of social club, communities and religious and children activities etc.

Financial Independence

59 percent of the working women financial independent reveals that they felt that more respect in the society where as only 41 percent of the working women financially independent did not agree. They have a feel of a perceptual experience of a stable financial is required to get a respect. The women felt that as a working woman being financially independent is very essential and also gains superior reputation and independence in the society but still is not in the family. In the case of working women who are in higher position there is a notion that women are able to achieve the high post because of social control and concludes that women characters rather than accepting her capability of achieving a position. Working women colleagues are more personal in the

criticism and gossip more on a colleagues character, standard of living, working women family matters, and salad dressing styles etc. But in general financial independent gives working women get more respect in the society as it enhances one's reputation, freedom from dependency, social security and it also helps them improve their economic and gregarious status also.

Conclusion

The present study highlights that working women are strained to leave their small children, husband, and other family members because of their work and they lack support from their own kin and kith. Therefore balancing family life and work life being away from family surrounding and as a single parent is very challenging for women working residing at PG's. The study reveals that the health conditions of working women are very weak and should be very conscious and is also an important task to maintain their health. Though financial independence working women gives more respect for the working women in the society. But at the same time they face problems and criticisms from their own working colleagues as they are residing away from home and sometimes both men and women from their own circle draw conclusion about women's character without any basis. In India, in spite of all developments still a particular boundary exists for women in general and working women in specific but with all difficulties she is proving herself in all sphere of her life and becoming stronger to adhere to handle any adverse situation in work and family life. The present study emphasis that the societal construction does not accept the new role of women and her thought ununderstood and distressed.

References

1. Aggamwala in sexism and patriarchy society, women empowerment, are household responsibilities holding women back from participating in the work force?
2. ethesis.nitrkl.ac.in
3. Essays, UK (November, 2018). Problems of working women.
4. The annals of the American Academy of Political and Social Science, Vol. 27, the improvement of labor conditions in the United States, May (1906), pp. 165-175.

5. Women's rights and gender equality Global development, Women are better off today, but still far from being equal with me.
6. Women empowerment: working condition of female employees in government offices, April 2018, Team Safalta.

Index

D

E

F

G

H

I

W

Y

Z